EVOLUTION,
HUMAN ECOLOGY,
AND SOCIETY

EVOLUTION, HUMAN ECOLOGY, AND SOCIETY

W. NORMAN RICHARDSON

THOMAS H. STUBBS

Macmillan Publishing Co., Inc.

NEW YORK

Collier Macmillan Publishers

LONDON

Copyright © 1976, W. Norman Richardson and Thomas H. Stubbs

Printed in the United States of America

Macmillan Publishing Co., Inc.
866 Third Avenue, New York, New York 10022

Collier Macmillan Canada, Ltd.

Library of Congress Cataloging in Publication Data

Richardson, W   Norman.
  Evolution, human ecology, and society.

  Includes bibliographies and index.
  1. Human evolution. 2. Social evolution. 3. Human ecology. I. Stubbs, Thomas H., joint author.
II. Title
GN281.4.R52   573.2   75-9701
ISBN 0-02-399660-9

Printing: 1 2 3 4 5 6 7 8   Year: 6 7 8 9 0 1 2

Dedicated to

Esther Stubbs
Don and Jill Goodman

preface

This book is intended to accompany courses in evolution, human ecology, general ecology, general biology, and other related offerings assuming an environmental or evolutionary awareness.

During the optimistic 1960s, a belief was generated and propagated by the scientific community to the effect that all man's ills would be subject to rectification through the application of his increasingly sophisticated technology. As misleading in its naiveté as it is disconcerting in its ignorance, this scientific chauvinism was responsible for furthering a dangerously simplistic view of our biological condition and persuading much of the public to accept the philosophy of the technological optimist. Now we know that technology alone is no solution, as the world struggles in the grips of overpopulation and severe environmental abuse. But where does this leave man in his evolution and survival as a species?

A consideration of man's past and present ecological dilemma is essential to discussions of his evolutionary future, for man is a biological organism and, like so many organisms in this stressed biosphere, he is currently responding to the stresses that are products of his own technology. As a species, he is subject to the pressures of natural selection, just as are bacteria and bison. However, he is unique in two respects. He manufactures the culture that affects his environment and himself, and he is now capable to some degree of directing his genetic future.

Commencing with his advance to the status of tool-using ape, more than 100,000 years ago, man propelled himself, however slowly at first, into realms transgressed by no previous animal.

Some 10,000 years ago, the thrust of the Neolithic revolution in agriculture directed his species and his culture toward the complexities of the present. To the increasing biofeedback on the evolution of his culture and technology, man has cumulatively added the effects of the revolution in mass communications, those of the Industrial and Scientific Revolutions of the eighteenth century, of the internal combustion engine and its concomitant culture, and of the use of atomic power. With all of man's rapid and complex cultural innovations, his impact on his own biology and on that of other organisms sharing the biosphere with him has been increased. It is unfortunate that biologists and cultural anthropologists often operate as though their studies bore no relation, for they are expressions of the same set of factors: our culture influences our biology and our biology influences our culture.

The authors believe that it is important to generate a widespread awareness that man is still a biologically evolving organism, and that this process has not been totally superseded by cultural and technological evolution. Whereas the latter is increasingly rapid and its effects more easily discernible, our biological evolution is still proceeding under the stresses of an increasingly degraded biosphere. Planned genetic engineering may offer some improvement to man as a species, but our expanding environmental abuses continue to have negative feedback on our genetic systems. The effect of environmental factors on human evolution may prove more important than technological achievements in determining our genetic future and the survival of our species. We are at the point where man has to outwit many of the products of his own technology and culture to insure his survival. Cultural evolution originally conferred upon man a tremendous survival potential in the context of adverse natural phenomena, resulting in the spread of his numbers over the globe into areas not intrinsically favorable to his survival.

Man's role in the alteration of his environment is in itself nothing new. There is evidence that he was a significant factor in the extinction of numerous large mammals, such as the woolly mammoth and the sabretoothed tiger, during his days as a hunter at the end of the Pleistocene era. From his Neolithic beginnings as an agriculturalist, man has altered the fauna, flora, hydrology, soil profile, and climate of vast areas. His expanding population and technology resulted in land use practices that changed lush forest regions into deserts, particularly in the Sahara.

We have become increasingly aware of the impact of man's culture and technology on the survival of other species, as well as on critical life support systems. Although man has eliminated many stringently selective factors, such as many bacterial diseases, from his environment, he has added others, potentially more selective. Thousands of chemical substances have been added to the biosphere in the last 100 years. These irradiants and pollutants foul our water, inhibit our enzymes, block our biochemical pathways, bring cancer to our bodies, and mutate our genes.

One of the most realistic arguments against technological solutions to such problems is that our own overpopulation tends to neutralize any beneficial effects of this technology. Overpopulation is certainly the undoing of the so-called "Green Revolution" in agriculture; technological answers to our social, economic, and political problems are also made impotent by overpopulation.

When Darwin popularized the phrase "survival of the fittest," he was referring to those individual animals that left the greatest number of offspring, not to the genetic fitness of a species. In those terms, man has been a spectacular evolutionary success. But does the accumulation of sheer numbers mean that we are winning the game of evolution, the only goal of which is survival? It is a paradox that, by our success in numbers, we are now threatened in our survival as individuals and as a species. What we now know that Darwin did not know is that the successful species is that which maintains an *optimal* number of diverse individuals. Sheer maximization of numbers does not win the game. We could be lemmings on a one-way trip to the sea.

In the preparation of this book, we have attempted to present a broad perspective on the dilemma man faces as a biological organism being overwhelmed by the accumulated debts built into his cultural advances. We believe that the deterioration of the biosphere portends strong selective pressures on mankind. The first three chapters deal with some evolutionary principles relevant to contemporary man and his biological and cultural evolution. However, this is not meant as a book on evolution; for those interested in further readings on that subject, a number of excellent references are available in the suggested readings list following Chapter 1. Nor is this intended to be a text in human genetics per se.

Biology, physical sciences, anthropology, and sociology have tended to operate academically as discrete areas of study with little or no interaction. However, our contemporary environmental concerns are multidimensional problems encompassing all spheres of human biology and culture. We do not believe that they should or can be separated. It is our hope that this book will meet the need for integrating perspectives, in describing how social problems can affect our biology, and how biological considerations in turn influence culture. For this reason, similar topics may appear in more than one part of the book. For example, intelligence is discussed in the chapter on sociological factors and again as a theme in itself, because of the need for a better understanding of the multifaceted concept of so intangible a quality.

Finally, we wish to emphasize that our use of the word *man* in this book refers to the human species, and is in no way meant as a sex-oriented reference. We subscribe completely to the equality of sexes, and would not intentionally convey an opposite impression.

We are indebted to the many people who helped us in the preparation of the text, although we assume total responsibility for the information contained herein, of course. Particular thanks are due to Dr. Don and Dr. Jill Goodman and Dr. Stephen Yarnell, with whom we exchanged numerous ideas. Mr. Charles Stewart and Joan Delaney at Macmillan patiently assisted in many ways. Ms. Elizabeth Owen, Ms. Dorothea Slater, and Mr. Wayne Whitmarsh struggled with the handwritten first copy and subsequent revisions. And we owe an expression of thanks to all of our friends in Panajachel, Guatemala, where we wrote much of the text.

W. N. R.
T. H. S.

contents

introduction: a synopsis

Quietly, in the still darkness of a protective cave, a group of large primates sat huddled in darkness. Outside, light was dissipating the night, and soon the band within stirred, peering out at the advancing dawn, its light soft over the expanse of an African plain. There were few of these creatures, and their world was a hostile, forbidding environment. However, they were well equipped to cope with adversaries. As incipient dawn evolved into full daylight, the small enclave of early men spread out over the warming plain. And they never stopped.

When early man entered into the initial stages of culture, he began to affect the course of his own evolution, albeit unconsciously, in ways more far-reaching than had any previous animal. Today his accelerated advances in science and technology present new and severe selective pressures on his genetic evolution, but provide him with possible tools for determining his genetic future. Man's contemporary culture both increasingly restricts and enhances his potential for survival. But man's biological integrity has been, is, and will continue to be the summation of his interactions with his culture and environment. Whereas the products of science and technology are affecting his genetic potential in numerous respects, man remains subject to the shaping influences of natural selection.

About 70 million years ago, during the Paleocene, a group of small, shrew-like mammals began living in the trees, enjoying relative success in their new niche, which offered more security from the numerous predators below. Through natural selection, various innovations in structure and function occurred to suit these mammals to an arboreal domain. Manipulative, grasping hands and feet were advantageous in leaping from limb to limb; one fall might serve as strong negative selection. Stereoscopic vision (for depth perception) was also an aid in negotiating trees; binocular vision was enhanced by a rotation of the eyes to the front of the skull, and by a reduced snout that would not get in the way. In the trees, sight and touch transcended smell and hearing as important senses, so there was a trend toward higher development of the cerebral cortex, as voluntary movements were necessary if vision and touch were to coordinate beneficially.

Thus the earliest primates evolved from a most inconspicuous progenitor. Other new characteristics evolved along with the arboreal lifestyle. Obviously, numerous disadvantages accompanied a large litter size for tree-dwelling animals. The number of offspring was reduced, while females devoted more time to the one or two they had. Also, in the relatively tropical climes where man's ancestors evolved, there was little to limit sexual receptivity to certain periods. Mating occurred throughout the year, a decided advantage for increasing the population of a species with a low birth rate.

In terms of the advancements that led to man, living in the trees had pronounced disadvantages. As it was, the African forests seem to have thinned out, giving way to a landscape of plains. Certain primates began to evolve away from the trees, among them the ancestors of man, equipped with the modifications which proved as positive on the ground

2

as they had in the trees. When the man-ape *Australopithecus* began using tools, groundwork was well established for the evolutionary pathway to modern man.

What is the nature of this process of evolution, which is constantly altering the biotic face of the earth? The total *biofeedback*, or *biocybernetics* (the science of feedback relations between living and nonliving elements of an ecological system), from the biological and physical environment effects changes within the structure and function of organisms over time. It is not a process occurring within individuals, but rather within groups of individuals known as populations.

As the world is not static, but a dynamic system of continuous change, living organisms must be dynamic as well, to cope with alterations of their environment. Generally, evolutionary changes are synergistic; organisms interact with each other and with their environment, each affecting the other to some degree. These changes may occur by an isolation of gene pools; a section of an animal population may be cut off from another, and over time—(perhaps thousands of years)—the formerly similar animals become less and less alike. And each time an animal sexually reproduces, there is a recombination of *genes* (the hereditary material) in the formation of *gametes* (reproductive cells). Also, agents in the environment—irradiation or chemicals—cause mutations within gametes, either increasing or diminishing the potential variation of an organism. Natural selection—Darwin's "survival of the fittest"—gives merits to those populations interacting most efficiently with the total environment, eliminating by one means or another the individuals least able to cope with the vicissitudes of a very stressful world.

If we construct an anthropomorphized analogy, evolution may be likened to a gambler (the process) who attempts to make his living (survive) by always betting (natural selection) on the winning horse (species). Regardless of what the gambler does, *chance* is still the predominant factor determining the outcome. There is no formula; a winning combination is just that, a fortuitous result that will remain valid only until the circumstances of environmental change cause its successful qualities to become obsolete. All living things subject to the pressures of natural selection usually change slowly over many thousands of years. No organism—not even man—is free of the influence of this process.

Physically, man is closely similar to several other primates. But man is unique in that he has culture, the sum of all socially transmitted behavior coupled with its physical artifacts. This culture, beginning with

3

the most inchoate of practices, such as the use of primitive tools, has evolved into a vastly complex network of interactions, increasing exponentially to the point that it is now a problem just to keep track of them.

At one time, most physical anthropologists believed that man's cultural heritage was the result of his large cranial capacity, and especially of the enlarged cerebral cortex. The fossil record of man clearly shows a progressively larger brain. The "ape-man" *Australopithecus* had a cranial volume of 450 to 600 cc (cubic centimeters), whereas a more recent ancestor, *Homo erectus*, had a capacity of 775 to 1,200 cc, and contemporary man, *Homo sapiens*, has an average of 1,450 cc.

What is probably true, in fact, is that brain size spurred incipient culture, and that culture increased brain size. In man's case, there was survival value in greater intelligence, so there was selective advantage favoring brighter individuals, both socially and biologically. And as man became more intelligent, his culture became more complex, so these two qualities coevolved, each aiding the other.

Whereas consistent tool-making was the first stage in the development of culture, there was a major gap between the making of simple tools and the perpetuation of a more complex culture. This was bridged by the advent of language, with the neuromotor expression of speech. Only when man had developed a language could he effectively pass along the details of cultural developments to succeeding generations, thereby allowing new individuals more time for making their own discoveries. With language, man became *Man*, giving to his culture a continuity which had never before existed. It is probable that the resultant feedback of speech and tool usage on man was primarily responsible for the threefold increase in his brain size.

What makes us "human"? Is it our ability to reason? Not entirely—certain chimpanzees have been shown to reason nearly as well as some men. We might well argue that speech was our vehicle to humanity. Chimpanzees and other primates may lack culture due not to a lack of reasoning ability, but to the lack of culturally transmitted speech and the concomitant ability to perpetuate patterns of culture. Speech reinforces the use of tools and other innovations of physical culture, and facilitates an increasing complexity of socially transmitted behavior.

Man's physical evolution has not, as some will argue, come to a halt. But whereas biological evolution tends to be an exceedingly slow process, and the effects of it usually are not readily discernible, our cultural evolution has been rapid, and is now at the point of curving around to affect drastically our physical being as well.

Man lingered on the threshold of cultural evolution for 100,000 years after initiating the use of tools. An accelerated cultural revolution, however, began only about 12,000 years ago with the dawn of agriculture, which caused a shift from mobile hunting and gathering groups to sedentary societies made possible by the presence of an increasingly predictable food supply. When his limited food source was developed into a *surplus* food source, man began his cultural ascent. Even with speech to transmit culture, man had to have surplus food before he had any time for exploring the scope of possibilities. With a stable lifestyle and food reserves, he had time to investigate expanding potentials for making life both more comfortable and complex. Social organizations such as religion were born, as well as craft specialization, leading to ceramics and textiles. Although speech may be considered man's principal root of humanity, certainly abundant food supplies provided the capacity for expanding the meaning of being human.

The degree to which man has changed his domesticated plants and animals over a period of 12,000 years is striking. The ancestors of our domestic cattle produced less than 600 pounds of milk per year, whereas a modern dairy cow in North America may give up to 9,000 pounds per year. The progenitor of today's chicken laid about fifteen eggs in a clutch, while a contemporary, genetically engineered chicken lays about 220 eggs per year. Many domestic plants are now dependent on man for propagation. If man has so radically altered those organisms with which he has evolved in relatively recent times, has he remained unchanged in the process?

Although basic genetic changes are easily observed in populations of fruit flies or bacteria, evolutionary aspects of human populations are not so easily discerned. Anyone can observe that there are tremendous variations within our species, on almost every character imaginable, but how do these variations arise? They originate by the same mechanisms causing variation among any other organisms: mutation, recombination (of genes), isolation of population segments, and the resulting effects of natural selection. But where is the evidence that man is still evolving?

A classic example of a physical character which has been significantly changed over a relatively short period, one having a strong genetic component, is that of height, which has increased markedly in many parts of the world over the past thirty years. The most obvious answer might

5

seem to lie in better nutrition, both prenatally for the mother and post-natally for the developing child. This is, in fact, a part of the reason. However, research in human genetics suggests that at least half of the increase in human height is the result of a change in mating habits among the parents.

During the past fifty years, our communications and transportation have rapidly improved, so people are far more likely to encounter and marry individuals from distant areas. In previous times, a majority tended to marry within a much more distinct group, usually selecting mates from their hometown, or a nearby community. This is no longer the pattern, mates being chosen from a vastly greater number of possibilities and on different criteria.

Within sexually reproducing organisms, a phenomenon known as *heterosis,* or hybrid vigor, tends to operate, in which the offspring of individuals more genetically distinct tend to demonstrate characteristics often quite different from those of both parents. In a study on the genetic basis of increased height, the height of adults was shown to be significantly and *inversely* correlated to the degree of inbreeding in the geographical region. Man apparently has, by increasing his mobility, increased his height.

However, what seems paradoxical is that while the offspring of un-related individuals tend to be physically superior as the geographical origins of the parents become more remote, the possibility of fetal loss also is greater. It has been shown that as gene pools are mixed even within interethnic marriage, the intensity of natural selection increases. In a study of Caucasian groups, it was discovered that fetal loss increased 2.5–3.0 per cent for each additional country of birth tallied from the great grandparental generation. Conversely, a lower fetal loss was shown to exist for parents with fewer countries in their genetic background and a small distance between parental sites of birth.

A common North American frog, *Rana pipiens,* was found to evidence similar qualities. This species has a wide range, encompassing most of North America, and may be encountered in a variety of environments at both high and low altitudes. Although they are all considered to be of the same species, there are many genetically isolated races. When frogs from widely diverse habitats were brought together and bred, the surviving offspring were normal in form and development. However, as the distance separating the ranges of the parent frogs increased, the rate of development of the embryo slowed, and the number of morphological and developmental defects increased.

There may also be significant genetic variation within a limited geographic area. In Wales, it was found that women of Welsh descent are less fertile than non-Welsh women, a condition probably genetic in origin. Modern Welsh form the last of the Celtic fringe, the remnants of the earliest people in Britain. Culturally they are fairly intact, having retained their language, and they tend to marry within their own ethnic group, leading to some genetic isolation and, accordingly, a gene pool different from that of the contemporary English population as a whole.

There even appears to be more of a genetic basis for behavior than previously has been assumed. A study conducted in a San Francisco hospital indicates that Chinese-American newborns are generally steadier and calmer than European-American infants. Many significant covariables were controlled in the study, so there is good reason to believe that the observed behavior differences are based on genetic contribution.

That man is an actively evolving species is implicit in these demonstrated genetic variations, suggesting that he is still responding, through natural selection, differentially to various selective agents (environmental stressors). Our biological and cultural evolution has produced definite selective factors operative on the human gene pool, some of which are certain to influence profoundly the future of man.

Under ordinary conditions, mutations are constantly occurring within species, and most of them are harmful. Although many mutations are deleterious in the short run, they may be useful in the long run, or elsewhere. But unequivocably harmful mutations fall by the wayside, being eliminated at about the same rate at which they occur, allowing the 1.0 per cent or so that are beneficial to advance evolutionary progress.

The circumstances of our times are not ordinary, and harmful mutations are now occurring faster than they are being eliminated as our environment is flooded with potentially mutagenic agents, such as DDT, mercury, and radiation. Although individuals may suffer or die from exposure to these, the real danger, biologically speaking at any rate, lies in mutations that alter the genetic potential of future generations, usually for the worse. In this century, the mutagens pervading our environment have been multiplied countless times, exposing us to many thousands of alien substances, most of which have not been analyzed as to their physiological or long-term genetic effects.

These agents are assaulting us through our air, water, food, and other media. No one knows yet which ones are potentially the most dangerous,

7

since in many instances the means by which genetic damage is caused are unknown. But the damage is documented. The difficulty in defining the potential genetic effects of many agents, such as food additives, is that although within the body they may not cause harm in themselves, they may be metabolized into substances that do.

An inherent problem in assessing the genetic impact of this flood of pollutants hinges partially on the intrinsic nature of research. It takes time, especially if all variables and interactions are to be tested. There are just no means for investigating thoroughly the effects of all environmental contaminants at this stage.

Even from known facts, definitive conclusions may not always be drawn. Since 1948, the Atomic Bomb Casualty Commission has been evaluating the effects of radiation exposure in survivors of Hiroshima and Nagasaki. In a study of 70,000 children conceived *after* the explosions, of parents who were present within a significant radius of where the bombs were dropped, no unequivocal effects of radiation were found, there being no evidence of high percentages of birth defects or gross abnormalities. But chromosomal abnormalities were found in persons who were exposed to the blasts *in utero* and among those who were exposed at the age of thirty or older. A markedly smaller head circumference resulting in mental retardation was the principal deformity found among those individuals exposed *in utero*, a condition directly correlative to the degree of exposure. Among the adults, effects have been shown to be leukemogenic.

Although the genetic outcome of Hiroshima and Nagasaki is not as conclusive as might be anticipated, an indisputable fact is that the effects of radiation, as with numerous other mutagenic agents, are cumulative within the individual. While those first two explosions may not have left so deep a mark on the human genome, what of increased radiation since then, coming from a variety of sources? It has been estimated that by the year 2000, 60 per cent of our (United States) energy will be derived from nuclear reactor plants. Charles Hyder, an astrophysicist at the NASA Godard Installation in Albuquerque, says that the AEC has predicted the United States will have 1,000 nuclear plants by 2000 A.D. Plutonium is the biggest hazard. One pound could kill 9 billion people and a nuclear reactor plant requires at least two tons for operation. By 2020 A.D., the AEC predicts 24,000 operating nuclear plants. An accident probability of only one in a million would result in one accident every forty years, which for a nuclear plant is one too many. We do know that there is some leakage from presently operating plants and that when nuclear power becomes a common energy source, considerably more irradiation will be released into the environment. It is inevitable that an increasing quantity of radioactive materials in our environment will adversely affect the human genome. And of no small consequence is evidence that higher levels of radioactivity will reduce the atmosphere's protective ozone content, causing higher rates of skin cancers. It has also been suggested that were there ever a nuclear holocaust, ozone in the atmosphere would be so drastically depleted that man, along with numerous other species, would not survive.

Obviously, these are risky stakes in terms of man's genetic future as well as his present safety. This seems a rather high cost for energy. Radioactive and chemical contaminants pervading our environment are probably the most influential selective agents on populations today. Many are subtle in effect, far less spectacular than radiation, and yet they affect our genes. Caffeine, for example, has been shown to be mutagenic. Ubiquitous in many societies, being consumed through coffee, tea, and cola, it is a relatively mild offender in contrast with many, but still it does affect us to an unknown degree.

With environmental degradation increasing, accompanied and accentuated by the pressures of overpopulation, one cannot help but ponder the fate of man, questioning his future in the face of catapulting problems. Many have turned for an answer to the science of eugenics, the theoretical improvement of man through genetic control.

Eugenics itself is not a recent idea, although many present and futuristic applications of it are. The early geneticist Hermann Muller, who studied the effects of X rays on genes at the turn of the century, recognized man's potential for controlling his future. He thought principally in terms of positive eugenics, such as selective breeding to enhance the number of desired characteristics in offspring, and negative eugenics, selective breeding designed to minimize undesirable qualities. The rules for even this kind of genetic control depend necessarily on a kind of here-and-now utility, as the notion of superior qualities is subject to change. The Platonic forms of "ideal" truth, beauty, and functionality do not exist, nor does the ideal genotype.

Possibilities within the field of eugenics have advanced to include genetic transplants, cloning, genetic "mate" selection from a gamete bank, and genetic microsurgery, the actual changing of hereditary information. While these are mainly futuristic in terms of a general application, other forms of eugenics, such as genetic counseling, artificial insemination, abortion, family planning, and voluntary self-sterilization are already commonly practiced. The technology for mammalian cloning already exists, and we are probably just a step away from that needed for genetic microsurgery.

With the capacity for complex genetic control looming directly ahead, we are plagued with an insistent question: what is a "good" genotype? That is, how should we decide which has the maximal potential for long-term survival in a future when unknown factors may place a different order of priorities on survival mechanisms? Genetic engineering will no doubt reduce genetic diversity within man, and by so doing, will decrease man's capacity for coping with change. What is designed today, in all good faith, may prove a thousand years hence to be a genetic Edsel. But then it may be too late.

In discussing contemporary man's developing skills in controlling his present and future genetic makeup, it is worthwhile to consider a belief generated by our contemporary culture, one amazing in its naïveté and disconcerting in its ignorance of the nature of crises besetting us. This notion is that our technology holds the answers to all of our problems. It does not. In Garrett Hardin's classic paper, "The Tragedy of the Commons," he refers to a class of "no technical solution" problems with which Earth is being confronted in expanding numbers. But technology has become our opiate. Margaret Mead has aptly pointed out the fallacy of the popular concept of "Spaceship Earth," since our world is not merely another piece of technological apparatus designed to do man's bidding, but an organic, closed system, little understood and of tremendous complexity, within which we must operate.

Relying on sophisticated eugenics, such as genetic microsurgery and molecular engineering, to mold a better man when the world is so incredibly polluted and overpopulated seems at present little more than game-playing. Before any serious consideration can be given to man's theoretical genetic future, we must curb the human population explosion. It is quite real, and if effective solutions are not found, then much of the technology which might better man will have to be suspended, since it is very consumptive of energy. If the human population is not controlled, and some cataclysm were to extinguish most of us, still the species would probably survive, complete extinction being relatively difficult to accomplish. But then our genetic pathways would be radically different from those we are now traveling.

Our environmental-survival dilemma is of man's own making, being the logical culmination of his technological abuses coupled with an excessive population and the added disadvantage of inefficient and fre-

10

INTRODUCTION: A SYNOPSIS

quently self-serving political institutions. We must experience an immediate shift from man the user, consumer, and manipulator to man the custodian and guardian if we are to have even a token chance of turning midstream in our presently disastrous course. We acknowledge the need for a collective conscience as obligatory to the integration of technology, human values, and survival priorities.

Although man's genetic potential *can* be engineered, it is highly improbable that his survival as a species will be ensured by it. Man has been directing his own evolution through biofeedback with his environment and culture at an increasing rate ever since the agricultural revolution. And yet, his survival now is more threatened than ever before. Even were we to stake our survival on the science and technology of genetic engineering alone, billions of dollars in economic resources would be preempted in this pursuit.

The quality of man, like the quality of an ecosystem, lies in his diversity. Just as the diversity of the world's ecosystems has been diminished by the impact of human populations, so has man's survival capacity as a genetically diverse, sexually reproducing organism been lessened. If we wish to ensure a maximal diversity of our gene pool, then we must maximize our environments.

• It is impossible at present to speculate with much accuracy on the total impact of the genetic changes occurring in our polluted environment. For much of the world's population, the promise of quality living may have to be abandoned. The future of man, at least as he knows himself, is a most uncertain one, fraught with a myriad of pitfalls of his own making.

11

section

I

chapter

1

THE REALITY OF EVOLUTION

The authentic Garden of Eden was the primordial sea, filled with highly complex molecules of organic matter long before the existence of any form of life. Within this organic soup were amino acids, the essential constituents of protein molecules. When over about 1.5 billion years ago—probably half of geological time—these organic compounds began to replicate themselves, then that vague threshold beyond which life may be distinguished had been crossed.

From its beginning life has been evolving in structure and function as the earth has undergone the gradual but extensive changes responsible for the diversity of living things. If the earth were not a planet of continuously changing surface, then the predominant life-forms we know today surely never would have come into existence.

Through the accident of evolutionary success, an advanced primate evolved to the status of a being we know as man, an animal characterized by numerous qualities distinguishing him from other living things, even his close biological relations. Since it is man that perceives and defines himself, he is frequently given to the satisfying concept that his species represents an evolutionary apex, rather than merely a point in a continuing process. Yet in fact, contemporary man is probably being more rapidly molded by evolutionary pressures than were his predecessors, as he is not only subject to Darwinian natural selection, but has created, both intentionally and otherwise, a multiplying legion of factors affecting his genetic endowment.

In biological classification, man is a species, an entity once considered a securely distinct form. Presently, however, most biologists concede that species, as taxonomic categories, are much less distinct than had been assumed, and that the classification of organisms is more a convenient manner for providing systematic reference than a rigid system of definitions. The reason that organisms—including man—are so uncooperative with the aspirations of classical taxonomists is that they *are* continuously changing. There are relatively distinct aggregates of organisms, defined most accurately by similar genetic and somatic expression, which we accurately may call species, but any one of these, however slowly, is constantly altering.

The Evolutionary Process

Evolution, the result of the total biofeedback from the biological and physical environment, affecting the genetics, structure, and physiology of a species over time, is as integral a part of life as any other vital process. There is no such thing as a static species; the world is dynamic and there is no choice but to interact as efficiently as possible with a changing environment or to become extinct. Essentially, evolution entails the progression from a generalized to a more specialized form; organisms are involved in dynamic change *with* their environment. As Loren Eiseley put it, in *The Immense Journey*, "things are still coming ashore." And they always will be.

On considering evolution, there is an easy tendency to think in terms

16

of guiding or directing forces, a misconception distorting the nature of the evolutionary process. No organism has evolved toward its present form by design; what it is, and what it may evolve to be, lies in the genesis of a biological feedback system controlled by environmental and biological parameters. The origin and success of an organism are the results of chance, not foreplan.

Evolution is not a process affecting individuals, but the populations of individuals recognized collectively as species. Each individual, a unique being not exactly like any other, is what it is by virtue of its own genetic endowments (*genotype*) as environmentally expressed (*phenotype*). Even identical twins, more alike than most other individuals, are not precisely the same. Yet collectively, members of a species are comparably alike, having most of the components of their genotype in common, having a phenotypic expression that is similar, and reproducing individuals by sexual or asexual means that are like expressions of the total genetic-environmental feedback. Thus the species concept is validated as a working tool.

The impressive variety found both within and among species is primarily a result of the phenomenon of sexual reproduction, whereby the hereditary material constituting the basis for variation and the evolutionary process undergoes scrambling—or recombination by *genes*, by whole *chromosomes* (the larger hereditary units of cells containing most of the genetic information), or their parts—in the formation of *gametes* (reproductive cells), so that each draw in the genetic lottery is potentially different from every other. The probability of two individuals possessing exactly the same traits is so small as to be statistically irrelevant. Because there is so much variation within a species, there exist great possibilities for variation within its components—populations—providing that sexual reproduction and random mating occur.

Natural Selection

The most popularized aspect of evolution is natural selection, which effects differential reproduction among individual members of a population. The result of natural selection is seen in the net response of the population to pressures of selection from the total biological and physical environment in which the organism lives. This response can be measured as a change in the distribution of hereditarily determined (genetic) traits in that population. The concept was employed by Darwin to present his theories of evolution to an unreceptive public, and resulted in the misleading popularization of "the survival of the fittest." In some respects, it is true that natural selection is the survival of the fittest, but only in terms of species survival. Nor does it suggest a "struggle to survive," in any conscious sense. In an evolutionary perspective, the adapted or "surviving" individual is the one who leaves progeny to contribute to the continuation of the species, and does not in any way refer to the striving of an individual, but only to its reproductive success. Natural selection may enable a species and the population(s) composing it to accommodate to changing conditions, in which those individuals most able to cope with environmental stresses are the

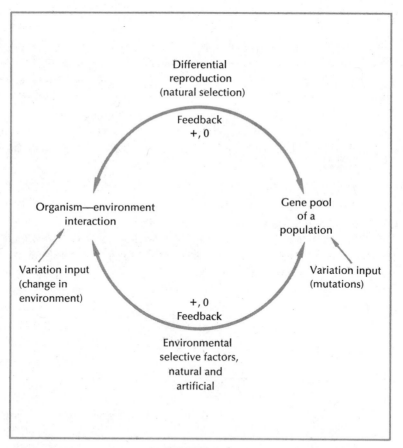

FIGURE 1–1

Simplified biofeedback interactions between the organism, its gene pool, and its environment. Note that feedback may be either positive, negative, or neutral.

18

ones most likely to produce offspring and therefore to survive evolutionarily. In essence, natural selection is the differential reproduction of different *genotypes*. In the true Darwinian sense of survival, someone of average or low intelligence, perhaps with a genetic deformity or two, who produces nine fertile children, is more "successful" than a genius in perfect health who leaves none.

There are four major aspects of the evolutionary process which must be understood in our discussion of human evolution: *natural selection, mutation, recombination,* and *isolation. Natural selection,* the adaptive population response of the survival of individual members best able to cope with the total environment, structures organisms through biological and physical pressures, and also structures relationships between species, sometimes enhancing the survival potential of members of these interactions. Natural selection cannot by itself induce evolution since there must be mechanisms for altering the genetic information between succeeding generations. Otherwise, when selective pressures prove too severe, a population would lack potentially adaptive genetic information and possibly die off instead of producing individuals able to cope with the new stresses. All that is really adaptive for the species is the gene frequency, the differential distribution of individual genes and gene combinations in the population.

Sources of Individual Variation

New genetic information must arise from the individual members of a population. By what mechanisms does such new and potentially adaptive information arise? One of these mechanisms is *mutation*, those changes in the genetic information transmitted to cells, which introduces alterations in the transmission of hereditary instructions. Mutations are occurring constantly, both spontaneously and as a result of a variety of inducing agents, but the great majority (99 per cent) are deleterious or productive of irrelevant changes. The majority of spontaneous mutations are probably recurrent in each generation and are either rejected or accepted into a population's *gene pool* (the summation of its individual genetic contributions) depending on whether or not, at any given time, the mutations are advantageous. By the persistent occurrence of mutations, a given population of organisms is provided with new genetic degrees of freedom and solutions for adapting to an evolving environment through a potential increase in the variability of the gene pool.

Individuals also contribute to the variation observed in the popula-

19

TABLE 1-1

Rates of Spontaneous Mutations

Organism	Mutations per Locus on the Chromosome per Million Somatic Cells or Gametes per Generation
Bacteria (*E. coli*)	0.001–10
Corn	1–100
Fruit fly	0.1–10
Man	1–100
Mouse	8–11
Viruses	0.001–100

From *Heredity, Evolution and Society* by I. Michael Lerner. W. H. Freeman and Company. Copyright © 1968.

tion belonging to their species in yet another way. *Recombination,* the mixing of genes or whole chromosomes into a variety of genotypes, rivals mutation as a source of diversity and accompanying evolutionary potential. A mutation produces changes in existing genes, whereas recombination causes a reorganization of them, by three distinct means. There may be a gene combination containing two different *alleles,* alternative expressions of a gene unit of the same gene. Or, a random mixing of chromosomes from the two parents' gametes may create a new individual. And there may be a mixing of a particular allele with genes not previously in contact with it by a physical exchange during *meiosis,* or gamete formation.

Recombination is often thought of as being important only in contributing to variation in the formation of gametes of potential individuals, but there are ways in which the process can act as a natural selective agent on *existing* variation as well as being a source of variation itself. An example of recombination as a selective agent in human populations, one which may prove to have an increasingly direct effect on the quality of our lives, is *infectious drug resistance,* a phenomenon that has been accelerating with the use of antibiotics. In 1955, a woman returned to Japan from Hong Kong with a case of particularly persistent dysentery. When isolated, the disease was shown to be caused by a bacterium of the genus *Shigella,* but had demonstrated resistance to four powerful drugs: sulfanilamide, streptomycin, chloramphenicol, and tetracycline. Thereafter an outbreak of dysentery, exhibiting the same resistant characteristics, swept through Japan. In 1959, Tomoichuro Akiba of Tokyo University deduced from characteristics of the bacterium that its resistance to the four drugs might have been transferred from an already multiply resistant *Escherichia coli*, a common bacteria within the human intestinal tract. Research bore him out, showing that the harmless *E. coli* with the aid of a virus had passed its quality of drug resistance to the dysentery bacterium in genetic recombination. This occurred in about twenty-four hours, a much shorter period than would have been required for the resistance to occur from new mutations (Watanabe 1967).

The implications of infectious drug resistance as a selective agent on human populations are disturbing in a world where the use of potent antibiotics has become a commonplace means for dealing with everything from a slight cold to fattening cattle. In many countries, mixing antibiotics with stock feeds has become routine. This procedure protects the animals from infectious diseases and promotes fattening. However, it has been shown that the use of antibiotics in livestock serves as a strong artificial selective agent favoring those microorganisms possessing drug-resistant factors, especially *Salmonella*, a genus of bacterium including a species which causes typhoid fever. When these animals are consumed by humans, the resistance factors are carried on to man in the bacteria-contaminated meat, and recombination of the resistant forms with the harmless *E. coli* occurs in his intestine. If the nonmedical use of antibiotics and synthetic drugs is not discontinued, we may ultimately be in danger of arriving at a point where antibiotics have lost their effectiveness and many disease-causing bacteria will acquire the capacity to resist available drugs.

Hybridization

Another facet of recombination as a source of potential variation highly relevant to the cultures of man is *hybridization*, defined by Stebbins, an eminent evolutionist, as the crossing between populations having different *adaptive gene complexes*. Any species, including those potentially involved in hybridization, has a complete genetic complement that enables it to survive under the summation of the selective pressures of its environment; thus, its genes are adaptive. Hybridization often results in an increase in the total potential adaptiveness of the new genetic entity, the *hybrid*, and thereby increases its survival value. Although there are other definitions of hybridization, this one is the most meaningful in

21

the context of evolution. It may involve populations of a particular species, or distinct species separated by isolating factors. When hybridization occurs, it usually results in offspring exhibiting most characteristics of the parents, and a few new ones as well. For the most part, the new adaptive gene complex of a hybrid progeny is inferior to the parents. But there may be a few individuals—one in a hundred, or perhaps one in a thousand—possessing an overall genetic superiority to the parental generation. These hybrids, as with the less than 1.0 per cent of beneficial mutations, are likely to survive and pass on their genetic content to succeeding generations, whereas the remaining 99 per cent, especially in environments identical to those from which the parents come, will fare poorly.

Usually under natural conditions, there are strong selective factors against the success of any hybrid population. First, as a result of incomplete gene or chromosome pairing in reproduction, the offspring of most hybrid animal crosses are totally or partially sterile so the possibility of segregating offspring from them is severely limited. But often plant hybrids are less restricted in their reproductive viability, and new plant species commonly arise in this way. Second, genotypes found even in the second generation of a cross from broadly different parents are highly variant, reducing the possibility that a superior hybrid will continue to breed true. For a hybrid to be successful under natural conditions, there must be a biological space (*niche*) available into which it fits better than either parent, total fertility must be restored without affecting the new gene combinations, and the new combinations must be constant enough to stabilize in nature.

With the beginning of man's cultural evolution, the *intraspecific* (within the species) hybridization of animals and *interspecific* (between species) as well as intraspecific hybridization of plants became integral tactics in his agricultural methods. Today, whether it took thousands of years or only the few required by modern knowledge of genetics, there are few widespread crops or stocks that are not the result of some sort of hybrid crossing. Earlier men unwittingly hybridized by choosing desired individuals for breeding; contemporary man does the same thing, aided by a vastly greater reservoir of information.

Response of Populations to Natural Selection: Adaptation

Populations respond to the pressures of natural selection by specific adaptations that can be measured in the frequency of heritable characters in that population. Selection is essentially anything that produces systematic heritable change in a population from one generation to those succeeding it. Following chapters discuss selection pressures operating on contemporary human populations, a principal focus of this book. Adaptations by populations to natural selective pressures may be the result of three types of selection: stabilizing, directional, and disruptive. *Stabilizing selection* favors the average phenotype of the mean environmental expression of the genetic constitution and selects against the extremes of that mean expression. *Directional selection* favors a phenotype not at the present mean of expression in the population and results in a shift, in time, in the mean. *Disruptive selection* favors phenotypes removed from the mean expression at a given time, and these new expressions form new means in the old population. All of these mechanisms of selection may operate within human populations.

Mechanisms of natural selection may wield change through the pressures of predation, climate, food supply, and other facets of biological and physical environmental stress. Man's pollutants, now pervading the biosphere, comprise physical selective factors affecting a myriad of life-forms, including man himself. But the results of these new stresses are not always readily observed, except, for example, in the DDT induced extinction of various species. A case in which adaptive success to severe stress *can* be seen is that of the Mediterranean fruit fly (*Drosophila melanogaster*), the victim of an extensive poisoning program directed against its proliferation when it began to enjoy explosive success in American fruit orchards. DDT, the use of which is now restricted in the United States, was sprayed from airplanes and distributed in other ways, to the detriment of an unknowable number of harmless and beneficial animals. The poisoning program may have endangered a few species of birds, but it *did* cause the development of a hardier fruit fly! The reproductive cycle of fruit flies occurs in a matter of days, and although the initial poisoning siege seemed to be eliminating the *Drosophila*, there were some mutations present for resistance to the effects of DDT. When the flies not having such resistance had died out, the only ones remaining were the DDT-immune individuals, which bred and passed on their capacity to cope with DDT to succeeding generations. The battle waged through poisons proved to be primarily a victory for the fruit flies. Projections of what man's outcome under this genre of stressors may be are considered in Chapter 4.

One of the first clues that man himself could create selective pressures as a result of his cultural activity came from a long-term study of the peppered moth, *Biston betularia* (Kettlewell 1958). Here is a classic example of an adaptive population phenomenon resulting from natural selection through a union of predation and man's industrial pollution. *Biston betularia* is found in northern Europe and North America. In 1848, about 1 per cent of this species' population exhibited melanism, a degree of dark pigmentation. The others were patterned in a light mottling that blended in with the lichen-covered trees of forests characteristically inhabited by the moths. Yet by 1898, 99 per cent were melanistic; only 1 per cent retained the original coloration. Why would a species, in what is evolutionarily a relatively short period, shift to a color possessed previously by a negligible percentage of the population?

In this case, the answer was found to lie in the effects of industrial pollution. During the mid 1800s, as the western world, and particularly England, began to experience industrialization and its accompanying pollution, certain organisms readily exhibited reactions to the changing atmosphere. Lichens are sensitive indicators of air quality, and in industrialized areas they succumbed to pollution, leaving the trunks of trees covered with dead lichens and soot. The pale moths, which had formerly blended into their background of grey lichens, stood out clearly in the altered environment, their contrasting bodies an invitation to hungry birds. The invitation was accepted, as diurnal birds hunting by sight easily picked off the undisguised moths. But the small number of

---

TABLE 1–2

Effects of Predation by Birds on the Peppered Moth *Biston Betularia*

	Light Form	Dark Form	Total
Nonindustrial area—1955 Dorset, England; vegetation not polluted by smoke.			
Released	496	473	969
Recaptured	62	30	92
Per cent recovery	12.5	6.3	9.5
Industrial area—1953 Burmingham, England; vegetation polluted by smoke			
Released	137	447	584
Recaptured	18	123	141
Per cent recovery	13.1	27.5	24.1

After H. B. D. Kettlewell (1956), *Heredity*, 9: 323–342; 10: 287–301.

---

melanistic individuals merged into the darkened tree trunks, and in time few members of the population retained the original color. The species was virtually saved by the presence of a single dominant gene for melanism. The reality of this conjecture was affirmed by the behaviorists Kettlewell and Tinbergen, who carefully observed differential predation on the two color variants of *Biston*. Motion pictures were also taken, illustrating that birds would invariably eat the lichen-colored moths and would frequently ignore melanistic ones only an inch or two away. Man, of course, is not subject to selection to any degree by predator-prey relationships unless one counts disease and one's fellow man among predators, but he is subject to a variety of selective pressures created by his culture.

Origin of Species

A classic question of evolutionists is, how does a population that has made a successful adaptive response to natural selective pressures become a discrete species? And how does a population that has achieved species status become further differentiated, enabling it to make additional adaptive responses to its environment, resulting in further speciation? These questions are better answered if we first consider what the general characteristics of a species might be.

As with man, all biological species possess a discrete complement of genes that are expressed in population characteristics. In many species, and especially man, these regional gene complexes are connected by interbreeding of populations. Population gene complexes are isolated to some degree from others by biological, behavioral, geographical or, in man, cultural mechanisms. The effectiveness of isolation mechanisms determines the degree of biological and systematic integrity of the species. In man's speciation, culture overcomes these barriers, leading to minimal isolation of population gene complexes and the biological integrity of a single species, *Homo sapiens*. The populations of man (races) have indistinct boundaries, and further speciation within the species is arrested by cultural and genetic infusion among populations. Another criterion of a biological species is that each occupies a niche not utilized exactly by any other species. In man, this niche is defined increasingly by his culture. Finally, a species is not static, both genetically and evolutionarily, but dynamic, as a result of mutation, recombination, and the continuous adaptive responses to a changing environment. It must be realized that the potential for further differentiation and specia-

FIGURE 1–2

Life on earth began in the sea, made a slow adaptation to expanding land masses, and eventually was manifest in the earliest terrestrial form—reptiles —from which arose mammals and, of recent arrival, man.

tion exists within every species, providing the barriers to gene exchange break down. When genetic isolation does occur, new potentially adaptive gene complexes may increase in frequency in the population, resulting in subsequent differentiation. When populations of the same species become separated, changes are manifested among them because of the genetic isolation. If a small population has been geographically isolated from the parent population for some reason, then the *potential* for variation is reduced because the group is limited in the introduction of new genetic material. Isolation is an important mechanism by which marked differences arise in formerly identical populations. The Galápagos Islands, a small archipelago west of Ecuador, host an array of isolated and highly specialized populations of birds and reptiles descended from species whose ancestors originated on the South American

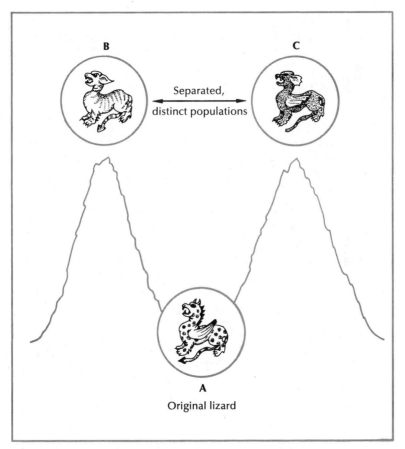

FIGURE 1–3

If the population of any species were to be isolated through the erection of geographic barriers, the separated groups would eventually become dissimilar to the point of breeding incompatibility. For example, if a population of high mountain-dwelling lizards existing within a continuous range were fractionalized by geologic changes separating the range, the formerly single species would in time become two or more, depending on the number of isolated populations arising.

mainland. Darwin's first major text on species origin was profoundly inspired by what he observed there. But speciation can occur in much less spectacular fashion. For example, a population of mountain-dwelling lizards, over a long period, may be divided by erosive forces separating a formerly continuous range. No longer able to share genes, the lizards would, over time, become increasingly dissimilar until finally, even were individuals from the separated groups to be reunited, they would no longer be capable of interbreeding.

The most impressive historical isolations were caused by the phenomenon of *continental drift*, the movement and subsequent separation of continental masses (see Colbert 1972). Geologists and physicists were long opposed to any theories challenging continental fixedness, but biological and geological evidence supporting continental drift is overwhelmingly in its favor, particularly when one considers the fossil records from the Triassic, Permian, and Pennsylvanian periods. These geologic drifts caused a great many populations to become separated from others with which they formerly had genetic continuity, thus affecting broad avenues of evolutionary direction.

Climate is also an effective isolating factor, since few animals are as adaptive as man in coping with a variety of external environments. For example, most reptiles, being unable to internally regulate their body temperatures, are restricted to relatively warm areas. Everywhere climate is in some way a limiting factor, restricting populations and affecting

---

TABLE 1-3

Isolating Mechanisms

---

1. Spatial isolation.
2. Genetic isolation.
   a. External reproductive isolation.
      i. Ecologic—mates do not meet.
      ii. Ethologic—mates do not meet.
      iii. Morphologic—mates meet but gametes are not transferred.
   b. Internal reproductive isolation.
      i. Gametes die—no fertilization.
      ii. Zygote dies—no implantation; spontaneous abortion.
   c. Postreproductive isolation.
      i. Hybrid progeny sterile—no gametes produced.
      ii. Hybrid progeny shows reduced reproductive viability.
      iii. Hybrid progeny's gametes incompatible with those of the parent gene pool.

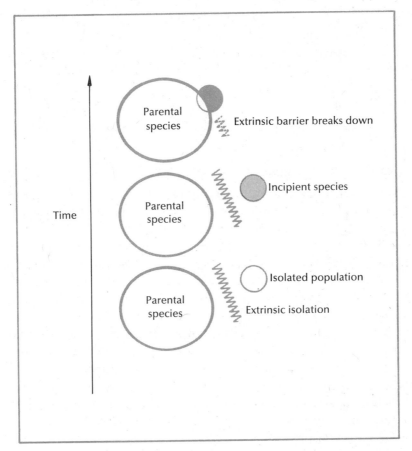

FIGURE 1-4

The role of geographic or behavioral isolation in the formation of species. When the external barrier breaks down, the isolated population (called an incipient or potential species) may merge again with the parent population as has been the case with the races of man. If the time-space isolation has progressed sufficiently, the incipient species may be genetically distinct from the parent species and gene exchange between the two may not occur after the breakdown of the extrinsic isolation barrier.

(After Terrell H. Hamilton, *Process and Pattern in Evolution*, New York, Macmillan Publishing Co., Inc., 1967.)

their form and development. Bergman's rule, which states that within a given race of warm-blooded animals, individuals farther from the equator *tend* to be larger, is illustrative of the shaping force of climatological variation. This rule has exceptions, but generally it has some validity. There is an advantage for a warm-blooded animal in a cooler climate to have less surface area per unit of weight, as this promotes heat conservation, and an increase in size will accomplish this. Over time, if segments of a given tropical race migrate far enough away from the equator, they will eventually become unlike those individuals remaining in warmer climes, as a result of physiological and morphological adaptation.

Culture As an Isolating Factor

Man has both consciously and unconsciously created means, which are shared by no other animal, for genetically isolating himself from other groups of his species. His culture, and the concomitant phenomenon of language (even among some other species vocal communication barriers are important) are more effective in isolating man than most geographical or climatic barriers because culture has allowed him to circumvent numerous obstacles imposed on other species. Although the effects of mass communication and increased mobility have accelerated a disintegration of some cultural boundaries, many are still pertinent.

Before this loosening of cultural restrictions, most people tended to marry within their own ethnic group and within a small radius of their hometown, causing the potential gene pool to be far more limited than it is today. Only a tiny fraction married into groups of varying racial, linguistic, and ethnic character. So the genetic possibilities were as limited, or more so in some cases, as if different groups had been separated by continents. Cultural sanctions are powerful restrictive forces, and have surely been a significant factor in molding the races of man.

In India, the caste system has long maintained severe restrictions among groups within the same culture. Hindu philosophy attributes character and abilities to one's forefathers, so the caste system is an attempt to keep individuals within their pre-ordained station in life. It also serves to isolate genetically subgroups within the population, as there is little probability of anyone from a higher caste wishing to marry someone from a low caste, or being allowed to do so (Dobzhansky 1973). Although this discriminatory and devitalizing system has been outlawed in India, it is still very much in effect. Operative legislation against deeply ingrained cultural practices is an extremely difficult undertaking, characterized more often than not by a superficial acquiescence hiding the continued practice of outlawed customs. These sorts of cultural isolation mechanisms are present to some degree in all societies.

Language, a unique facet of human culture, distinct and relevant to our development, has been an important isolating factor, causing by its prodigious diversity barriers between cultural groups in all parts of the world. In many respects, language determines the tone of a culture; by the existence of many languages and dialects, cultural diversity is heightened, but so also is genetic isolation.

A variety of other examples might be employed to demonstrate the genetic significance of isolation. Any barriers of time and space, whether physical or cultural, resulting in the prevention of breeding between different populations or subgroups within a population, will eventually lead to an increasing distinction between the separated groups. Man himself is not immune from this, as can be observed readily in the variety of geographical racial types composing the human species. There are many other aspects of the evolutionary process, more relevant to nonhuman populations, which will not be considered here, such as predator-prey relations, mimicry, other agonistic adaptive phenomena, and adaptive radiation of populations in relation to food source. For reading in these areas, consult Stebbins or any other of the evolution texts suggested at the end of this chapter. It is the aim of this text to focus on those mechanisms structuring the adaptations of human populations.

Base Line for Measuring Evolution

For many years before and after Darwin, evolution could be inferred only from measurements of past diversity in the fossil record and from existing diversity in contemporary populations. There was certain evidence of continuous change in extinct and extant species, but no means for measuring this change in present populations. If one assumes that evolution operates in the presence of mutation, recombination, natural selection, and gene flow, what sort of model could be established for the theoretical population in which these factors were absent and no evolution occurred? Such a model represents a steady state population. It assumes that all individual members have the opportunity to mate at random, or that the population in its reproduction is *panmictic*. Panmixis is rare in most biological populations and is unknown in human populations. The unchanging gene pool—the summation of the genes in that population at a given time—in the absence of mutation, recombination, natural selection, and new gene input comes to an equilibrium state. Genotypic equilibrium for a particular heritable character exists in the population when the two alternative expressions of the same gene

31

(alleles) *a* and *a′* occur in the individuals of the population in combinations *aa*, *aa′*, and *a′a′* and in the frequencies *a* = *x* and *a′* = *y*. The Hardy-Weinberg rule defines the relationship between allele frequencies and zygotic proportions.

This equilibrium is a theoretical statistical phenomenon and can be expressed by the expansion of a binomial, such as

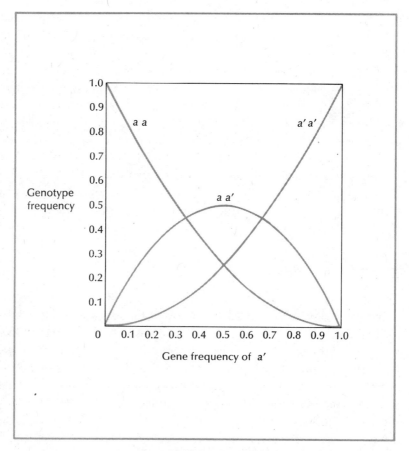

FIGURE 1–5

Theoretical relationship between genotype frequency and gene frequency for two alleles in Hardy-Weinberg equilibrium. Such a situation rarely exists in natural populations as they are subject to continuous selection, mutation, recombination, and gene elimination, as well as potential spatial and behavioral isolation.

(After D. S. Falconer, *Introduction to Quantitative Genetics*, New York, Ronald Press, 1960.)

$$(x + y) = 1 = x^2 + 2xy + y^2.$$

The maximal value for allele sets aa, here represented by x^2, is 0.25, as it is for $a'a'$ represented by y^2. When like allele sets are expressed in the same genotype, they are called *homozygotic*, which denotes contributions by like gametes. The maximal value for allele set aa' (the genotype) is 0.50. This allele set represents different alleles of the same gene expressed in the same genotype and is termed *heterozygous*, denoting contributions by unlike gametes.

While such equilibria can be demonstrated for some traits in human populations, especially in blood groups, for many traits they cannot be shown. The reason is simply that natural selective pressures, spontaneous and induced mutations, recombinations within and between genotypes, and cultural isolative factors disrupt the equilibrium. Hardy-Weinberg describes only a base line situation in which there is *no* evolution. It is not our intent to describe theoretical population genetics of man. These topics have been treated extensively elsewhere. What is presented in the following chapters is a consideration of contemporary and future evolution in human populations with an examination of those selective pressures, both natural and man-created, that are acting to shape the evolving populations of man.

Diversity

We may assume that no form of life is a stable entity, destined to remain forever as it now exists. The influence of natural selection, acting through genetic isolation, mutation, and recombination, will continue its kaleidoscopic effect on the biosphere, a realm of perpetual change. Those species failing to cope adequately with the exigencies of environmental stresses will die out and be replaced by organisms more suited to contend with new conditions. As long as there is genetic diversity and a changing biosphere, their interactions will result in evolutionary change; nothing is static. This includes man, who from his lofty tower of anthropocentric perception tends to look upon himself, for reasons cultural or religious, as exempt from the evolutionary principles affecting other organisms. Although the phenomenon of his culture has affected the course of his evolution, and may have an even more profound effect in the future, he will continue to be a product of organic evolution. Man is not immune to the action of environmental stressors—including those of his own making—and it is by no means inconceivable that before the total annihilation of life on earth, he will be replaced by some more adaptive—and perhaps more sensible—form of life, either through his own evolution, or as the result of his ultimate extinction.

Suggested Readings

Avers, Charlotte J. *Evolution*. New York: Harper and Row, Publishers, 1974.

Colbert, Edwin H. "Antarctic Fossils and the Reconstruction of Gondwanaland." *Natural History* 81 (1972): 66–73.

Dobzhansky, Theodosius. *Genetic Diversity and Human Equality*. New York: Basic Books, Inc., 1973.

Eaton, Theodore H. *Evolution*. New York: W. W. Norton & Company, Inc., 1970.

Ehrlich, Paul R., and Richard W. Holm. *The Process of Evolution*. New York: McGraw-Hill Book Company, 1963.

Eiseley, Loren. *The Immense Journey*. New York: Random House, Inc., 1957.

Grobstein, Clifford. *The Strategy of Life*. San Francisco: W. H. Freeman & Co., 1974.

Hamilton, Terrell H. *Process and Pattern in Evolution*. New York: Macmillan Publishing Co., Inc., 1967.

Hendrickson, Walter B. "An Illinois Scientist Defends Darwinism: A Case Study in the Diffusion of Scientific Theory." *Transactions of the Illinois State Academy of Sciences* 65 (1972): 25–29.

Kettlewell, H. B. D. "A Survey of the Frequencies of *Biston betularia* (Lep.) and Its Melanic Forms in Britain." *Heredity* 12 (1958): 51–72.

Lerner, Michael I. *Heredity, Evolution, and Society*. San Francisco: W. H. Freeman & Company, 1968.

Mayr, Ernst. *Populations, Species, and Evolution*. Cambridge, Mass.: The Belknap Press of Harvard University Press, 1970.

Miller, Stanley L., and Leslie E. Orgel. *The Origins of Life on Earth*. Englewood Cliffs, N.J.: Prentice-Hall, Inc., 1974.

Pianka, Eric R. *Evolution Ecology*. New York: Harper and Row, Publishers, 1974.

Savage, Jay M. *Evolution*. 2nd ed. New York: Holt, Rinehart, and Winston, Inc., 1969.

Stebbins, G. Ledyard. *Processes of Organic Evolution*. 2nd ed. Englewood Cliffs, N.J.: Prentice-Hall, Inc., 1971.

Vermeij, Gurat J. "Biological Versatility and Earth History." *Proceedings of the National Academy of Sciences, USA* 70 (1973): 1936–1938.

Watanabe, Tsutomu. "Infectious Drug Resistance." *Scientific American* 217 (1967): 19–27.

chapter

2

EVOLUTION OF MAN

Conjecturing on the point at which our prehominid ancestor became *man* is a pastime more suitable to philosophers than to evolutionists, as it is a question dealing essentially with semantics rather than relevant aspects of our evolutionary history. There is no particular demarcating line in our evolutionary past at which man's predecessor transcended its animal qualities to achieve a unique status, even though this notion is fostered either directly or indirectly even by some biologists and anthropologists. Although man is unique in numerous fascinating respects, so are many other animals. Cultural evolution, setting man distinctly apart from other animals, is a function of increased interactions with material artifacts and language, which also resulted in greater brain volume. As a species, man continues to be a product of organic evolution.

The Development of Evolutionary Thought

When Charles Darwin (1809–1882) published *The Origin of Species* in 1859 (see reference in Chapter 9), his ideas met with derision even by the scientific community because they were in opposition to the teachings of a uniformly religious culture. It was disturbing enough to consider his claims that life had not always been as it then existed, but of greatest impact was his assertion that man himself was an evolving, changing organism, a revelation challenging the accepted belief that man was an entity completely distinct from other animals, created in the image of a supreme God. Religious men did not like the concept of God resembling an orangutan or chimpanzee.

One of the more widespread misconceptions generated when Darwin published *The Descent of Man* in 1871 is that man descended from a monkey. What Darwin *did* claim is that man evolved from a hominoid; he did not evolve from a monkey or any other extant primate, as they are themselves the products of evolution, and many are structurally more specialized than man. We comprise a fascinating species in that a predominant feature, an enlarged brain (primarily the cerebral cortex), ultimately permitted man to reach his present cultural and intellectual condition and apparently set him apart from other animals. Along with a few skeletal modifications this is all that distinguishes him from modern primates. In many other respects, man is relatively generalized.

Although Darwin is sometimes credited with originating the concept of evolution, he was not the first person to realize that life had undergone changes in arriving at its present forms. The Greeks believed in the transition of organisms from an aquatic to a terrestrial existence. However, Aristotle (384–322 B.C.), whose influence on categorization of natural history phenomena has persisted until the present, was not a believer in evolution, and his views served as a major inhibition to the growth of evolutionary thought. Later medieval philosophers' speculations revolved around the moral nature of man, while progress in scientific thought floated in a limbo of repression. But Charles Darwin's own grandfather, Erasmus Darwin (1731–1802), speculated on the reality of evolution, believing that all life originated from a single source. His thinking no doubt influenced that of his grandson. The French biologist Georges Buffon (1707–1778) suggested an evolutionary process accomplished by the inheritance of acquired characteristics, and Jean Baptiste de Lamarck (1744–1829) put forth the first comprehensive theory of evolution, also placing importance on the inheritance of acquired characteristics, a process that does not in fact occur. Even Darwin's main thesis, that of evolution by the means of natural selection, had been suggested by at least three pre-Darwinian authors, all of whom Darwin had read: Edward Blythe and Patrick Mathew, who were British, and Charles Wells, an American. Their ideas were flawed, but nonetheless must have had an effect on Darwin's postulations.

The reason for Darwin's fame is that he was the first man to describe accurately the process of natural selection, detailing it in his lengthy treatise on species origin which was published at a time when the intellectual climate of England and the rest of Europe was becoming increasingly receptive to the fact of evolution. Another naturalist, Alfred Russell Wallace (1823–1913), arrived at a theory of evolution via natural selection at about the same time and independently of Darwin, but he did not produce so detailed an analysis. One reason that it was becoming increasingly difficult for scientists to scoff at evolution was that with the industrialization of England and a subsequent mining for coal, rich fossil beds were discovered. These findings were countered somewhat by the *catastrophists* who claimed that fossils were the remains of animals killed off during certain catastrophes in the earth's geologic past. Their reasoning, however, dissipated under the pressure of an accumulating fossil record demonstrating a logical progression of forms.

Even the conceptualizations of these two brilliant naturalists were somewhat tangled in the webs of ethnocentrism and religious dogma. Darwin believed that man had arisen by means of the same natural principles involved in the development of any species, but he harbored a certain scorn for primitive cultures, believing that such people were far inferior to Europeans in intellect and several levels lower in the evolutionary progression. Wallace disagreed with this, spurning so ethnocentric a viewpoint. Although he maintained that all races of men were basically intellectual equals, at the same time he excluded man from his otherwise logical scheme of evolution because he perceived him as an immutable and divine creation. This sort of dichotomous thinking is difficult to understand in terms of our contemporary perspective, but during the time of Wallace and Darwin, evolutionary thought had begun only an incipient advance. It is not surprising that even thoughtful scientists chose to cling to certain archaic doctrines.

Darwin was unable to explain the cause of the tremendous variation in biological organisms because he knew little about heredity, although he made many observations on hybridization of plants and animals. It is often suggested that the answer to the mechanism of hereditary variation was provided by Gregor Mendel (1822–1884), a Czechoslovakian monk, from his studies on *particulate inheritance* (single gene-determined characters), but this is not entirely true. Mendel's ideas were unknown to Darwin and were rediscovered by the geneticists Correns, DeVries, and Tschermak in 1900. This rediscovery did not, however, lend immediate support to the theory of evolution, but placed it in some doubt. It took the cumulative studies of the ensuing sixty years—in basic descriptive, biochemical, and population genetics—to support fully the correlation between variation in natural populations and its basis in particulate inheritance. The reason for a lack of immediate complementation of the two ideas was that Mendel had studied characters, such as tall and dwarf pea plants, which, as differences between populations, are rather uncommon. Most of the characters that are expressed as variations between natural populations are determined not by single gene expressions, but by whole complexes of genes. Ultimately the resolution of this apparent but unreal conflict came through a more complete understanding of the complex relationships between genes, manifest characters, and their expression in biological populations.

The Rise of Man

Despite repression of the growth of knowledge, evolutionary thought gained credence, and today no reputable scientist would deny the evolutionary strategy in regard to man or any other organisms, whatever he might believe the reasons behind the process to be. An extensive fossil record indicating that organisms have changed gradually in form leaves no room for valid objections. Although the fossil record of man is not as complete as it hopefully will be one day, there is more than ample evidence to illustrate the ascent of modern man from a protohuman primate. What, then, were the conditions giving rise to the primates and eventually modern man?

In the Jurassic period, when the insects and flowering plants known as angiosperms evolved together, the aspect of the world underwent major changes. A landscape dominated by ferns, cycads, and gymnosperms gave way to one of seed-bearing trees and other angiosperms more similar to those with which we are familiar today. Then during the Paleocene, about 70 million years ago, as the new lines of mammals were becoming differentiated, certain groups began living in these trees, a lifestyle probably offering more protection. Their interactions with the angiosperms caused a selection for plants with seeds offering better food sources. As

FIGURE 2–1

Modern tree shrews, *Tupaia*, are reminiscent of the supposed insectivorous progenitors of man and other primates.

the animals eating seeds assisted in their dispersal, an exchange evolved initiating the development of fruits, which today are important in the diet of many animals, especially primates.

One group of these early mammals, primarily insectivorous and differing little from others of the initial mammalian stock, developed characteristics distinguishing them as primates. These small, quick, and curious animals, superiorly competitive despite their relatively small size, profited from an omnivorous inclination, devouring the angiosperms' developing food sources as well as insects and probably small reptiles. An opportunistic diet is still characteristic of most primate species, few of which are entirely herbivorous, but none of which are strictly carnivorous. The tree shrews (*Tupaia*), which *may be* the most primitive of existing primates, are illustrative in many ways of their progenitors of 70 million years ago and bear more resemblance to a large shrew or peculiar rodent than to any popular stereotypes of man's relations.

In their adaptation to an arboreal existence, our dawn antecedents began to acquire characteristics marking an inchoate step toward the evolution of man. For a successful life in the trees, innovations in structure and function were subject to natural selection, as the requirements for survival had changed. Among most terrestrial mammals, the sense of smell is a predominant one, but an arboreal habitat demands selection for the development of acute vision. Stereoscopic vision, which allows for increased depth perception, evolved as olfactory senses declined. There was probably a rapid selection for stereoscopic vision, because a young animal moving through a forest canopy with frequent misjudgments of depth perception would be less likely to survive and produce a progeny than one better equipped for coping with a gymnast's existence. One long fall could be a strongly negative selective factor. For the enhancement of stereoscopic vision, a rotation of the eyes to the front of the skull was beneficial, as was the reduction of snout size so that it would not interfere with forward vision. Although man's ancestors ultimately descended from the trees, many features of their arboreal life have been retained, including the nature of vision and the poor sense of smell.

Arboreal adaptations initiated the development of an opposable thumb and forefinger, a structure useful in grasping branches and indispensable to the creation of man's past and present material culture. These adaptations served to increase the size of the cerebral cortex, coordinating sight and voluntary movements. This neural predominance is retained among land-dwelling apes and man. The authentic garden of

40

Eden for the origin of life was the primordial sea, but for the origin of higher primates specifically it was the forest canopy because those particular qualities leading to the evolution of contemporary man would not have arisen in the absence of arboreal demands.

Other problems associated with living in the trees caused a selection for further qualities generally characterizing primates. Although a large litter size was an advantage on the ground, due to the high rate of predation on smaller animals, it may have been an encumbrance to arboreal efficiency. The logistics of manipulating tenuous passages or of fleeing from enemies was accentuated by having numerous young. Of course, nesting animals can deposit their young in a hidden recess, keeping them there in relative safety until they have matured beyond a helpless stage. But primates were relatively mobile, a consequence of their omnivorous food habits, and selection probably favored individuals having fewer young, which were cared for more intensively over a longer period. The extended developmental period coupled with the habits of living together in groups, a tactic providing for mutual assistance in protection and food-finding, possibly acted to strengthen the cohesiveness of bands and to further incipient stages of social organization that eventually gave rise to human culture.

The evolution of man would not have occurred, we may be certain, if primates had remained in the trees, for there is little technological potential in an arboreal habitat in terms of raw materials, and the necessities giving a driving impetus to cultural development were not as severe. But fortunately (or unfortunately, perhaps) the forests in southern Africa where early man evolved seem to have thinned out, being separated by savanna country. Adapting to this, our prehominid antecedents moved away from an arboreal life, but retained a prehensile grip, increased neuromotor coordination, stereoscopic vision, a small litter size, and year-round sexual receptivity. Added to these adaptations was a bipedal posture with its concomitant modifications of pelvic and limb structure, a form allowing a reasonably fast gait and, most significantly, freeing the manipulative hands for exploratory behavior. These characteristics had their reward (that of greater survival potential) in increased food-getting and fecundity. The advanced primate that would someday give rise to early men did not, of course, suddenly swing out of the trees and set about the business of becoming man. The return to a strictly terrestrial existence was doubtlessly a slow one, having only tenuous selective advantages. The preceding distinctive physical features coupled with a preexisting social organization gave prehominids (pre-men) nu-

41

FIGURE 2–2

An Australopithecine on an African plain. *Australopithecus* was probably a good runner, pursuing its game in small bands.

merous advantages in competing for survival on the African plains, where man probably originated and began his successful dispersal throughout the world. A possible transition stage from apes to hominids is represented in some East African fossil remains known as *Dryopithecus*. Living in an area of savanna country, where clusters of trees were separated by open grasslands, this species may have initiated the ascent to man.

Fossils of the order Primates are rare, being found to any degree no earlier than the later Cretaceous. Likewise the fossil record of man is relatively scant. When Darwin wrote *The Descent of Man*, there were few human fossils of any kind available, so his information was necessarily speculative in nature, although he felt certain that supporting evidence would be discovered in the future. The first hominid fossils brought to public attention were discovered in 1856 in a grotto of the vale of Neander near Dusseldorf, Germany, by a schoolteacher and amateur archaeologist, Johann Karl Fuhlrott. At a meeting of eminent scientists in 1857, the remains were presented for consideration. But Rudolph Virchow, a famous European anatomist who was present at the gathering, declared upon examining the find that the bones were those of an individual born with a skull deformity, and who had been afflicted with rickets in youth and arthritis in old age. His analysis caused the summary dismissal of further discussion. Another skull, which had been found in 1848, one similar to that discovered by Fuhlrott, was presented to the Royal College of Surgeons in 1868. Other bits of evidence trickled in, until finally the validity of Neanderthal Man (*Homo neanderthalensis*) was generally accepted, a milestone in the progress of human evolutionary theory because the existence of a hominid unlike modern man had been solidly supported. Since then, many Neanderthal remains have been found in Europe and similar specimens in North, South, and East Africa, the Near East, Russia, China, and Java.

The second major fossils of human origin were uncovered by Eugene Dubois, who as a medical student in Amsterdam became convinced that the human species arose in tropical Asia. He obtained an assignment as an army surgeon in Java. The presence of Pleistocene fossil beds caused him to believe that Java would be an appropriate place to start his explorations. Soon after his arrival, he did find some fossil teeth and the top of a skull too large for an ape but too small for a modern man. Then a year later, he found the thigh bone of a fossil man, giving it the name *Pithecanthropus*, or as it is now known, *Homo erectus*.

It is probable that southern Africa, not Asia, was the birthplace of the human species. The first hominid fossil in that area brought to the attention of science was received in 1924 by Raymond Dart, then a newly appointed professor of anatomy at the University of Witwatersrand in South Africa. It was the skull of an "ape-man," as he termed it, which he tagged *Australopithecus africanus*, from *australis* (south) and *pithecus* (ape). His conviction that the skull represented a prehuman ancestor was not widely shared by other scientists, most of whom believed that

Dart had the skull of a large prehistoric ape—an interesting find, but nonetheless an ape. Twelve years later another skull of *Australopithecus* was found by Robert Broom in a lime quarry at Sterkfontein, near Johannesburg. It was from an adult, and obviously similar to Dart's skull, although as the result of some details of tooth structure he named it *Australopithecus transvaalensis*, a designation now considered invalid, as it is at most a distinct race.

Hominid Classification

As increasing fossil remains of early men accumulated, there was an overzealousness on the part of researchers in designating classifications. Every time a new fossil man was discovered, especially in a different geographical area, it was liable to be placed into a distinct genus or at least defined as a separate species. The physical anthropologist L. S. B. Leakey classified some early finds from the Olduvai Gorge under the taxa *Zinjanthropus boisei* and *Homo habilis*, which are now considered specimens of *Australopithecus africanus*, *A. robustus*, *A. boisei*, and *A. (or Homo) habilis*. Although Leakey included *habilis* in the genus *Homo* (Leakey *et al.*, 1964), David Pilbeam (1972) believes that it should be assigned to the genus *Australopithecus* because of a brain volume closer to that of *Australopithecus africanus* than to *Homo erectus*, and other features of the cranium, dentition, and mandibles. *Australopithecus habilis* was probably very similar in build to *A. africanus*. The genus *Pithecanthropus*, along with the Peking Man (*Sinanthropus*) and remains found in Algeria, which were labeled *Atlanthropus*, are all considered varieties of *Homo erectus*. Although one might argue that these latter fossils warrant a species distinction, they are at least members of the genus *Homo*, and as no really clear differentiation has been substantiated on the specific level, for the sake of clarity, they are here included as *Homo erectus*, as their similarities are more profound than their differences.

Whereas at present it may be oversimplifying matters, there is a trend among physical anthropologists to consider the human fossils thus far uncovered as falling into two genera and seven species: *Australopithecus africanus*, *A. boisei*, *A. robustus*, *A. habilis*, *Homo neanderthalensis*, *H. erectus*, and *H. sapiens*. A recent discovery in Kenya by Richard Leakey, son of L. S. B. Leakey, places hominid remains as far back as 5 million years, whereas prior remains had been dated at only about 900,000 years. And the recent discovery of a hominid, well within the

44

cranial capacity (800 cc) of *Homo erectus*, which appears to be 2.5 million to 3 million years old, may considerably alter our view as to how long contemporary man's immediate antecedents were present.

The skull of *Australopithecus* is quite distinct from modern man, having a much heavier jaw, a receding chin, prominent eyebrow ridges, and, of most significance, a cranial capacity about one third (600 cc) the size of *Homo sapiens* (1,400–1,600 cc). A. *robustus*, a larger and possibly more herbivorous animal than A. *africanus*, was superficially less similar to man than its smaller relation, which weighed about 50 pounds. The structure of the latter's pelvis and feet suggest that it stood upright much of the time and that it was a good runner, an obvious advantage in pursuing herds of hooved mammals.

Australopithecines had an average brain size somewhat less than that of a gorilla, but it is important to understand that the brain size is less

FIGURE 2–3

Drawing of the head of a young *Australopithecus africanus*, discovered in Bechuanaland, based on a skull reconstruction by A. Forestier.

(Courtesy of the American Museum of Natural History)

important than the composition of the brain itself, especially in the development of the cerebrum. Changes in the internal organization of the brain and an increase in the size of individual neurons seem to have been key factors in the development of human intelligence. The little australopithecines, weighing about a quarter as much as a gorilla, had relatively larger brains and were probably considerably more intelligent than contemporary apes. The question of intelligence is of particular interest in a discussion of human evolution, as one school of thought contends that the evolution from early man to modern man was influenced by superior brain size, and that other human characteristics followed an enlarged brain. The opposite opinion is that brain size increased as a function of physical and cultural traits and feedback. As the social order of man's ancestors became more complex, there was presumably selection for individuals of higher intelligence, a trend which in itself would have fostered a more complex social structure. One might say, in essence, that rather than man inventing tools, the tools invented man. We know that australopithecines made effective use of tools, but some form of tool was no doubt used by prehominids. Even chimpanzees demonstrate a rudimentary knowledge of tool usage in their employment of sticks to capture termites. An animal using stones or sticks as tools and weapons tends to have a selective advantage over those not doing so, and accordingly there is a tendency for the development of that capacity with a correlative increase of the cerebral hemispheres related to these actions.

It should be clear, then, that contemporary man arrived at his present station in the biological world through the same mechanisms of evolution affecting any other organism, as well as through the influence of his culture. From the primitive mammal that took to the trees 70 mil-

TABLE 2–1
Cranial Capacity of Man and His Relatives

Species	Chronological Range of Existence in Thousands of Years	Range of Brain Size in Cubic Centimeters
Homo sapiens	50–0	900–2,100
Homo neanderthalensis	150–40	1,200–1,500
Homo erectus	1,000–500	700–1,200
Australopithecus spp.	2,000–600	300–600

lion years ago, dryopithecine apes, forerunners of modern types, were firmly established more than 30 million years ago. From them developed a form eventually giving rise to the earliest man, or near-man, *Australopithecus*. The development of a high intelligence proved an evolutionary

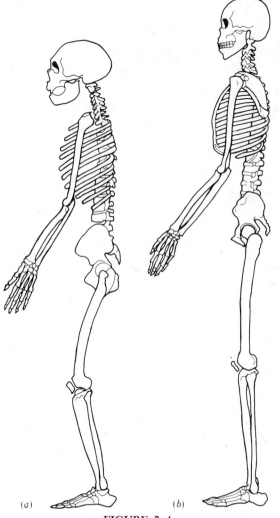

(a)   (b)

FIGURE 2–4

Skeletons of a Neanderthal man (a) and a modern man (b), illustrating some morphological changes, especially in the skull and posture.

(Carl P. Swanson, *The Natural History of Man*, © 1973. Reprinted by permission of Prentice-Hall, Inc., Englewood Cliffs, New Jersey.)

FIGURE 2–5

Cave drawing of a bison at Altamira, Spain. Such paintings represent attempts by early men to integrate aesthetics into their developing cultural fabric.

(Courtesy of the American Museum of Natural History)

strategy useful to the survival of an organized and cooperative hunting animal, and the growing intelligence, in turn, ramified the structure of social organization to the point that contemporary man has reached a level at which he can use his genetic endowment purposively to affect his own genetic future.

Homo erectus was a dominant form in Africa and Eurasia, perhaps for several million years, until the appearance of modern man (*Homo sapiens*) about 200,000 years ago. A brain similar to contemporary man's (1,200–1,400 cc) and a fairly complex tool industry characterized *H. erectus*; different races, such as Java Man, Peking Man, Olduvai Man, and Heidelberg Man, possessed distinctive tool-making traditions, the beginning of cultural diversity. By the time *H. sapiens* had fully assumed the status of a species, the foundations of human culture had been deeply established.

Suggested Readings

Bates, Marston. *Man in Nature*. 2nd ed. Englewood Cliffs, N.J.: Prentice-Hall, Inc., 1964.

Day, M. H., and R. E. F. Leakey. "New Evidence of the Genus *Homo* from East Rudolph, Kenya. 1." *American Journal of Physical Anthropology* 39 (1973): 341–354.

Kelso, A. J. *Physical Anthropology.* 2nd ed. New York: J. B. Lippincott Co., 1974.

Leakey, L. S. B., Jack Prost, and Stephanie Prost, eds. *Adam, or Ape.* Cambridge, Mass.: Schenckman Publishing Co., 1971.

Leakey, L. S. B., P. V. Tobias, and J. R. Napier, "A New Species of the Genus Homo from Olduvai Gorge. *Nature* 202 (1964): 7.

Leakey, R. E. F., and B. A. Wood. "New Evidence of the Genus Homo from East Rudolph, Kenya. II." *American Journal of Physical Anthropology* 39 (1973): 355–368.

Lestrel, Pete E., and Dwight W. Read. "Hominoid Cranial Capacity Versus Time: A Regression Approach." *Journal of Human Evolution* 2 (1973): 405–411.

Napier, John. "The Antiquity of Human Walking." *Scientific American* 216 (1967): 52–64.

Pilbeam, David. *The Ascent of Man.* New York: Macmillan Publishing Co., Inc., 1972.

Poirier, Frank E. *Fossil Man: An Evolutionary Journey.* Saint Louis, Mo.: C. V. Mosby Co., 1973.

Radinsky, Leonard. "The Fossil Evidence of Anthropoid Brain Evolution." *American Journal of Physical Anthropology* 41 (1974): 15–27.

Stebbins, G. Ledyard. *Processes of Organic Evolution.* 2nd ed. Englewood Cliffs, N.J.: Prentice-Hall, Inc., 1971.

Swanson, Carl P. *The Natural History of Man.* Englewood Cliffs, N.J.: Prentice-Hall, Inc., 1973.

Washburn, Sherwood L. "Tools and Human Evolution." *Scientific American* 203 (1960): 63–75.

chapter
3

AN OVERVIEW OF CULTURAL EVOLUTION

The essence of man is his culture, which as the sum of his artifacts, social patterns, and language has assumed a myriad of diverse forms. The beginnings of the cultural experiment are rooted in the social organization and tool-using habits of prehominid ancestors of the australopithecines. In using a stone to secure food by killing game or perhaps just to crack nuts, these hominoids had an energetic and assumedly productive advantage over individuals using only their hands, and the survival of the genotype of the former was favored. The growth of cul-

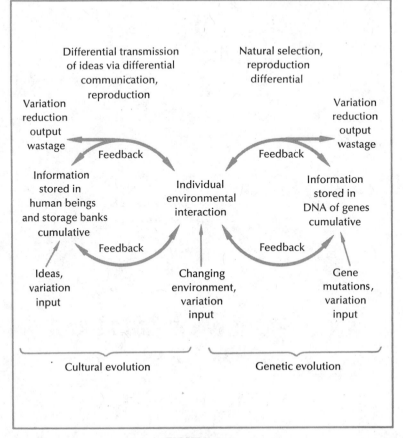

FIGURE 3–1

A simplified biofeedback model illustrating the interactions between genetic and cultural evolution in human populations. All inputs, outputs, and feedbacks can be positive, negative, or neutral.

(After C. J. Bajema, *Natural Selection in Human Populations*, New York, John Wiley & Sons, 1971.)

tural man was synergistic with the evolution of physical man, the elements of culture interacting with physical developments in a progression of mutual feedback.

Anatomical Feedback

In minute steps through hundreds of millenia, natural selection operated on a certain line of prehominid apes to favor those having the greatest reasoning powers associated with the conceptualization and use of tools for food gathering and weapons. Because the brain increased in size so dramatically from australopithecines to modern man, especially in those areas involving neuromotor, associative, and coordinative functions, we may assume that the expansion of coordinative reasoning prowess continued to be an advantage in survival. In relation to a contemporary man's cranial capacity, that of earlier men, such as *Homo habilis* (or *Australopithecus habilus*), was small, but these early men did cooperate in food-getting, a sign of some social cohesiveness.

Human material culture would not have been possible without simultaneous adaptation of the hand. Although it is in some ways generalized, in many respects the hand is a highly specialized organ and has been responsible for man's ability to accomplish detailed, mechanically sophisticated work. Without a perfectly opposable thumb, many cultural activities would be difficult or impossible. John Napier, a physical anthropologist, has suggested that a progression of the hand's development may be observed in living primates, in increasing degrees of complexity, in these species: tree shrews, tarsiers, New World monkeys, Old World monkeys, and man (Napier 1962). The tree shrews (sometimes classified as Insectivores), possibly the most primitive of primates, occupying forests of the East Indies and Malaysia, have only a rudimentary manual capability and must use both paws in grasping objects. Tarsiers, small primates found in the East Indies, are able to bend their digits toward the thumb, which has a limited degree of opposability. The New World monkeys' thumbs are opposable, but imperfectly so. Old World monkeys exhibit a true opposability, which is even more perfected in man. Our closer modern simian relatives are not considered in the sequence, as their hands are specialized for swinging from branch to branch.

The significance of the changing form of the hand in cultural evolution is evident upon examination of the two major working positions of human hands. In one position, which Napier refers to as a *power grip*, the tool is placed between flexed fingers and the palm, with the thumb reinforcing the pressure of the fingers. In the *precision grip* a tool is held between the thumb and one or more fingers. It is this latter position that enables us to accomplish tasks of a sensitive nature, from playing the violin to performing surgery. The modification responsible for true opposability, without which a precision grip would be impossible, is the saddle joint at the articulation of the thumb metacarpal (a palm bone) and trapezium (a wrist bone). This allows the thumb to rotate at 45° around its own longitudinal axis and thus to have opposability with the

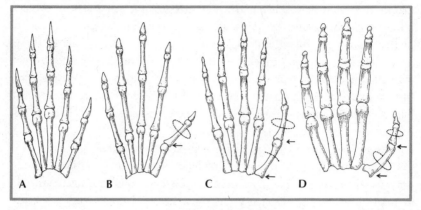

FIGURE 3–2

Hands of living primates, all drawn same size, show evolutionary changes in structure related to increasing manual dexterity. Tree shrew (A) shows beginnings óf unique primate possession, specialized thumb (*digit at right*). In tarsier (B) thumb is distinct and can rotate around joint between digit and palm. In capuchin monkey (C), a typical New World species, angle between thumb and finger is wider and movement can be initiated at joint at base of palm. Gorilla (D), like other Old World species, has saddle joint at base of palm. This allows full rotation of thumb, which is set at a wide angle. Only palm and hand bones are shown here.

(From "The Evolution of the Hand" by John Napier. Copyright © 1962 by Scientific American, Inc. All rights reserved.)

four digits. There is no evidence that australopithecines' hands were as flexible as those of modern man, but opposability was probably advanced.

Language

A major aspect of culture as we know it is language (Stopa 1973). Whether or not australopithecines had a language is a question necessarily remaining in the realm of speculation, but they may have had at least a complex organization of vocalizations. *Homo erectus*, whose culture was considerably more advanced than that of *Australopithecus*, left enough evidence in the form of tools to suggest an oral tradition necessary to their manufacture. This supports the proposition that language, without which the expressions of human culture would have been restricted, existed at that time. With language we can communicate specifics, down to very great detail, not only in the present but also in reference to the past and future. And we are able to communicate abstract ideas, a process that would otherwise be difficult.

Language differences in the human population comprise a major factor in genetic isolation. Over 2,800 languages are currently spoken, and there is a vast range of vocabulary and structure. Their relationship to the ways in which individuals of varying cultures relate to the world is complex, because one's perception of reality is in certain aspects necessarily a product of the structure of one's language.

The tools of *Homo erectus* are of a complexity suggesting a verbal transmission of information from one generation to another. There are stone axes, some with handles, chipped expertly from flint and carefully sharpened. They exhibit progressive advances in design and also a growing sensitivity to aesthetics, judging from the finished quality of some later ones. The techniques of making these flint tools are more complicated than a novice might suppose, as any anthropologist who has trained himself in this occupation can attest. Although it is not inconceivable that each generation could have learned from watching, there is a greater probability that some verbal teaching was involved. Language did not just appear to enhance the cultures of *Homo sapiens*, but developed along with other human attributes in early men, so it is entirely logical to assume that *Homo erectus* had language, and possibly more than one.

Language must already have been a part of human culture by the time of modern man. In Europe the Neanderthals (*Homo neanderthalensis*) are known to have interred their dead, a sign of cultural cohesiveness and some manner of religious beliefs. They also left cave paintings and beautifully fashioned tools, a basis for believing that aesthetic appreciation was by then a part of man's culture. By the time *Homo sapiens* assumed predominance, some foundations for modern man's cultural complexities already existed: language, social cooperation, aesthetics, religion, and tool technology.

Pre-agricultural Man

The cultural complexity of man was limited as long as most time and energy were consumed in obtaining enough food to survive. The impetus to our cultural development has its roots in the selective value of rudimentary cultural traits, such as the use of primitive tools, which gave populations a greater survival potential. But cultural possibilities are restricted in groups of men who are hunters and gatherers, as a result of a lack of population density and social specialization. Contemporary men having the least in the way of material culture are hunters and gatherers, such as the vanishing Kalahari Bushmen and the Australian aborigines.

Australian aborigines migrated from Asia to their harsh environment at least 30,000 years ago during the Pleistocene, and perhaps earlier (Mulvaney 1966, and Dortsch and Merrilees 1973). Their material culture was as impoverished as that of any Paleolithic people. In Australia, flint for making durable tools and weapons was scarce, and there were no horned animals to provide hard organic tools. It is not possible to know how extensively bones might have been used, since the highly acid Australian soil disintegrates them. And the ubiquitous termites consume any wooden artifacts. The archeological record reveals no tombs or grave goods, dwellings, or ceramics, nor were there any cultivated plants or domesticated animals except the Australian dog, the *dingo*. The sig-

FIGURE 3–3

Australian Aborigines have retained one of the most materially primitive cultures of any extant peoples.

(Courtesy of the American Museum of Natural History)

nificance of raw materials for the development of a complex material culture cannot be overstated; despite the existence of an intricate religious and social organization, their physical culture is one of the most impoverished. It is a temptation, in considering a group with so poor an archeological record, but which has been described in detailed anthropological records ever since Europeans arrived, to trust in anachronistic concepts. But it is only an inference, and not a fact, that the aborigines of today are representative of those in the past.

Agriculture

Hunting and gathering continued as the human mode for a long time after the use of tools had become well-established. About 12,000 years ago, men initiated the *Agricultural Revolution*, a change in lifestyle that created the basis of modern culture in that it freed men from the eternal quest for food and caused the establishment of more permanent dwelling sites. The term *revolution* is misleading in that it implies a rapid shift to agriculture; it was a revolution only in terms of its eventual effect on human population and culture. The Fertile Crescent of Asia is frequently cited as the birthplace of agriculture, but present evidence suggests that the experiment occurred independently in various parts of the world. Southwestern Asia may have been the point of spread in the Old World, but agricultural practices arose at about the same time in Mesoamerica, the Andes, China, southeastern Asia, and very likely, as a result of limited archeological excavations, in areas of which we are unaware. When considering preliterate history, it is important to remember that archeological records come from a tiny percentage of the world's land surface, usually arid regions where artifacts are well-preserved, and that sequences defined are always subject to these limitations. That men began agriculture in unrelated parts of the world within a relatively close time span suggests that it was a predictable outcome of the conditions of cultural development and climatic changes.

In the fertile hills and low mountains of southwestern Asia, green from plentiful rains both in summer and winter, wheat and barley grew wild at elevations of 2,000 to 4,300 feet. At first, grains were harvested from wild plants, but later incipient cultivation began, perhaps in a manner no more complicated than the sowing of seeds in particular fields. Small settlements became permanent, as people realized that they could take advantage of a predictable food source, a factor adding to the stability of social groups. The two earliest permanent agricultural villages known in that area were Jarmo in Iraq and Tepe Sarab in Iran, occupied by at least 7000 and 6500 B.C., respectively (Braidwood 1960). Flint sickle blades have been found as artifacts from other early cultures of Palestine, and milling and pounding stones are present from early sites in Kurdistan and Palestine, but none are conclusive evidence of established agriculture, as these implements might have been used in the collection and preparation of wild grains.

In the cultivation of wheat, the most important early crop in Asia, man has produced a plant that depends on him for propagation. Wild wheats must scatter their seeds, and on ripening the grain spikes become brittle, the seeds easily breaking off. But in a few wild plants, there is one recessive gene causing the production of seeds that do not easily fall off the spike. In nature, such individuals do not reproduce well because the seeds remain on the spikes, yet these plants, retaining most of their grain, were the ones chosen by early men harvesting wild wheat. Accordingly, selection was for plants having the toughest grain spikes, a condition that would almost prevent reproduction were man not present to disperse the seeds. From the earliest stages of agriculture, men have been selectively breeding from the varieties they prefer, merely by choosing the seeds of plants exhibiting useful qualities.

In Europe, oats and rye were added to wheat and barley as basic crops. Although these grasses became staples, when men settled in permanent villages they began to experiment with other plants, some of which proved adaptive to domestication, such as lentils and millet. Rice became a staple in India and parts of Asia, a lamentable choice due to its low protein content.

In Africa, grain cultivation is assumed to have been adopted about 7,000 years ago. Barley and emmer were cultivated as staples in the lower Nile Valley. At this time, referred to as the Makalian wet phase, much of the Sahara was well-watered and bush-covered. As that region experienced increasingly arid conditions, as a result in part of ecological upsets from man's agricultural practices, grain agriculture was pushed farther south into more humid tropical areas during the post-Makalian dry phase, about 3000 B.C. Today, millet has become an important crop throughout much of Africa.

In the New World, the shift to agriculture involved a slow evolution from a hunting and gathering existence, principally in Mesoamerica and the Andes, to one primarily dependent on corn, or maize. Cultivated varieties are even more dependent on man for progagation than wheat because the corn seed grains are enclosed in a tough husk. This change appears to have been more gradual than in the Old World, occurring from about 7000 to 1000 B.C. (Coe and Flannery 1964). By the time of the Spanish conquest, there were more than 150 varieties of corn under cultivation from Chile to the Valley of the St. Lawrence. The ancestor of corn was long thought to be teosinte grass or *Tripsacum*, but Mangelsdorf, who studied the evolution of New World corn, provided evidence through breeding experiments that neither of these grasses could have been progenitor to corn and suggested that corn was descended from nothing more mysterious than a type of corn. Since then, other discoveries have supported him. Pollen cores taken from the swamp on which Mexico City is located yielded corn pollen 80,000 years old, about 50,000 years older than the earliest previously accepted date for man in the New World. A cave at Coxcatlán, in the state of Chiapas, had twenty-eight separate occupation levels, the earliest of which dates back at least 10,000 years. Excavations from 1961–1964 yielded over 1 million remains of human activity, among which were more than 1,000 animal bones, including those of extinct Pleistocene antelope and horses, and 80,000 plant remains; of these 25,000 were of corn. The cave was inhabited almost continuously during this 10,000 year period; that is a better record than any Old World site offers. The details available in this uninterrupted archeological record show the people of the Tehuacán Valley to be among the first to evolve from a primitive economy of food-collecting and hunting to become primarily agriculturists. By 5000 B.C., still only 10 per cent of the food was obtained from agriculture. Fifteen hundred years later, agricultural food had risen to 30 per cent, and domesticated animals, the dog and the turkey, were present. At this time, cultural growth began an exponential increase. By 2300 B.C. there were hybridized varieties of corn, and pottery. It is worthwhile to note, although the correlation may not be conclusive, that no culture lacking pottery has achieved agricultural competence. The complexity of village life and religion accompanied by a growing sophistication in pottery-making were companion effects as agricultural practices improved (Mac-Neish 1964).

The Tehuacán Valley, where corn was developed, serves to illustrate certain relevant aspects of the shift from hunting and gathering to agriculture in the New World. The pre-agricultural people of Tehuacán probably lived much as did the nineteenth century Shoshone of the Great Basin of the southwestern United States. While that area is generally thought of as desert, and most of it truly is, there are microenvironments, from salt flats to high piñon pine forests. Rather than thinking of the Shoshone as inhabitants of the desert, it would be more accurate to examine them in terms of seasonal movements among vertically and horizontally differentiated microenvironments. Variations in the microenvironments, or niches, which comprise a more general macroenvironment, are key factors in the survival of hunting and gathering people, and are highly relevant in considering the growth of agriculture.

The Tehuacán Valley is a hilly, arid region consisting of four major microenvironments (Coe and Flannery 1964). There is the *alluvial* (river formed) *valley floor*, essentially a level plain offering good possibilities for agriculture dependent on rainfall. Rocky slopes of limestone were good for growing maize and tomatoes and for trapping rabbits. The Coxcatlán *thorn forests* yielded wild fruits, deer, peccaries, and rabbits. And the *eroded canyons* were productive ground for hunting deer. In the long period during which corn, followed by squash and beans, became increasingly significant, the Tehuacán people followed a cycle of seasonal hunting and gathering within microenvironments of the valley.

Any shift to agriculture has probably followed this basic pattern of adapting a few plants from particular niches, while continuing to take advantage of energy sources offered in all microenvironments until the agricultural crops are stabilized and productive enough to completely eliminate the need for supplements. Mangelsdorf has suggested that the ancestors of cultivated plants may have been more mutable, a condition making them more susceptible to hybridization and artificial selection (Mangelsdorf 1952). It has been argued that from an ecological standpoint, the important fact is not that man planted wheat (and presumably other domestic crops), but that he moved it to new niches, thereby changing the pressures of natural selection. He thus allowed for more deviations in phenotype, and eventually selected for characters not beneficial under natural conditions.

The story of plant domestication offered by the archeological records of Tehuacán in Mesoamerica and by Jarmo and other sites in the Old World is probably typical, but we have no record of any kind from many regions of the world. The development of agriculture was not a universal phenomenon, as attested by existing cultural groups that still lack it, such as the aborigines, and the great number of people who were without agriculture until they acquired it through cultural diffusion within the last several hundred years. Once adopted, it is not necessarily considered the ultimate economy. The inhabitants of certain coastal communities in Peru apparently gave up agriculture whenever fish became plentiful and became farmers again only through necessity (Lanning 1965).

Animal Domestication

Established agriculture and its resultant settled communities provided a basis for the second phase of agricultural evolution, that of animal domestication. This process took place chiefly in the Old World, occurring to a significant extent first in Iraq and Iran, where there were wild goats, sheep, cattle, pigs, horses, asses, and dogs. In contrast, the New World had few domesticated animals; in Mesoamerica, there were only the turkey and the dog, and in Peru there were guinea-pigs, vicuñas, alpacas, and llamas. The Old World diet, especially in Europe, centered around a few staple grains and meat, whereas in the New World, the diet centered on corn and a much greater variety of plants, but less meat and correspondingly less protein.

Animals were probably kept as pets at first, and their domestication stemmed from this habit. When adults were killed, their young were occasionally brought to the village and reared, perhaps being nursed by a human mother, a practice still prevalent in some cultures. The young animals undoubtedly served a broader function than that of village pets, having value as a food source and also as decoys for living game of the same species. A tame goat staked in a field might allay the fears wild goats harbored about feeding in too close a proximity to human dwellings. The readiness of animals to breed in captivity must have varied among individuals and species, and in time the wisdom of maintaining captive stock of animals receptive to domestication became apparent.

The process of domestication results in a strengthening of particular characteristics and a weakening of others. Domestic animals exhibit more divergence from the ancestral lines than one could expect to occur under the conditions of natural selection. Without being aware of the principles of natural selection per se, men have induced radical changes in their animals as well as plants by a pragmatic culling of individuals of less use and the breeding of those having currently desirable qualities. In many cases, a dependence on the stewardship of man, nearly as binding as that found in wheat or corn, has grown out of domestication, particularly in some of our bizarre pets such as toy poodles. On the other hand, many survive with minimal difficulty when returned to the wild. Hogs, for example, seem to have few problems in adjusting to

61

freedom, and within several generations tend to revert to their ancestral morphology.

Apart from the obvious accentuation of physical qualities useful to man, the hereditary reorganization of a wild species' behavior and its subsequent conversion into a tame animal were probably the most basic and important results of animal domestication. Docile animals were preferred to others having aggressive or otherwise incompatible personalities, and the resulting selection for breeding of individuals that interacted agreeably with men led to a genetic reorganization of behavioral traits, leading to a change in the neuro-endocrine mechanisms regulating the animals' physical processes.

The genetic reorganization of behavioral characteristics as a consequence of domestication has been shown to be of greater significance than merely resulting in a tame animal. According to Belyaev (1969), mutation rates in animals depend primarily on a balance of hormones, especially between the adrenocorticotropic (ACTH) and sexual hormones. A decrease in the hormone production of the suprarenal glands, which lie just over the upper end of the kidneys, results in an increase in mutations. Behavioral changes caused by domestication are accompanied by a suppression of suprarenal production, so the frequency of mutations is correspondingly accelerated, allowing a greater variability among animals subject to domestication. Under the conditions of natural selection, there is a tendency toward the stabilization of a phenotype. But artificial selection varies the ways in which mutations are expressed by disintegrating the controls on the "wild" phenotype. Mutations that would be suppressed in the context of normal competition are selected for, producing the broad range of variation evidenced among domestic animals. An example is man's ubiquitous companion the dog (*Canis familiaris*), selected over thousands of years for suitable behavioral traits but also for a spectrum of physical types, technically of the same species, ranging from tiny Chihuahuas weighing two pounds to Great Danes weighing 200 pounds. When returned to a wild state, those that can survive at all tend to revert in succeeding generations to a stabilized phenotype similar to that of wild canids.

Demography

There is general agreement that modern civilization rests upon the pillar of successful agriculture and the corresponding free time acquired with it. A sharp rise in the human population can also be shown to correlate with the advent of agriculture, and it frequently has been stated that man's population was limited by food scarcity, which was alleviated with agricultural food surpluses. Edward Deevey, a demographer, doubts that preagricultural men suffered much from a scarcity of food, but rather that their way of life imposed a population limit (Deevey 1960). The wandering existence of hunters and gatherers is not conducive to large populations, as too many small children create an obstacle to efficient mobility. The problems inherent in large numbers of small children would have been no less to the nomads of 15,000 years past. The probability, then, is that the sudden population growth attending the agricultural revolution was more the result of increased sedentariness than of surpluses of food. Population size should not be considered a correlative with the development of present culture, except to the extent that a minimal population limit is necessary for the diverse nature of our existing material culture.

Science, Industry, and Technology

Since the advent of agriculture, the human species has enjoyed a spectacular proliferation. Deevey's estimates place the numbers of man during the tool-using stage at a plateau of about 5 million, or 0.1 person per square kilometer of land surface. From the initiation of agriculture until the *Scientific-Industrial Revolution* of 300 years ago, our population increased to one person per square kilometer. In the 300 years following the rise of science and industry, up to the present, the population has grown to more than sixteen persons per square kilometer. A uniform rate of doubling quickly leads to incredible numbers, and it may be seen from these figures that our own rate of increase is even greater than that, with the rate itself increasing. In 8,000 years, human numbers increased by a factor of ten, an impressive gain. Then in a mere 300 years, they were sixteen times greater.

What were the conditions of the scientific-industrial period allowing so impressive a multiplication? Nutrition and medical knowledge were improving, and correspondingly more children in a family could be expected to reach maturity and to reproduce. Adults were living longer, through the effects of both medical advances and improved nutrition. In England, a simple shift from woolen to cotton underclothing resulted in the abatement of plague as a factor in population reduction. The wool had created a warm, hair-like covering for the propagation of plague-carrying lice, a condition not simulated by looser cotton garments. The sum effects of these small advances—a better understanding of medical techniques, nutrition, and means for lessening the impact of environmental stress factors—spread throughout the world and resulted in an exponential growth of population.

The rebirth of science began early in the seventeenth century, given the thrust of Galileo's belief that authority and knowledge should not necessarily rest in the established bodies of church and state. Although Galileo was finally forced to capitulate publicly to the views of the Roman clerics, his dissension aided in the eventual weakening of the authority of the church, paving the way for further independent inquiry into science. Vestiges of church control over free thought still exist even in this century, however, such as the prohibition against birth control devices by the Catholic church.

During the eighteenth century, scientific inquiry was active throughout Europe. Newton stood out in math and physics, Lavoisier in chemistry, and Linnaeus in the natural sciences. There was a brief suppression in France during the revolution of 1789–94, but the opposition was primarily against assumed church control because most scientists of that period were either clergymen or nobility. Of the three estates acknowledged during that period (clergy, nobility, and peasants), only the former two were considered privy to knowledge. Also, there was no state support for scientific endeavors, and the only individuals having the finances and time for such pursuits were either wealthy or supported by the church.

Effects of the Scientific-Industrial Revolution, felt primarily in Europe and parts of the United States at first, have affected the quality of life in positive and negative ways. First lamented by Oliver Goldsmith in his poem "The Deserted Village," there was a displacement of local populations to the cities, where younger individuals could find more work and a greater variety of entertainment, a pattern continuing today in underdeveloped countries. Aside from the resulting demographic and social disruptions accompanying the shift from village life, cities offered only a minimal quality of life to factory workers. Only recent improvements have upgraded conditions for the mass-production employee.

Thermal pollution began with the textile mills in England, altering the state of exposed aquatic habitats. During this period the unchecked exploitation of nonrenewable natural resources began with the need for coal, metals, oil, and other materials. Atmospheric pollution first became a problem at this time and has increased both in extent and severity, now approaching potentially disastrous levels.

Many of the advances of the past 300 years have made life a more comfortable and rewarding experience, freeing us of miseries once accepted as natural in the course of living. Citizens of developed countries have, for the most part, a quantity of materialistic comforts denied even to a medieval king. It is not these luxuries that are to be condemned, but rather their cost in terms of ecological disruption and the resultant degradation of life imposed on future generations. Overpopulation, of

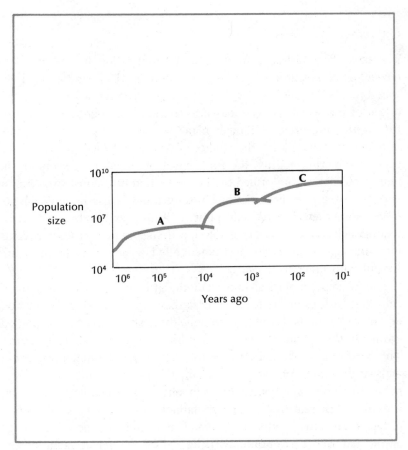

FIGURE 3-4

Population growth as a result of human cultural advancement. Increment A results from Paleolithic and Mesolithic tool innovation and use; B is a result of the Neolithic transition to agriculture; and C results from recent advances in social, technological, and medical areas.

(From "The Human Population" by Edward S. Deevey, Jr. Copyright © 1960 by Scientific American, Inc. All rights reserved.)

65

course, is going to be a key factor in the problems that our descendants must confront. But even apart from that reality, the material cultures of developed nations have been rampant in waste and excess, deriving a bulk of their resources from countries in which only a fractional percentage of the inhabitants will ever realize any benefits from the exploitation of their ecosystems. Whereas the potential seemed limitless, the actualized effects of science and industry have not been all to the good.

Contemporary Factors

The scientific-industrial revolution was a foundation for the *medical-technological revolution* of the 1900s, during which antibiotic drugs were brought into use and rapid gains were accomplished in the application of physical laws. We may also consider that period the time of the *atomic revolution*. Although man's knowledge of radioactive substances commenced with the studies of Marie and Pierre Curie at the beginning of this century, the full impact of the atomic revolution in human culture was unleashed by the detonation of the first two nuclear devices on the Japanese cities of Hiroshima and Nagasaki on August 6, 1945. Since then, theoretically positive as well as negative aspects of thermonuclear power have been developed, such as nuclear reactor plants for providing energy. Even most potentially beneficial uses, however, are fraught with inherent dangers.

The principal biological impact of the atomic revolution on human culture is with us in the form of more than twenty years' accumulation of radioactive fallout from thermonuclear test explosions, distributed unequally throughout the world according to varying weather patterns. The chief effects of radioactive substances in the biosphere include a massive disruption of living systems in the proximity of nuclear detonators. And the replacement of metabolic chemical units in living organisms is caused by radioactive fallout; an example is strontium replacing calcium in vertebrate bones. The much higher potential energy of the radioactive strontium particles causes the replacement of the lower potential energy element calcium, a condition that leads to leukemia and bone cancer. The most far-reaching effect in terms of human evolution concerns the potential of these high-energy atoms to act as mutagenic agents on genetic material by changing the sequence of DNA-RNA protein. Ionizing radiation from our solar system, and from the galaxy of which our system is a small part, continuously penetrates the atmosphere, a protective shield of water and gases, and acts as a mutagenic agent on all living things. But the increase of radiation levels resulting from thermonuclear explosions and leakage from nuclear power generators is accelerating the rate of mutations, portending unforeseeable changes in living systems, as will be discussed in subsequent chapters.

Another revolution in the advance of science occurred in the early 1950s when chemistry and biology came soundly together as a result of the studies of James Watson and Francis Crick, who theorized and demonstrated the structure of the hereditary material of which most living things are composed: DNA. Their discovery progressed to an increased understanding of the biochemical nature of life processes, and made possible the advances leading to the sophisticated eugenics already influencing man's genetic future, and which will become a more significant force when advanced techniques are made practicable.

Finally, a word is due on the effects of mass communications on man's culture. The growth of information transfer has affected societies on every continent. Information transmission is almost instantaneous, allowing people to observe wars on their televisions while eating dinner, or to see slow-motion replays of murders. There is considerable debate as to the psychological effects of so great an access to visual horrors. Does it sensitize people to atrocities, or does it foster callousness? Whichever the case, the instant communication of information, through visual and auditory means, is unlikely to decrease. A major impact that may be attributed to mass communications is an increasing homogeneity of culture, the result in large part of western ideals of material culture being thrust on other countries through movies and television.

Man's cultural evolution has progressed from the use of simple stone tools into an era of sophisticated technology understood only by a small fraction of the individuals enjoying its products. We have more material comforts and may expect a greater longevity than did our ancestors. Yet we are accumulating a debt, evident in the conditions of a polluted, deteriorating environment. It has been estimated that a third of the world's population is suffering from malnutrition, and still our numbers are surging forward. Deevey has suggested that in each of the three major revolutions prior to the 1940s (tool-making, agriculture, and science-industry) there were intrinsic population limits. Although we have made stunning cultural advances during the past fifty years, we are now entering a period in which the negative feedback aspects of our modern tech-

TABLE 3-1
Major Periods in Human Cultural Evolution

Period	Years Ago	Cultural Advancement
Mass communi-cations	15	Mass media/culture information
DNA	25	Understanding of the molecular basis of life
Atomic	30	Development of nuclear power
Industrial	150	Industrial revolution in western Europe ·
Iron	3,500	Beginnings of recorded history; iron
Bronze	5,000	Urbanization; use of copper and tin
Neolithic	14,000–7,000	Agricultural transition
Mesolithic	14,000–10,000	Domestication of animals; water transport
Paleolithic	1,000,000	Tools; cave paintings

nology—pollution, overpopulation, agricultural and spatial limitations —will enforce a limit to our present population, perhaps through the effects of war, famine, and social deterioration.

A modification of man's behavior is more important now for his future survival than the proliferation of his technology. In the past, the ethic has tended to be one of individual competition and advancement. We must evolve to a new cultural era of cooperation, rather than one of increasingly partitioned individualism, if man is to survive in populations of large numbers. A time of technological, environmental, behavioral, and cultural symbiosis is necessary if man is to cope successfully with the encroaching crises threatening his very civilization. Technological solutions alone are not going to be sufficient. *The Limits to Growth* (see Suggested Readings, Chapter 12), a book resulting from computer studies on man's critical problems, predicts that in their present course the world's technological civilizations are destined to collapse, not through slow deterioration, but with an inalterable suddenness. This gloomy projection is not absolute, but it underlines the urgency of international cooperation. Man is technologically in a better position to improve himself culturally and biologically than he has ever been, while at the same time he is in a precarious position resulting from his own technology. If man does not in some manner establish congruity with his environment, then those cultural mechanisms that have provided so great a buffer against the natural world will deteriorate, exposing our species once again to the effects of precultural natural selection.

Suggested Readings

Belyaev, D. K. "Domestication of Animals." *Science Journal* 5 (1969): 47–52.

Binford, Sally R. "Late Middle Paleolithic Adaptations and Their Possible Consequences." *Bioscience* 20 (1970): 280–283.

Braidwood, Robert J. "The Agricultural Revolution." *Scientific American* 203 (1960): 130–148.

Coe, Michael D., and Kent F. Flannery "Microenvironments and Mesoamerican Prehistory." *Science* 143 (1964): 650–654.

Deevey, Edward S. "The Human Population." *Scientific American* 203 (1960): 88–96.

Dortsch, C. E., and D. Merrilees. "Human Occupation of Devil's Lair, Western Australia During the Pleistocene." *Archeology and Physical Anthropology in Oceania* 8 (1973): 89–114.

Heiser, Charles B., Jr., "Some Considerations of Early Plant Domestication." *Bioscience* 19 (1970): 228–231.

Kearney, Hugh. *Science and Change: 1,500–1,700.* New York: McGraw-Hill, 1971.

Lanning, Edward. "Early Man in Peru." *Scientific American* 213 (1965): 68–76.

Lynch, Thomas F. "Harvest Timing, Transhumance, and the Process of Domestication." *American Anthropologist* 75 (1973): 1254–1259.

Mangelsdorf, Paul C. "Evolution Under Domestication." *American Naturalist* 86 (1952): 65–77.

Mulvaney, D. J. "The Prehistory of the Australian Aborigine." *Scientific American* 214 (1966): 84–93.

Napier, John. "The Evolution of the Hand." *Scientific American* 207 (1962): 56–62.

Stopa, R. "Hominization." *Journal of Human Evolution* 2 (1973): 371–378.

Weiner, J. S. *The Natural History of Man.* New York: Doubleday, Anchor Press, 1973.

chapter 4

MAN'S INFLUENCE UPON THE ATMOSPHERE

Climate and Evolution

Before man evolved into a cultural being, climatic stresses were a more significant directive of his evolution than they are today. Clothing, housing, and other cultural innovations giving man an edge on cold, heat, and humidity have ameliorated the keen edge of climate as a selective factor, but it still exists as one. In present times, man is confronted with an increasing variety of atmospheric pollutants representing stresses on

71

the human gene pool, and which, additionally, alter climate. A growing layer of dust particles in the stratosphere may be causing a significant lowering of the earth's temperature and an accompanying alteration of climatological patterns. A variety of substances in the lower atmosphere, products of human cultural activity, are toxic to the physiological well-being of man and other organisms. Excessive carbon monoxide, lead, asbestos particles, and a growing list of other substances belched forth from human civilization comprise an ever increasing burden, creating significant stresses on human populations and affecting their contemporary evolution.

Any organism must operate within a critical temperature range. Man has achieved a greater versatility than other species as a result of his cultural practice of insulating himself with clothing and effective shelters. For the past million years or more, as contemporary man was evolving, the earth's climate has been relatively harsh, being generally cooler than during the previous 500 million years (Dorf 1960). There have been several *ice ages*, or *glacials*, during which the land masses of Europe and North America were largely covered with great sheets of ice, interspersed by warmer periods known as *interglacials*. Man living under these rigorous conditions was subject to severe selective pressures, as the physiological requirements in extreme cold demand more specific adaptations than those necessary when warmer temperatures prevail.

The earth's climate is a markedly dynamic aspect with which all organisms must cope. Because the last million years have comprised a relatively stressful climatic period, especially in Europe, Asia, and other more northerly regions, has man therefore been physically influenced by the complexities of cold climates? The dispersal of the human species from tropical savannas continued to occur during glacial times, and even today races of man living under materially primitive conditions are capable of coping adequately with somewhat discordant environments. Until very recent infusions of technology, Eskimos survived the rigors of a barren, frozen land with relatively primitive accessories; in many respects, they still do. Man has proven by his survival to be a highly adaptive species, occupying a far greater variety of habitats than any other animal. This is in part the result of the development of material culture—housing, clothing, and energy capture—which has aided in overcoming the exigencies of living much of the year in sub-zero temperatures. But only recently has man perfected mechanisms of total thermal protection, most of which were unavailable to the primary inhabitants of arctic lands, severe deserts, and tropical habitats. Physiological and morphological adaptations were surely involved in the adjustment to a way of life compatible with the climates occupied by more primitive man (Scholander 1954, Schreiber, 1964).

The problems of heat dissipation must have been extremely important

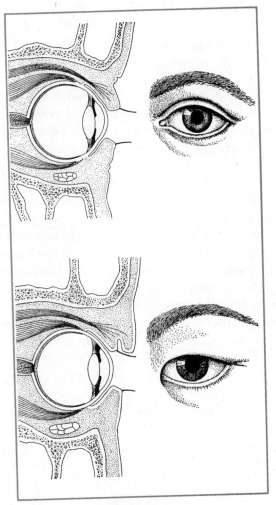

FIGURE 4–1

"Almond" eye of Mongoloid races is among latest major human adaptations to environment. The Mongoloid fold, shown in lower drawings, protects the eye against the severe Asian winter. Drawings at top show the Caucasian eye with its single, fatty lid.

(From "The Distribution of Man" by William W. Howells. Copyright © 1960 by Scientific American, Inc. All rights reserved.)

to Arctic aborigines. Clothing and housing were cultural adaptations, but were not in themselves sufficient to negate the severity of the environment. The igloos of Eskimos, noted for their insulative effectiveness, are a comparatively recent invention; former Eskimo housing of caribou skin construction was far less warm. It is reasonable to assume that in man, as with any other species faced with a similar problem of survival, the individual with the physique and physiology tending to discourage heat loss would have a survival advantage over individuals lacking these genetically determined qualities. And by the same token, races of man living in tropical areas would be expected to benefit on a population basis from adaptations resulting in rapid heat dissipation. In either example this may be shown to be the case among extant primitive peoples, although arguments exist among physical anthropologists as to the relative importance of physiological versus morphological adaptations.

In relation to morphological adaptations to climate, there have been numerous contentions centered on two *ecological rules*, which have been subject to extensive misinterpretation. One of these, Bergman's Rule, states that "races of warm blooded vertebrates from cooler climates tend to be larger than races of the same species from warmer climates." The other, Allen's Rule, maintains that in cooler climates extremities tend to be reduced, thus minimizing the surface area and accompanying heat dissipation. In either case, the effect is to increase the mass relative to surface area, a condition causing the retention of more body heat. Although earlier proponents of these rules applied them to species as well as races (subspecies), contemporary supporters emphasize that they are valid only in terms of intraspecific (ecological race or subspecies) variation.

It has been argued that physiological adaptations, not morphological, are responsible for the adjustment to cold climates. The supporters of this view can readily find contradictions to Bergman's and Allen's Rules. What is often overlooked, by taking an all-or-nothing interpretation that is biologically invalid, is that the phenotype or functional morphology of a species is the result of different and often conflicting selective pressures. As an example, the European mole (*Talpa europea*) decreases in size in its northerly range. In this case a sparser food supply is the limiting factor (Mayr 1956). But the existence of many exceptions does not negate the functional validity of these ecological rules any more than the existence of numerous exceptions to a basic color pattern of a highly variable species denies the reality of a predominant color phase or pattern. Contradictory selective pressures may often be at work among populations of a widely distributed species. Physiological adjustments, such as vascular constriction in extremities to control heat loss, may be more

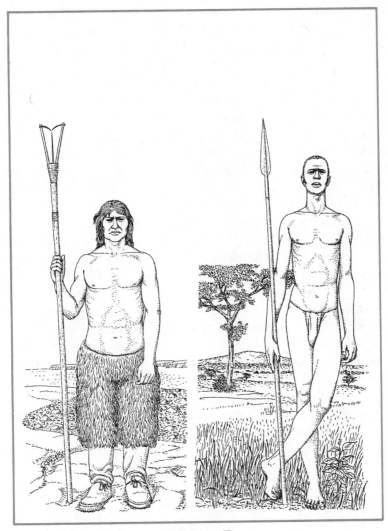

FIGURE 4–2

Human adaptation to climate is typified by Nilotic Negro of the Sudan (right) and arctic Eskimo (left). Greater body surface of Negro facilitates dissipation of unneeded body heat; proportionately greater bulk of the Eskimo conserves body heat.

(From "The Distribution of Man" by William W. Howells. Copyright © 1960 by Scientific American, Inc. All rights reserved.)

important, but intrinsically there is no disagreement between such adjustments and selective factors affecting morphologies that represent more complete adaptations of intraspecific populations. Reflections of these ecological phenomena may be seen among populations of man, as with the slender equatorial Masai and the stocky, arctic Eskimo. Rather than contradictory, physiological and morphological adaptations are manifestations of a continuum of adjustment to environmental stress. Any characteristic conferring a greater survival potential will be manifest in positive selection and in time will accumulate in populations as physiological-morphological adaptations.

A third point of view strongly denies the validity of either of the biological mechanisms of physiological-morphological adaptation when applied to the human species by declaring that cultural factors have transcended the selective pressure of external physical stress from the environment to the human organism. As mentioned previously and discussed in detail subsequently, this does not appear to be the case. Culture has affected man's adjustment and often created new selective pressures, but it has not in the past or present superseded the importance of environmental stress in relation to climate or other ecological circumstances. The artificial microclimates created by man's technology vary greatly from one culture to another, as does their adaptive survival value. Protection from the cold is far more effective in middle-class housing in the United States than it is in many of the other developed countries, such as Britain, where heating still tends to be inadequate to the degree that some pre- and postnatal mortality is surely the result (Schreider 1964). Although certain cultural innovations of technologically developed countries may afford protection from stressful extremes of climate, by no means are these factors eliminated as selective on a worldwide basis; the poor of many countries are unable to afford the expensive amenities of protective clothing and shelter. In essence, it is an unsupportable contention that in contemporary human evolution cultural factors have surpassed the stresses of environment on a world scale, however great cultural influences may be locally.

As climate has been of importance in the physical adaptations of man, so has man been a factor in the alteration of world climate. In the past this biofeedback interaction between man's cultural activity and his environment was accomplished primarily through his agricultural practices, which continue to be a significant element in the total contemporary problem of climatic change (Ehrlich and Ehrlich 1972). One manner in which agriculture may affect the climate of an area is by bringing about changes in the natural vegetation. This is frequently hastened through the laterization of soils, a condition common in many tropical areas of the world, and by the primitive agricultural tradition of moving on to a new plot when the usefulness of the old has been exhausted (McNeil 1964). Lateritic soils are composed of a heavy clay layer, often twenty to thirty feet deep, overlain by a shallow layer of tillable topsoil. When the protective natural vegetation is removed and the extremely thin layer of topsoil is eroded by agricultural practices,

FIGURE 4-3

Tropical rain forest, rather than providing fertile agricultural land, usually grows on low-nutrient soil, and when cleared tends to become agriculturally worthless, or, at best, depaupered.

(Photo by Thomas H. Stubbs)

the exposed iron-rich clay is converted by oxidation into a rock-hard material useless for agriculture and support of vegetation by the endemic plant community. Extensive loss of vegetation cover alters the hydrology of areas and was probably man's first climatological-ecological impact on soil and plant communities. In the past, laterization of soils has been a problem of agriculture in tropical areas—Angkor Wat in Cambodia is built partially from lateritic brick—and is one of the most imminent problems confronting agriculture in tropical countries today. As human population pressures mount throughout the world, more and more tropical lands are cleared for agriculture. The deforestation of much of the Amazon Basin in Brazil, a world environmental and climatological catastrophe that is presently continuing, may well transform northern Brazil from one of the most productive areas of the earth in terms of plant and animal diversity and oxygen production for our biosphere into the laterized Sahara of the New World. The Brazilian Nature Conservancy has been warning the Brazilian government of this potential disaster, but to no avail in the face of an ardent program to develop for agriculture this largest remaining expanse of jungle in the world.

FIGURE 4–4

Eroded hills in Veracruz, Mexico. Where there was lush jungle, corn now struggles to keep a foothold.

(Photo by Thomas H. Stubbs)

That deforestation appreciably changes the climate of an area is evident in the historical example of North Africa's Sahara. Northern Africa was the fertile grainery of the Roman Empire (Walker 1974); today the Sahara is the world's largest expanse of desert, encompassing an area as large as the United States. It may be difficult to conceive of thousands of square miles of dense rain forest such as that of the Amazon Basin being reduced to a desert or xeric community within a few hundred years, but exactly that future looms as more than a remote possibility.

Decreasing global temperature, partly a result of contemporary man's cultural activity, is responsible for the climatic changes and increasing pressures on human populations now occurring in northern and central Africa as a result of a continuing extension of the Sahara by thousands of square miles. The Sahel Region on the southern edge of the Sahara has long been precariously dry, but until recently there was enough rainfall to support sparse natural vegetation and small herds of cattle, camels, and goats kept by nomadic tribes such as the Fulani and Taureg. During the wetter months, a subsistence agriculture of sorghum and millet existed as a staple food supply for thousands of small villages. Then the rains failed, and by 1973 the desert had crept sixty miles farther south and encompassed a vast acreage, where parched sand now shifts among the ruins of abandoned villages and covers the bleaching skeletons of thousands of camels and cattle.

Weather in the Sahel has been governed in the past by movements of bodies of cold polar air. During the spring and early summer, the polar masses receded northward and drew temperate air masses from the south up to the Sahel. Moist air belts bringing monsoon rains followed. In the fall the polar air masses, announcing the beginning of the dry season, would advance southward again. This pattern provided enough water to allow a sparse population of men and domestic animals to eke out a living from a land that, although not generous, was sufficient.

It now appears that the climatological pattern of centuries may be changing, and that the polar air masses are no longer moving northward in the spring and summer. In all probability, this situation is the result of the decreasing worldwide temperatures, resulting in an expansion of cold air masses that has caused the northern limit of monsoon rains to recede (Walker 1974). Rain still falls in the Sahel, but during the last several years, it has lessened dramatically. In Boutilimit, Mauritania, a town deep in the Sahel, 200 ml of rain could be expected from July to September, but in 1973 only 41.6 ml were recorded. Rainfall in Rosso, on the Senegal River, lessened from an anticipated 530 ml to 164.5 ml.

The natural selective, political, and humanitarian consequences of this drought inevitably are going to multiply. There are about 50 million people within the African drought belt, and at least a third of them are severely affected. Estimates on the number immediately facing starvation vary from 5 to 10 million. In reality, one can do little more than guess, so extensive is the tragedy. Politically, an area of the world already beset by tensions is being driven into further conflict as the unrest caused by starvation and disease adds further complexity to a seemingly insoluble ecological problem. Even if massive revegetation projects could be accomplished in time to avert disaster for those millions of men and domestic animals presently on the brink of starvation—and they could not—such efforts would be to no avail unless adequate rains return. In the light of the present it appears that the Sahel is lost to man, and that large numbers of the human species formerly living in balance with a precarious ecosystem are doomed to death from starvation or any of a number of diseases, from tuberculosis to typhus.

It is worth noting in relation to the problem of the Sahel that well-intentioned but ecologically misguided efforts by international agencies have compounded the seriousness of the Sahel drought. The United States Agency for International Development built 1,400 wells over the past fourteen years, removing water as a key limiting factor on the size of animal herds. As a result of more domestic animal production, the human population also exploded. Desert ecology is fragile, and the increase in the number of men and their grazing herds caused a deterioration of the already sparse vegetation of the Sahel to begin. Now there is no food for the animals; livestock have eaten everything in sight, compounding the effects of the drought. Bodies of cattle lie bloated from the water of the well sites, but starved for lack of grazing forage in the parched, overpopulated landscape. While human factors of misguided agriculture and animal husbandry have precipitated the crisis, there is evidence that the roots of the problem lie in particulate atmospheric pollution and the resultant change in world climate, as will be discussed subsequently in this chapter. It is also argued that the Sahel tragedy is the result of inevitable secular climatic change. It seems plausible that both points of view have merit, and that the Sahel drought was brought about by a combination of factors.

As in the Sahel of North Africa, domesticated animal grazing has been responsible for vegetative and climatic change throughout the world. This is especially true of herd animals such as sheep and goats that pull up shallowly rooted grasses covering marginal desert lands. In arid regions, where these domesticated animals tend to survive and thus assume economic importance, their feeding habits promote soil erosion by the removal of sparse ground cover. Records from the last century indicate that many areas in the now devegetated Navajo lands of New Mexico and Arizona were once grassland communities before they were progressively denuded by an ever increasing number of sheep and goats kept by the Navajo over the last 100 years.

The farming of marginal lands, made increasingly possible during the last few decades through intensified irrigation practices, tends to be accompanied by increases in the salt content of soil as well as by minor climatological alterations; this salt buildup constitutes a serious problem in the context of world agriculture. In West Pakistan more than 5 million acres of land, or about 18 per cent of the total cultivated, have been lost to agriculture and man for this reason. Irrigation of marginal desert lands causes salts to be pulled up to the surface through capillary action, eventually attaining a concentration prohibitive to plant growth. In Egypt, this dilemma has been circumvented by effective drainage of salted lands, but in countries such as West Pakistan, where such technology is lacking, the loss of land to salt deposition places a heavy burden on an area incapable at best of enough agricultural production to sustain a rising population. Yet the ecological impact is of a more pervasive and long-term nature than merely the removal of land from agricultural production. The communities of xeric plants originally present will not return when agriculture has been abandoned, as the heavy salt concentrations prohibit the growth of them as well. In such areas there is limited rainfall, and the salts will not leach out in the time spans relevant to the course of contemporary civilizations. More deserts and dustbowls are thus created on a worldwide basis.

These barren deserts may be expected to contribute through wind erosion of soils—as with the dustbowls of the Oklahoma-Texas area of the 1930s—to increasing concentrations of dust particles in the stratosphere. Presently, dust clouds from the Sahara drift for thousands of miles and have been known to produce haze over the state of Florida. It is impossible to know at present what the total environmental effect of increasing stratospheric dust may be, but it definitely creates a slight shield against the sun's rays reaching our biosphere and is responsible in part, along with soil dispersal from cultivation by mechanized agriculture, for the cooling trend indicated for the past three decades. Ironically, the majority of particulate matter added to the atmosphere from functional farmlands comes, not from the marginal desert areas of the world, but from the richer soils where agricultural practices are visibly successful. Mechanized agriculture has increased man's food supply tremendously in the last thirty years, but it has resulted in the loss, through deep, extensive, and repeated plowing and exposure, of topsoil that is blown away to be trapped in the layers of the atmosphere. The advent of agriculture gave man tremendous freedom from previously severe selective pressures on food supply and human population growth. In the light of current practices (in both the developed and underdeveloped countries) meant to increase the food supply for an ever-growing human population, man's agriculture may well become a selective force on his populations once again by creating, paradoxically, a world of cool deserts of low productivity. Man, through contemporary agricultural practices, is altering both land-use potential on a global scale and long-range climatological patterns. It is foolish to assume with complacence that human evolution is beyond the forces of selection of the natural world when our own agricultural systems, especially those in more northern hemispheres such as the wheat producing regions of Canada, the U.S.S.R., and China, may be limited by man-induced climatological changes within the next hundred years.

Evidence has been accumulating that the atmospheric levels of carbon dioxide (CO_2) have been rising as a result of the products of human cultural activity, especially industrial burning and use of internal combustion engines (Revelle and Suess 1967). It has been postulated that the increasing CO_2 content of the atmosphere should have resulted in a warming trend, but if in fact the rise of CO_2 levels was responsible for the warming tendency apparent from the beginning of the Industrial Revolution up to the 1940s, then another component of the atmosphere, particulate contamination, has overcome the warming effect (Schaeffer 1969). It may well be proven that the accumulating dust layer in the stratosphere is creating an effective blockage of the sun's irradiation and has resulted in a counter-cooling. Whether the net cooling effect will remain mild is of more than passing interest. A few degrees up or down the thermal scale may seem inconsequential on a global level, but those few degrees may cause major changes. The last ice age resulted from a drop of only 7–9°C (Aynsley 1969). In light of this we should not brush off the consequences of atmospheric alterations of climate. The increase in dustiness or turbidity of the atmosphere has been documented. Data from the Moana Loa Observatory in Hawaii, several thousand

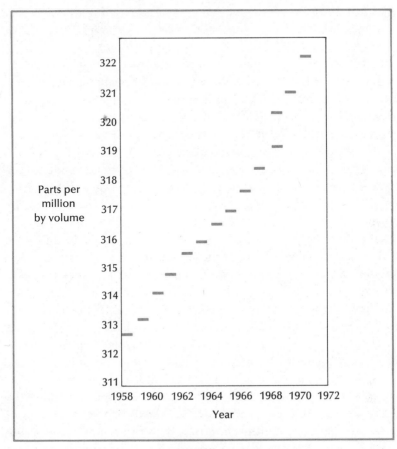

FIGURE 4-5

Increasing carbon dioxide concentration in the atmosphere as measured at the Mauna Loa Observatory in Hawaii. The present increase averages 1.5 parts per million/year. The source of this increase in CO_2 is combustion of fossil fuels.

(After Lester Machta, "The Role of the Ocean and Biosphere in the Carbon Dioxide Cycle." Paper presented at Nobel Symposium 20 "The Changing Chemistry of the Oceans," Göteborg, Sweden, August 1971.)

miles from predominant sources of global air pollution, indicate a long-term increase. Air turbidity has increased nearly 60 per cent over Washington, D.C., nearly 90 per cent over Switzerland, and elsewhere the accumulation of atmospheric particulates has been rising at an approximate annual rate of 10 per cent (Aynsley 1969). This shield acts not only to cut off a portion of the sun's radiation reaching the earth, but excess dust initiates cloud formations that can alter patterns of precipitation.

In 1973 the North Atlantic's ice cover was greater than it had been for the previous sixty years. It is a sobering speculation that our own cultural activity may be hastening the coming of another ice age or at a lesser effect bringing on a period of much colder weather that will have a significant impact on the world's agricultural production.

Dust accumulation in the atmosphere has an effect on rainfall patterns because the solid particles serve as nuclei for cloud condensation. Depending on weather conditions in a local area, either clouds or fog may be formed. The altered weather conditions are, however, locally determined.

At La Port, Indiana, a town about thirty miles to the south of the steel production centers of Gary and South Chicago, precipitation has increased. During the fourteen years prior to 1965, La Port's precipitation increased in all respects; there was 31 per cent more rain, 38 per cent more thunderstorms, and 245 per cent more hailstorms. The rainfall was shown to increase in apparent correlation with the production rates of the Gary mills (Changmon 1968). However, under other circumstances, particulate matter may result in a decrease in rainfall. This is caused by the condensation of many small droplets which, if no additional moisture is available in the air to give them weight, remain in the air as clouds. In Queensland, Australia, rainfall has been reduced as much as 25 per cent in areas downwind from sugarcane fields that are burned as part of the harvesting process. The burning produces thick clouds of smoke that collect and retain the water vapor in the air, thus reducing rainfall (Warner 1968). The decrease has not occurred in peripheral areas unaffected by the smoke.

Automobiles have become a notorious factor in air pollution in the United States. One of the unseen effects of the auto emissions that acts to alter climate is that the smog particles cause formation of ice crystals in clouds (Schaeffer 1969). Lead additives in gasoline combine in the car exhaust and in the atmosphere with the small number of iodine molecules continuously present. The result of this chemical interaction is the formation of ice crystals in winter skies over urban areas, with a resultant depression of air temperature.

The vapor trails of high-flying aircraft serve as the source of another atmospheric catalyst. Aircraft spew large amounts of CO_2, water vapor, and particulate matter into the stratosphere. The wispy cirrus clouds thus formed by the tailings of aircraft have increased the cloud cover between North America and Europe by as much as 5–10 per cent. Dr. R. A. Bryson suggests that with the increase in supersonic jet travel, this cover could increase up to 100 per cent! So great a potential effect in just one area from a single source illustrates the vulnerable nature of our atmosphere in relation to climatic change. Fortunately, rain and snow act as natural cleansers on the lower layers of the atmosphere, but apparently they may not be effective enough against the barrage of pollutants continuously being thrust up by our civilization to prevent ensuing climatic change. And the particles in the stratosphere are not subject to any natural cleaning action, as they are beyond the reach of lower climatic conditions.

Human interference with the atmosphere may yield effects more acute than the direct ills caused by pollution. It has been suggested that continued deforestation and oceanic pollution adversely affecting phytoplankton might result in a reduced global oxygen supply. This does not seem likely (Broecker 1970), but another possibility warranting equal concern is that atmospheric ozone may be reduced (Cutchis 1974). Ozone, which shields the biosphere from excessive ultraviolet radiation, could be significantly depleted as the result of nitrous oxides infused into the earth's atmosphere by fleets of stratospheric spacecraft. Increased levels of radiation also reduce ozone. A nuclear holocaust could devastatingly lessen the atmospheric ozone content to the point of extinguishing much life on earth. The mildest outcome would be a rise in the incidence of skin cancers.

Poisons in the Air

We must add to this scenario of the future the reality of present air quality acting as a factor on human natural selection. Our atmosphere is currently being inundated with a variety of poisons and corrosives introduced through industrial activity, agriculture, transportation, and other sources. Pollutants in the atmosphere easily spread over great distances by following wind currents far from the source. While individuals in heavily urbanized areas are the most directly affected, it is no longer possible to breathe genuinely unpolluted air anywhere in the world simply because the effects of local air pollution have become global.

These atmospheric pollutants are meaningful selective factors on contemporary human populations, as they act on perinatal and older prereproductive age groups as well as on postreproductive citizens. During

(a)

(b)

Figure 4–6 (a, b, c)

The formation of smog over Los Angeles. Many urban areas have levels of air pollution high enough to initiate or exacerbate emphysema, possibly lung cancer, and a variety of other human ills.

(L.A. County Air Pollution Control District, Courtesy of the U.S. Environmental Protection Agency)

(c)

the ten year period from 1950 through 1959, deaths from emphysema among males in the United States rose from 1.5 per 100,000 to 8.0 per 100,000 (Haagen-Smit 1969). Bronchial asthma, which affects prere-productive individuals, is frequently aggravated by air pollution. In 1946 a form of asthma, correlative with the heavy industrial pollution on the Kanto Plain, began occurring among American troops and their families stationed in Tokyo and Yokohama. In New Orleans, asthma attacks have been linked to burning at the city dump, as well as with other air pollution sources. Air pollution has also been shown to correlate with outbreaks of upper respiratory infections.

Studies at the University of Southern California School of Medicine have demonstrated the antagonistic effect of air pollution on patients suffering from bronchitis and emphysema (McDermott 1961). One hundred patients were observed, first while breathing Los Angeles air, then while breathing air purified with charcoal filters. When breathing the purified air, patients evidenced marked improvements in lung func-tioning. Significantly, several days of breathing purified air were neces-sary before changes were detected, suggesting that the pollutant's effects on bronchopulmonary tissues are longer lasting than those produced from cigarette smoking.

Several occurrences of the last few decades demonstrate the severity of intense air pollution and the rapidity with which varying age groups

87

in human populations respond. The town of Donora, Pennsylvania, situated on a bend of the Monangahela River, is surrounded by high hills. The air is burdened with the waste of blast furnaces, steel mills, sulfuric acid mills, and slag processing plants. Ordinarily, the smog would lift each day at noon, but in October 1948, a temperature inversion occurred over most of the United States, including Donora. The pollution was held over the city, and by the third day of unabated smog, 5,910 persons had been reported ill. More than 65 per cent of the residents sixty-five years and older were reported affected, and about half were in serious condition. A heavy rain fell after the third day and dissipated the smog and the epidemic of bronchial illness, but twenty died as a result of the contained pollution (Fletcher 1949).

A troubling aftereffect of the Donora smog episode is that for the decade thereafter, those individuals who had become ill and then recovered were afflicted with a higher incidence of mortality and illness than those who were present at the time of the inversion but apparently unaffected. A degree of this impact may be attributed to heart and lung disease antedating October 1948. Possible population genetic effects are not determinable.

Hospital and death records also attest to the tolls of air pollution in New York City from 1952–1962. The London "black fog" of 1952 resulted in an excess mortality of 4,000–5,000 within a single week (McDermott 1961). In most of these cases of numerous deaths associated with a sustained smog layer, the individuals counted as victims had a previous record of bronchopulmonary disease. And it is interesting that hospital patients suffering from bronchitis began to show symptoms of discomfort six to twelve hours before the smog inversions had become generally apparent.

Localized and worldwide atmospheric pollution is creating stresses on the human species that are difficult to measure quantitatively. Those already demonstrated should be considered valid samplings of widespread problems. We are confronted with knowledge, both empirical and intuitive, that is sufficiently impressive to prompt needed changes. Smog in some urban areas of the United States has been above tolerable levels for years and remains as an abiding problem. In 1970 a proposition appeared on the general election ballot in California calling for a diversion of a percentage of gasoline taxes into mass transit systems and pollution control. It was defeated. Human well-being and survival may be threatened when individuals will not alter their lifestyles even though confronted with overwhelming evidence that the excessive use of autos in congested areas constitutes a health hazard. Although the "energy crisis" of 1973–1974 caused a slight slowdown in the use of individual autos, their use returned to the usual level when gasoline became more readily available. Unfortunately, on a global level, even a 50 per cent reduction in the number of automobiles operating would represent a minor impact on pollution if all other air-contaminating sources were allowed to operate at their present rates.

How will human populations respond to these newly created selective pressures? Certainly their effect will be seen in an increased mortality among urban populations. One might suppose that were smog levels unabated, a trend might be seen toward smaller body size, as observed in populations living at high altitudes where smaller quantities of oxygen is a limiting factor. Prenatal and postnatal mortality would become apparent selective pressures. Individuals whose physiologies are better able to cope with air liberally supplied with toxic additives would be favored. Regardless of the means by which our species accommodates itself to these unnecessary stresses, extensive individual discomfort and health care costs necessarily will be included.

In their pervasive influence throughout our environment, air pollutants aim a wider range of blows than those directed against the human organism; our economics and aesthetics are affected as well. These pollutants, particularly fluorides, affect the productivity of cattle and damage agricultural crops. Smelters in British Columbia, emitting an average of 600 tons of sulfur per day, caused the eradication of pines and firs within a radius of several miles from the source. In Mexico City, where air pollution is probably the worst in the world as a result of the altitude and increased production of CO_2, 100-year-old eucalyptus trees are dying. Orchids and other epiphytic plants cannot be raised commercially in most metropolitan areas as they are acutely sensitive to air-borne poisons. Damage to vegetation has become so widespread in southern California that experts can now determine the agent of pollution by the appearance of the agricultural plant crop. All biological organisms, including man, responded to environmental stresses. Even were we unconcerned with the blighted landscape resulting from smog, the economic factor of air pollution is consequential to world agriculture; losses alone are estimated to be in excess of $500 million annually (Ehrlich and Ehrlich 1972).

Exposed materials from fabrics to metals deteriorate more rapidly and

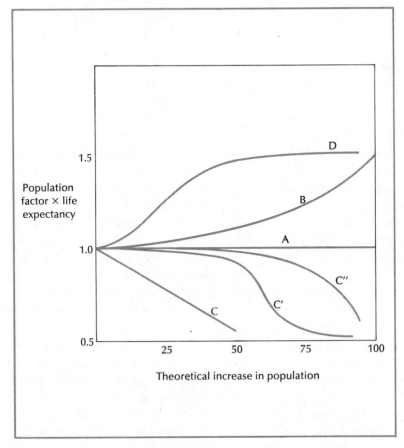

FIGURE 4-7

Possible effects of total environmental pollution on average human lifetime. As conclusive evidence is lacking in many instances, the above figure projects several different curves. Curve A assumes no effect on lifetime by pollution (normal life expectancy is multiplied by 1.0). Curve B assumes an improbable but theoretically possible enhancement of lifetime with increasing environmental pollution (normal life expectancy is multiplied by a greater number than 1.0). Curves C, C′, and C″ reflect differing assumptions concerning the extent of deleterious pollution effects. Curve D assumes a positive accommodation to pollution.

(After D. H. Meadows, et al., *The Limits to Growth*, Universe Books, New York, 1971.)

need cleaning more frequently. Ozone from smog causes rubber to crack (an assay of smog activity), and the sulfur oxides from smog cause the deterioration of paints. The degeneration of buildings and materials is hastened, as illustrated by Cleopatra's Needle, which has deteriorated more since its arrival in New York City in 1881 than it had in Egypt during the previous 3,000 years.

Air pollution costs are many; biological, aesthetic, and economic. It is regrettable that the latter is often the only one carrying enough impact to precipitate change. Estimates of financial costs to U.S. society for fouling its own nest are placed at $12 billion annually (Haagen-Smit 1969), disregarding the less quantified human costs. Yet only a tiny fraction of this amount is invested in attempts to overcome the problem of air pollution. A priority of values, in this case, has been shown to be wanting.

Even with the most stringent of controls, however, air pollution cannot be expected to diminish, because of the same factor producing so many other stresses on humanity: overpopulation. Consider the example of Los Angeles, a metropolitan sprawl encircled by the mountains and the sea. Frequent temperature inversions, occurring about seven out of every sixteen days, create a trap for polluted air, holding it down over the city. Four hundred years ago, the Spaniard Juan Rodriguez Cabrillo reported that the fires of the Indians in what is now the Los Angeles basin rose to a height of 400 feet, spreading then in a haze over the valley. In addition to the pollutants contributed by 4 million cars and industry, Los Angeles is gifted with an abundance of sunshine that acts on the mixture of oxygens, nitrous oxides, and hydrocarbons to produce photochemical smog. Since 1960 there has been no improvement in the air quality of the Los Angeles basin despite strict enforcement of laws by local government. Although there are restrictions on industry, coal burning, garbage disposal and incineration, and auto emissions, and even effective forest fire control in the area, air pollution has been increasing, damaging vegetation hundreds of miles to the east of the city. Why, as controls have become more effective, has pollution worsened? The answer is that there are more people in the basin; even if the amount of smog produced per capita has lessened, the increase in population has more than compensated. Air pollution will continue to be a strong selective factor on human populations in urban areas until there is stabilization of population growth and demographic shifting. On a world basis, the surging tide of humanity gives no indication of receding, but rather of multiplying beyond the environmental carrying capacity of its own ecosystem. If modern technology increases proportionally, those factors causing climatic changes and atmospheric pollution will be difficult to contain even at the present levels, much less to reduce. The biologically selective consequences cannot but manifest themselves increasingly. Man as a population surely possesses the genetic capacity to adapt to pollutants, but there is no reason to suppose that this capability is infinite. The human species is going to be taxed and tested more with the passing of every year if atmospheric pollution is not in some way controlled. There is every reason to believe that the stresses imposed through these factors in the future are going to have even more significance as influences on the selection of the human genotype.

Other Toxins in the Environment

As well as the environmental pollutants resulting from agriculture, industry and urban growth, man has introduced a variety of other stress agents into the ecosphere, such as radiation and various chemical poisons, from food additives to insecticides. Although many of these chemical substances apparently act to shorten the lives of postreproductive adults, and therefore are not selective in the sense of eliminating individuals before they are able to reproduce, there is evidence that many of these agents are mutagenic and potentially selective on all age groups in the population. A difficulty in assessing the extent of selection exerted by many of these chemical pollutants is that their total effect cannot be known. Our environment is so pervaded by a myriad of potentially mutagenic substances that definitive studies on the genetic and health risks presented by them all would prove to be nearly impossible. Even caffeine, so pervasive in our society in coffee, colas, and other beverages, has been indicated as an agent of chromosome damage (Weinstein et al. 1973).

The organochlorine compound DDT (dichlorodiphenyltrichloroethane) is perhaps the best example of a poison introduced in the optimism that its benefits to man would be far-reaching, outweighing potential liabilities. And in many respects this has been true. DDT has been employed successfully throughout the world to kill crop-damaging insects and to eradicate insect-borne diseases, especially malaria, which once caused 750,000 deaths per year in India alone. The treatment of large areas with DDT, beginning in the early 1940s, caused impressive reductions in the death rates of some underdeveloped countries. In Ceylon, the death rate was halved in a ten year period (Davis 1956). Yet ironically, less than three decades after the inventor of DDT received the Nobel Prize in 1948, many countries are outlawing its use. What was at first accepted as a multidimensional boon is now seen as a bane of similar proportions, causing more damage than benefit. It has even been argued, sidestepping humanitarian perspectives, that DDT's universal usage merely accelerated the ticking of the human population bomb. It is important to emphasize the distinction between deaths caused by disease *before* the use of DDT, and those deaths and genetic damage resulting from DDT itself. Disease eliminated weaker individuals of a population. The deleterious effects of DDT, as with any mutagenic agent, are to cause death and changes in the genetic constitution of man, to detrimental ends in almost all cases. Unfortunately, it is not patently simple to "prove" to skeptics that DDT causes death in humans, as the adverse effects are manifested indirectly, through cancer (Falk et al. 1965) and other pathologies.

DDT also serves as an illuminating example of the far-reaching effects that may occur from the wholesale use of environmental poisons. What began to occur, as a few unheeded voices had warned in the 1940s, was that the insects for which DDT was intended began to develop resistance. This is what happened with the fruit flies mentioned in Chapter 1. When the poisoning was initiated, the results were dramatic, but in any treated population there were always a few individuals possessing a natural resistance to the stressor that served as the population bases for strains of DDT-resistant insects.

Unfortunately, populations of vertebrates are not, on the whole, as resiliently adaptive as are invertebrates. The indiscriminate use of DDT has had devastating effects on birds and other wildlife, frequently killing great numbers of an insect population's natural predators, while the insect species renewed itself in full force from a few resistant individuals. In remote villages of Borneo, for example, the World Health Organization sprayed the insides of huts with DDT to eliminate flies potentially carrying disease. The weakened and dying flies became easy prey to geckos, small lizards common in tropical dwellings, which then sickened and fell victim to the village cats, which in turn became sick and began to die. As the cats became fewer, rats began to invade the villages, possibly bringing with them fleas harboring plague. To avert the possibility of a plague epidemic, disgruntled cats were dropped by parachute into the Bornean villages in an attempt to restore the balance that had existed before the interference of DDT (Smith et al. 1974).

The insidious quality of DDT is that, unlike other more immediately toxic substances, such as parathion, it does not readily break down into a harmless state, but instead may be carried along the entire length of a food chain, resulting in ecosystem disruption, as in the Bornean villages. When DDT is sprayed over pasture land, it will be consumed and concentrated by grazing cattle. With each higher step in the food chain, the quantity of DDT increases. When a human consumes contaminated meat or milk, he is receiving a dose of pesticide which will become even more highly concentrated over a period of time. By virtue of our position in the food chain, human milk is more contaminated with DDT than is cow's milk. According to the National Institute of Public Health in Sweden, human milk there contains 70 per cent more than the maximally accepted levels of DDT and related compounds. This amount is undoubtedly higher in the United States, where usage of DDT has always been far greater than in Western Europe. Dieldrin, another organochloride, is present at levels ten times higher than the accepted maximum in the milk of American and British mothers, and in Australian mothers it exists in quantities thirty times greater (Lofroth 1968). Babies drinking this milk are receiving very large doses of such poisons, which are potentially mutagenic. The organochlorides are not metabolized but stored in adipose tissue. If an individual happens to lose a great deal of weight, as in a crash diet, excessive quantities of organochlorides are released into the system and the dieter may suffer poisoning symptoms.

In accommodating ourselves to an environment pervaded with poisons, we are facing a dilemma requiring decisions on priorities. The poisons are already loose in our external and internal environment, and the situation is unlikely to improve much in the near future. Should we stop drinking milk and consuming animal fats because of the DDT contained in them? Should mothers refrain from breast-feeding their babies because of the very high levels of DDT passed on by this mechanism, in the process depriving their children of a psychologically important routine? These are difficult questions. Nutritional value, immunological benefits, and maternal contact provided by breast-feeding are factors to be weighed in assessing the high intake of DDT by nursing infants.

A fact often overlooked is that chemical pesticides are not confined to their areas of application. DDT concentrations are present in the tissues of men living on all parts of the globe whether or not organochlorides are locally used. This is significant testimonial to the ease with which pollutants are dispersed even when their application does not direct them into the atmosphere. For this reason, a diet of "organically grown" produce, cultivated without the aid of pesticides and chemical fertilizers, and usually sold at rather high prices, is not a realistic alternative, comparative analysis having shown no significant differences in the organochloride contents of commercially and organically grown fruits and vegetables. The explanation is simple—DDT and other toxins are ubiquitous at this point, and constitute inescapable stress factors on the fertility, mortality, and development of human populations. It is hoped that viable alternatives, such as biologically controlled crop production, will be employed more frequently. But a part of the success of using nontoxic pest controls must be a change in attitude on the part of the consumer, who has become accustomed to purchasing produce of a nearly flawless appearance. When consumers realize that the lack of pesticides in their food is preferable to an illusion of perfection, then rational human behavior will have triumphed. In the interim, commercial food growers are going to continue to use poisons, and we have little choice but to live with them until their environmental effect is dissipated with time, particularly in countries where agriculture has

FIGURE 4–8

The spraying of a peach orchard with parathion, a toxic insecticide. Excessive and indiscriminate use of pesticides has created a significant stress upon many organisms, including man.

(Photo courtesy of the U.S. Department of Agriculture)

reached the status of large industry. Potential genetic risk, whatever it may be, is the price the human population is now paying for years of distorted priorities. If the money that has been invested in the development of chemical poisons had been diverted instead to research in the field of biological controls, although the results might not have been as rapid nor as spectacular, the long-range effects would have been more wholesome for both man and the fragile ecosystem that he is so deleteriously affecting.

Measurement of the concentrations of DDT and other poisons would be extremely difficult, if not impossible, to obtain on a worldwide basis, but some statistics are available. Data obtained by S. Oden and his associates in Uppsala, Sweden, indicate that a total of about 1,250 metric tons of DDT compounds are distributed in Swedish soils. They have also found that organochlorides in the atmosphere, because of fallout in rain and snow, are being distributed in heaviest concentrations in those areas where the most food is grown.

Considerable controversy exists over setting a maximal safety level for the intake of DDT. Exposure to DDT and similar pesticides can be evaluated by analyzing adipose tissue, in which they are stored. Currently, from 5 to 27 ppm (parts per million) of DDT compounds are found in persons living in countries where its widespread use is common. From the known ratio of oral intake to storage in adipose tissue, it may be assumed that these individuals have a daily intake of less than .001 mg. per kg. of bodyweight, a quantity 10 per cent or less of that recommended as a safe level by agencies of the United Nations. However, at this point we must enter the arena of controversy. Studies with other vertebrates indicate that the levels now recommended as safe for man are about twenty times higher than they should be, a discrepancy meaning, if it is true, that the concentrations in men, rather than being comfortably on the low side, are about ten times too high. Evidence from studies with animals indicates that low doses of DDT taken orally increase the frequency of tumors, and that even smaller amounts will cause hepatic enzyme induction, which results in steroid hydroxylation. In other experiments, a concentration of 3 ppm was found to inhibit an essential enzyme in the heart muscle, and 5 ppm caused the necrosis of liver cells. Only 2.5 ppm of dieldrin or chlordane effected similar results.

Even if the figures given by the United Nations were accurate, a significant number of people are consuming levels even higher than the United Nations' recommended maximum of .01 g. per kg. of bodyweight, primarily from milk. If these recent studies are more representative of truly safe concentrations than those given by the United Nations, then Swedish babies are drinking 1,400 per cent more DDT than is theoretically safe, instead of 70 per cent of suggested levels. The picture is even more grim with American mothers, whose milk may contain levels of 0.15 to 0.25 ppm, placing the content at five times or more than that allowed for the interstate shipment of cows' milk. And adult Americans, containing about 12 ppm on the average, would be considered unfit for consumption, as the maximum allowed for meat in the United States is 7 ppm.

TABLE 4–1

Mean Concentrations of DDT * in
Human Body Fat in Parts per Million

Population	Year	Number in Sample	DDT (ppm)
United States	1942	10	0
United States	1950	75	5.3
United States	1955	49	19.9
United States	1954–1956	61	11.7
United States	1961–1962	130	12.6
United States	1962–1963	282	10.3
U.S. (all areas)	1964	64	7.0
U.S. (New Orleans)	1964	25	10.3
U.S. (white, over 6 yrs.)	1968	90	8.4
U.S. (nonwhite, over 6 yrs.)	1968	35	16.7
Alaskan Eskimo	1960	20	3.0
Canada	1959–1960	62	4.9
Canada	1966	27	3.8
United Kingdom	1963–1964	65	3.3
Germany	1958–1959	60	2.2
Hungary	1960	50	12.4
France	1961	10	5.2
Israel	1963–1964	254	19.2
India (Delhi)	1964	67	26.0

* DDT is expressed as DDT and its breakdown product DDE converted to DDT equivalents.

In the United States, differences in DDT concentration are directly correlated with occupation (agricultural workers), frequency of application in a particular area, and other socioeconomic factors.

From *Population, Resources, Environment: Issues in Human Ecology*, Second Edition, by Paul R. Ehrlich and Anne H. Ehrlich. W. H. Freeman and Company. Copyright © 1972.

The wide-ranging dispersal of DDT became apparent in 1965 when it was reported that DDT and two of its toxic metabolites, DDE and TDE, had been found in two varieties of Antarctic animals—Adelie penguins and crab-eater seals (Ruzicka and Tatton 1967). More traces of DDT compounds were reported from other birds and mammals. The Antarctic findings were especially newsworthy because of that continent's isolation and relative freedom from the influences of man. Cape Horn in South America is the nearest land mass to the Antarctic, and that is 1,000 kilometers distant; most other land masses are at least 2,000 kilometers away. That DDT resulted from local pollution seemed improbable. The human population there is minute, limited to a maximum of 4,000 researchers and explorers on an area of 13 million square kilometers. By a general international agreement, no ecosystems in the Antarctic are to be disturbed by the introduction of alien species or by the use of insecticides. Even considering the odds of broken treaties, there are no insect pests on that continent, and the use of pesticides would therefore be pointless. Careful studies have revealed that DDT and some related organochlorides must have been spread to the Antarctic by way of the seas and the air. The reasonable deduction is that not a square foot of the earth's surface would necessarily be free of pesticides by virtue of isolation. It is plausible to suppose that groups of Amerindians, nomadic peoples who practice only primitive agriculture, living in the remotest sections of the Amazon Basin are carrying in their bodies traces of pesticides originating with cultures thousands of miles removed. The disturbing element in the DDT chain is that it is so readily passed on from the body fat of one organism to that of another, as it is not biodegraded. The use of DDT, which is still widespread, is a practice allowing the continuous input of a persistent artificial stress factor into our heavily burdened environment and gene pools.

DDT and its metabolites are a major problem as a result of common usage on a worldwide scale, but many other poisons are also entering the ecosystem and causing stress on our genetic resources. Another group of chlorinated hydrocarbon compounds, the polychlorinated biphenyls (PCBs), have been found to be a widespread pollutant, the effects of which are relatively unknown. They are released into the environment in vapor from storage containers, from factory smokestacks—along with other industrial wastes poured into streams, rivers, lakes, and the ocean—and are also added to atmospheric particulate matter as rubber tires are worn down. Like DDT, PCBs have been shown to exist in the milk of nursing mothers, but in this case, we have much less knowledge of the potential effects. Are they mutagenic, carcinogenic, or neutral? Do they affect certain organ systems or shorten life spans by causing organ malfunction? Unfortunately, the environment is being polluted more rapidly and by far too many substances to allow a complete compilation of data on the effects of these chemicals.

It is probable that the deleterious effects of our accumulating poison load are being felt in more respects than have been conclusively proven. Aside from those already mentioned, numerous other pathologies are indicated. DDT in high doses increases the incidence of cancer in mice, and it does not seem unreasonable to assume that this is also true of man. In doses of 10 ppm—less than that contained in the bodies of most Americans—DDT causes the production of excessive amounts of certain liver enzymes that break down many prescribed drugs, negating their effectiveness. And of particular interest to anyone concerned with genetic consequences is that DDT affects the sex hormones of rats and birds, altering their reproductive physiologies. Whether or not this is true in man is not yet known. Further evidence directly relating to humans is even more disquieting. Alan Steinbach, a neurophysiologist at the University of California at Berkeley, believes that DDT is an irreversible nerve poison in man, as well as in the insects for which it is intended. Correlations have also been shown to exist between high levels of DDT in human adipose tissue and certain causes of death. Concentrations were notably higher in the fat of patients who died from softening of the brain, cerebral hemorrhage, hypertension, portal cirrhosis of the liver, and various cancers than in patients dying of infectious diseases. While more conclusive evidence is needed to prove that these correlations are definitely related to DDT levels, the data as they presently exist surely offer no reasons for optimism to anyone. When operating in the realm of environmental poisons, a policy of accepting innocence until there is absolute proof of each and every harmful effect is socially irresponsible and biologically reckless. The necessary research is often difficult and consumptive of a far greater amount of time than it takes to irrevocably poison the earth.

Radiation: The Ultimate Stress?

It is possible that the introduction of chemical poisons, including those meant only for the good of mankind, has resulted in biological harm surpassing whatever benefits may have accrued. But there is another kind of pollution, invisible and equally insidious in its effect, beside which all others pale in comparison. Ionizing radiation, a recent introduction as a pollutant, is more surely destined to affect life on earth for the worse than any other poison that man has yet unleashed. As Sheldon Novick emphasized in *The Careless Atom* (1969), our environment has a limited capacity for radiation, one which can be overextended only once. Radiation is the first pollutant to have been monitored successfully in its dispersal over the planet as a result of the relative ease with which radioactive materials can be traced. But monitor it is about all we are able to do, since there are no means for cleansing the environment of radiation introduced by man, except the cathartic effect of time.

It is disturbing to know that radiation is an expanding hazard within our ecosystem, but equally disquieting is the relative complacency with which the hazard is accepted. No environmental shock that man has perpetrated on his planet has a potential even approaching the destructive powers of excessive radiation, yet confronted with our own possible twilight, the development and testing of nuclear weapons, thus far primarily responsible for radioactive pollution, continue despite efforts by rational men to achieve universal cessation of these tests. Every major nation and a number of smaller ones seem to feel the need to stockpile nuclear weapons.

The hazards of radioactivity are too lightly treated. The main source of radioactive contamination of our environment in the past has resulted from explosions of nuclear devices, often in relatively remote areas, Hiroshima and Nagasaki excepted. Now a new threat looms as an imminent source for present and future nuclear contamination, an accessory of man's attempts to provide enough power to maintain his civilization at its present rate of consumption, or even to expand that rate. Nuclear reactor power plants are intended only for man's improvement, yet in their proliferation lies a forbidding portent for the genetic future of man (Curtis and Hogan 1969).

Nuclear fallout is perhaps the most serious contemporary aspect of ionizing radiation, but it may soon be challenged in severity by the problems associated with nuclear power plants. Exposure from X rays and other clinical radioactive devices surpasses that of fallout, but these mechanisms are at least controllable. Fallout, on the other hand, is not; and if weapons testing persists, then the levels of atmospheric radiation will become greater. So far, the worldwide genetic effects of fallout are estimated to have been only a small fraction—perhaps one per cent—

of that attributable to cosmic rays and other natural sources, yet it has been calculated that these increases have resulted in the births of 2,000 to 12,000 genetically defective babies and have caused 25,000 to 100,000 cases of leukemia and bone tumors. To the individuals involved, the effects are far from miniscule.

What is the nature of the fallout itself? When a nuclear device is exploded, various unstable radioactive isotopes are produced from many elements, decaying at differing rates by the emission of beta particles. *Local fallout* is that composed of the heavier concentration of particles that come to earth in the immediate vicinity of the explosion. *Tropospheric fallout* is composed of lighter particles and may be carried for many miles, being deposited over a wide radius. *Stratospheric fallout* consists of those radioactive particles, produced by devices of one megaton or more, that become trapped in the upper atmosphere and eventually circulate throughout the world.

The effectiveness of a radioactive isotope as a contaminant depends largely on its half-life, the length of time it takes half of the radioactivity to diminish. Some isotopes have half-lives of only a few seconds, minutes, or days. But others have much longer half-lives, remaining in the environment for many years. A common radioactive isotope of particular interest to man is strontium-90, which has a half-life of twenty-eight years; another, cesium-137, takes thirty years to lose half of its radioactivity. These long-lasting isotopes present a serious menace as they settle onto the earth, adhering to plant material, which is in turn consumed by animals, including man.

The primary dangers from excess radiation are the development of cancers, tumors, leukemia, and accompanying mutagenic effects. On an individual basis, the former three are of far greater concern, but in a discussion of the projected effects of radioactivity on the human population as a whole, the weight would have to be transferred to the latter. Individual suffering from nuclear weapons testing cannot be too strongly condemned. The genetic deterioration of the species, however, gives an even greater cause for concern, as it will lead to a geometric increase in personal suffering and to tremendous social costs, such as the burdens created by physical and mental birth defects.

Just how "safe" is the testing of nuclear weapons? As has been discussed, smaller particles with long half-lives are destined for global distribution despite the location of the test site. Anyone who would deny that these isotopes are harmful is purveying misinformation intentionally, or is naïve professionally. Even the rain of local fallout is much less

101

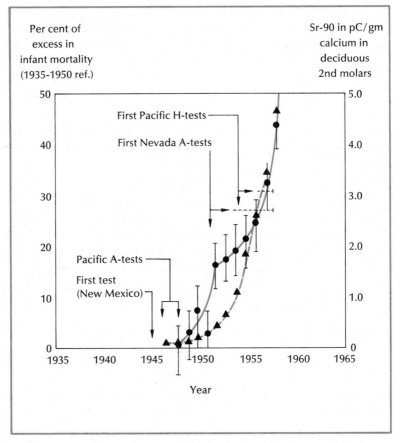

FIGURE 4-9

Per cent of excess in infant mortality (0–1 year) in Missouri calculated with respect to the 1935–1950 trend (solid line) and increasing strontium-90 concentration in teeth (dotted line).

(After E. J. Sternglass, *New Scientist*, 43 (1969), 178–181.)

predictable than it should be if the safety of potentially affected human groups is of any real interest. This fact was first brought to attention by the results of Project Bravo, a nuclear bomb test on the Bikini Atoll in the Pacific. The radioactive isotopes were carried much farther than had been anticipated, through the interference of high winds, and covered several thousand square miles with a radioactive dosage lethal to man. The radioactivity from Project Bravo had been expected to spread out over a large area of the Pacific, but to dissipate rapidly to undetectable levels. However, fish purchased from Japanese markets were tested and shown to possess levels of radioactivity significantly higher than those that should have been present at the anticipated rate of dilution. The reason for these high levels lies in the nature of radioactive materials, which become concentrated as they progress to higher levels in a food chain. Radioactive particles in the water are taken up by phytoplankton and zooplankton, which are consumed by larger zooplankton organisms, which are themselves consumed in turn by fish. With every step in this energy progression, the radioactivity is further concentrated until, in larger organisms, especially those having a partially or totally carnivorous diet, the amount of radioactivity is quite high.

Man, a large predator at the end of many food chains, ingests greater concentrations of radioactive isotopes than would a smaller herbivore. However, the avoidance of food products from animals high on the food chain, as is advisable with DDT concentration, is not necessarily a viable solution in avoiding radioactivity, as can be lucidly illustrated by the example of milk, conceded to be the single largest source of strontium-90 in the human diet. The strontium-90 replaces calcium in human metabolism, often initiating bone cancers and leukemia. It might seem that the most effective way to avoid an excessive intake of strontium-90 would be to delete milk products from the diet. But here we are faced with a biological catch-22. Although milk is a prime carrier of strontium, plant material carries even more. If a person were to abandon the use of milk and milk products, then the body must of necessity receive all its calcium from the more highly contaminated plants.

Another dangerous isotope ingested in milk is radioactive iodine-131. Its half-life is quite short—about eight days—and for a time it was considered to be of minimal concern to man. However, it is now known that in the few days during which iodine-131 represents a hazard, it may enter man through a simple food chain. The radioactive particles fall with rain or snow on plant material that is consumed by cattle, which pass the radioactivity on to humans in their milk. In man, the iodine becomes concentrated in the thyroid gland, a control center for the body's metabolism. It has been demonstrated that relatively low levels of radioactivity may cause tumors in the thyroid; and further, the toxic manifestations of the exposure may not be evident for ten years or more.

Illustrating the pervasiveness of radioactivity in the environment, a concentration of the isotope cesium-137 was found in the bodies of Alaskan Eskimos. Cesium behaves metabolically like potassium, found in all body cells, and it is readily absorbed into all living systems. In

Alaska the cesium fell to earth in rain or snow and was taken into the tissues of nutrient-hungry lichens where it was concentrated. During the barren winters, lichens are a major food source for caribou, which are in turn the primary diet of the Eskimo. After consuming the cesium-laden lichens, the caribou were eaten by the Eskimos, in whom the cesium was stored at a concentration double that found in the herbivorous caribou.

It is not possible to predict a given quantity of radioactive isotope contamination that will result from the consumption of any given food material, such as milk, because differing conditions determine the final concentration. If iodine-131 happens to fall on a range during a period when cattle are being given large amounts of supplementary feed, the contamination will be relatively less than if the cattle are dependent on natural forage. The individual physiologies of the cows will make a difference in the quantity of iodine given with the milk. It is true of any food that the degree of radioactive contamination will be subject to the vagaries of a multitude of influencing circumstances. But the complete perspective is that on which we should focus—the contaminants are in the environment, and we are ultimately receptacles for them to a greater or lesser extent.

We know only a small fraction of what there is to know about the effects of radioactive fallout. This is unfortunate since often the only way to have a problem taken as seriously as it ought to be is to have proof of its severity. Nor is it yet known what long-term damage results from the proximal exposure to an atomic explosion of adults or children *in utero*. With the detonation of a nuclear weapon, tremendous quantities of heat are produced at temperatures approaching those of the sun, within thousandths of a second. Everything in the immediate vicinity is vaporized, so long-term effects do not exist. Burns and mutilations may afflict close-range survivors, but what is the somatic and genetic expression of this sudden and powerful radioactive dosage over a period of many succeeding years? The Atomic Bomb Casualty Commission has been studying this question since 1948, tracing the histories of survivors of Hiroshima and Nagasaki (Miller 1969). Their findings are not conclusive in many respects, partially as a result of the difficulty of ascertaining that any given condition is unequivocally a consequence of the nuclear explosions. Some of their figures, however, give little reason to assume coincidences. Thirty-three out of 183 children exposed before birth had microcephaly, an abnormally small head size, and of these 15 were mentally retarded. Of the 15 mothers producing retarded children, 14 were 1.3 miles or less from the center of the explosions. Also of the 100,000 survivors who were closest to the explosion, there is an annual death rate eleven to twelve times higher than that of an unexposed control group. Among the survivors, about half the deaths result from leukemia. Chromosomal abnormalities were found in about a third of the survivors, but their significance is unknown; let it suffice that the probability that such abnormalities would be detrimental is far greater than the possibility of any benefit. Further, there is evidence that aging was accelerated among the survivors (Anderson, et al. 1974). In a group of forty-three Marshall Islanders exposed to radiation when the wind shifted after an explosion on Bikini, twenty-three have chromosomal irregularities. While it may be impossible to offer any precise statistical comparisons, it is an entirely valid supposition that genetic effects from radiation are almost always detrimental, since that is the case with mutations in general.

The fallout from nuclear explosions clearly represents a hazard to the welfare of man, probably to a greater extent than has been credited. Somatic effects are lamentable, as they produce untold suffering among perhaps hundreds of thousands of individuals, but subsequent genetic expression may prove to be of a vastly greater import.

A secondary mechanism for making radioactivity ubiquitous in the environment is the nuclear power plant, a source of energy destined to become commonplace throughout the United States and much of the world. Nuclear reactor plants may very likely become the primary source of global radioactive pollution. Intended solely for the benefit of man, their potential for usefulness is regrettably countered by a greater potential for harm. The plants are sometimes referred to as "non-polluting" because they do not produce the visible atmospheric contaminants that accompany the use of fossil fuels. But the radioactive waste products that are presently an inescapable accompaniment to their use may well be the greater of the two evils. The Atomic Energy Commission has proposed the solidification of radioactive fission waste products to be stored in empty salt mines. Even were there no potential for hazards emanating from the storage sites—but there are—the transportation of these waste materials incorporates some rather outstanding dangers. So extensive is the projected use of atomic energy, it has been estimated that by the year 2000 there will be 3,000 six-ton trucks in transit at any given time, carrying the nuclear wastes to disposal grounds. Surely no rational person would maintain that these trucks will be immune to accidents, with an ensuing leakage of radioactivity into the environment, endangering individuals within a variable radius.

There is an inherent danger in the plants themselves, which as man-made devices are subject to flaws. To err is human, but to err in a nuclear reactor plant may also be fatal, not only for those persons employed there but to others within a radius of many miles. Despite the claim of the Atomic Energy Commission (absorbed now by the Energy Research and Development Administration) to an excellent safety record, there have been some near misses that could have resulted in colossal tragedies. In the years preceding 1964, there were twelve accidents in reactor plants, involving serious damage to installations, exposure to radiation of individuals, and radioactive leakage. Some exceeded the "maximum credible accident," the Atomic Energy Commission's unrealistic standard for safety, defined as the worst that could occur in the absence of human error and with all safety devices operating flawlessly. In 1966, an accident at the Fermi Plant near Detroit exceeded this standard, although by chance there were no injuries (Ehrlich and Ehrlich 1972). Since the safety mechanisms *are* subject to flaws, and because humans *do* commit errors, to consider the probability of accidents in the absence of these two factors appears to be a meaningless speculation.

The Atomic Energy Commission predicted that by the year 2000, 60 per cent of the energy requirements in the United States will be met by nuclear power generated from 1,000 plants. Plutonium will be the major hazard, at least in terms of the possible aftermath of a serious accident. One pound of plutonium could kill 9 billion people, and a single plant requires about two tons for operation. The years subsequent to 2000 will witness an even greater proliferation of atomic power generators if the AEC's estimate of 24,000 operating plants by 2020 is even moderately accurate. At that number, an accident probability of one in a million would result in one accident every forty years. These are risky stakes, even for supplying the energy necessary to maintain our economy. Accidents within nuclear plants presage ultimately more serious consequences than do any other civilian installations.

Aside from the statistical probability that devastating accidents will accompany a profusion of nuclear power plants, there is another danger, more subtle but at least as significant in its effect on the biosphere and man's genetic integrity. This danger is the small but continuous quantity of radioactive isotopes leaking into the atmosphere and water. Presently

106

there are no economically feasible means of containing isotope leakage, and we are told that this must be accepted as a part of the price for nuclear energy. It is a price, sadly, without a figure; we know that there will be a cost, but that cost will not be revealed until we are committed to the bargain.

Emissions of a single isotope, krypton-85, could within the next century elevate the general radiation exposure of the population in the United States to 60 per cent of the maximum allowed by standards set by the National Committee on Radiation Protection and Measurement. As krypton-85 is but one of the 200 isotopes that will be released in low but steady levels from fission reactors, what will the cumulative addition of so great a number be on the biosphere? No one knows, nor is there currently any prospect for eliminating this menace as a by-product of fission plants. Although optimists maintain that the future advent of fusion reactors will solve these problems, F. L. Parker of the International Atomic Energy Agency has cautioned that radioactive tritium seeping from these installations may engender a greater peril than the leakage of isotopes from fission plants. In view of the grave risks to man intrinsic in the widespread use of nuclear power, it is questionable that wisdom has motivated its development as an alternative energy source. Perhaps if equivalent capital had been invested in research on solar energy devices, we would be advancing toward a safe, effective, inexpensive, and permanent supply of energy as a surrogate for the exhaustible fossil fuels.

What are "permissible" levels for the radioactive isotopes pervading our environment? It may be argued legitimately that none are, because no levels could be considered safe to man's health and genetic welfare, as the increase in radioactivity inevitably carries with it a potential for harm. But that is a moot point as fission reactors are most unlikely to be abandoned as an energy source. The evidence indicates that levels established as safe by the Atomic Energy Commission are not, and that new and realistic standards need to be set. The medical physicists J. W. Gofman and A. R. Tamplin of the Lawrence Radiation Laboratory of the University of California, in a report condemning currently acceptable levels, have urged revised guidelines, "absolutely above reproach and question," emphasizing that excessive radiation may lead to dire consequences for the future of the human race.

The politics of atomic energy control in the United States is open to criticism as a result of the somewhat contradictory nature of its structure. While the Energy Research and Development Administration is obliged to promote the use of nuclear power and does so zealously, it also serves the role of regulator, a function that will necessarily be at odds from time to time with its former capacity. We have no reason, from past performance, to suppose that the ERDA will assume an Olympian perspective on issues arising from the conflict of interests inherent in serving both as promoter and regulator. Early in the 1950s, the AEC attempted to attach minimal importance to the possible effects of atomic fallout. The agency's more recent activities have leaned in the direction of selling atomic power to the public as an indispensable and safe answer to energy shortages, while subduing any reference to the dangers that are inseparable facets of atomic energy development. Atomic power is *not* clean, in spite of the fact that emissions are invisible and therefore more easily ignored than those from traditional sources. Any attempts by knowledgeable individuals to convey this impression must be taken as calculatedly misleading.

Unless some radical and fully unexpected change attenuates the proliferation of nuclear power, increasing levels of radioactivity are inseparably linked to the future. How will the human genotype be affected? There is no way of predicting this except by logical inference from what we already know about the effects of radioactivity on our genetic constitutions. Present knowledge does not form the basis for an encouraging outlook. As useful as atomic energy may be, unless means are devised for eliminating the leakage of isotopes, the cost is more than likely to prove, over time, to have been far greater than the benefits. And even were emissions totally prevented, the ever-present shadow of major accidents arising from human error would still loom as an insoluble risk built into nuclear power development and man's coevolution with his technology.

A degree of genetic deterioration may have to be accepted as a part of man's future, at least for the time being. There is no reason to suppose that heightened levels of radioactivity can be other than detrimental to man. This is not to say that the resulting mutations might not be occasionally beneficial, but the statistical odds are heavily in favor of at best useless, or at worst damaging genetic changes. A rising incidence of leukemia, aplastic anemia, tumors, and other illnesses associated with higher level of radioactivity is a depressing prospect. Added to this is a higher rate of fetal wastage and mutation-caused birth defects. How can one assess the costs of human suffering? It is true that any advance has its accompanying dangers. Automobiles are responsible for thousands of annual deaths by accident, but few have suggested banning them for this reason. There is a difference, however; no one is forced to drive, and many choose to stay at home when risks are high, as during holiday periods. It is a question of unavoidable risk and magnitude; excessive radiation affects every living thing to an unknowable degree. Nuclear power may not be worth this hidden cost.

Of more future concern than individual pathologies are the mutagenic properties of radioactive isotopes. An ascending incidence of mutation can only result in a lowering of the fitness of the species. Mutations are indeed the stuff of evolution, but in excess they are maladaptive, encumbering us with the biological and social costs of mongoloids, microcephalics, brachycephalics, and other genetically produced deformities that are in no conceivable way beneficial.

Yet the fallout and isotope emissions from man's experiment with nuclear power are with us. The rain of radioactivity is pervading the world and is increasing. A silent, unseen rain, it is presently showering the earth with a conceivably more intense stress than man has met previously in his brief history.

Suggested Readings

Alexander, M. "Nonbiodegradable and Other Recalcitrant Molecules." *Biotechnology and Bioengineering* 15(1973): 611–647.

Anderson, Robert E., Charles R. Key, Tsutomu Yamamotu, and Todd Thorslund. "Aging in Hiroshima and Nagasaki Atomic Bomb Survivors: Speculations Based upon the Age-specific Mortality of Persons with Malignant Neoplasms." *American Journal of Pathology* 75 (1974): 1–11.

Aynsley, Eric. "How Air Pollution Alters Weather." *New Scientist* 44 (1969): 66–67.

Azevedo, M. D. "The Past, Present, and Future of the Biosphere." *Actualidades Biologicas* 44(1972): 128–173.

Battan, Louis J. *Harvesting the Clouds: Advances in Weather Modification.* New York: Doubleday and Co., 1969.

Broecker, Wallace S. "Man's Oxygen Reserves." *Science* 168(1970): 1537–1538.

Brown, A. W. A. "Insecticide Resistance Comes of Age." *Bulletin of the Entomological Society of America* 14(1968): 3–9.

Bryson, R. A. "Is Man Changing the Climate of the Earth?" *Saturday Review* 50(1967): 52–55.

Changmon, Stanley A. "La Porte Weather Anomaly, Fact or Fiction?" *Bulletin of the American Meteorological Society* 49(1968): 4.

Cihak, Robert W., Toranosuke Ishimaru, Arthur Steer, and Akira Yamada "Lung Cancer at Autopsy in A-bomb Survivors and Controls, Hiroshima and Nagasaki, 1961–1970: I. Autopsy Findings and Relation to Irradiation." *Cancer* 33(1974): 1580–1588.

Comar, Cyril L. "Biological Aspects of Nuclear Weapons." *American Scientist* 50(1962): 339–353.

Cooper, D. F., and William C. Jolly. *Ecological Effects of Weather Modification.* Ann Arbor: University of Michigan, School of Natural Resources, 1969.

Crecelius, Eric A., and David Z. Piper. "Particulate Lead Contamination Recorded in Sedimentary Cores from Lake Washington, Seattle." *Environmental Science and Technology* 11((1973): 1053–1055.

Curley, August, and Renate Kimbrough. "Chlorinated Hydrocarbon Insecticides in Plasma and Milk of Pregnant and Lactating Women." *Archives of Environmental Health* 18(1969): 156–164.

Curtis, Richard, and Elizabeth Hogan, *Perils of the Peaceful Atom: The Myth of Safe Nuclear Power Plants.* New York: Doubleday, 1969.

Cutchis, P. "Stratospheric Ozone Depletion and Solar Ultraviolet Radiation on Earth." *Science* 184(1974): 13–19.

Davis, Kingsley. "The Amazing Decline in Mortality in Underdeveloped Areas." *Journal of the American Economics Association* 46(1956): 305–318.

Davison, A. W., A. W. Rand, and W. E. Betts. "Measurement of Atmospheric Fluoride Concentrations in Urban Areas." *Environmental Pollution* 5(1973): 23–33.

Dorf, Erling. "Climatic Changes of the Past and Present." *American Scientist* 48(1960): 341–364.

Ehrlich, Paul R., and Anne H. Ehrlich. *Population, Resources, Environment.* 2nd ed. San Francisco: W. H. Freeman and Co., 1972.

Falk, H. L., Sandra J. Thompson, and Paul Kotin. "Carcinogenic Potential of Pesticides." *Archives of Environmental Health* 10(1965): 848–858.

Fiserova-Bergerova, Vera, Jack L. Radomski, John E. Davies, and Joseph H. Davis, "Levels of Chlorinated Hydrocarbon Pesticides in Human Tissue." *Industrial Medicine and Surgery* 36(1967): 65–70.

Fletcher, Robert D. "The Donora Smog Disaster—A Problem in Atmospheric Pollution." *Weatherwise* 2(1949): 56–60.

Flohn, Hermann. *Climate and Weather.* New York: McGraw-Hill, 1969.

Fowler, W. B., and J. D. Helvey. "Effect of Large-Scale Irrigation on Climate in the Columbia Basin." *Science* 184(1974): 121–127.

Haagen-Smit, A. J. "Air Conservation." *Scientia* 163(1969): 359–367.

Hersh, Seymour. *Chemical and Biological Warfare.* New York: Doubleday (Anchor Book), 1969.

Holmberg, Mats, and Jon Jonasson. "Synergistic Effect of X-ray and UV Irradiation on the Frequency of Chromosome Breakage in Human Lymphocytes." *Mutation Research* 23(1974): 213–221.

LaBarre, N., J. B. Milne, and G. B. Oliver. "Lead Content of Snow." *Water Research* 7(1973): 1215–1218.

Lerner, I. Michael. *Heredity, Evolution, and Society.* San Francisco: W. H. Freeman and Co., 1968.

Lewis, E. B. "Leukemia, Multiple Myeloma, and Aplastic Anemia in American Radiologists." *Science* 142(1963): 1492–1494.

Likens, Gene E., and Herbert F. Bormann. "Acid Rain: A Serious Regional Environmental Problem." *Science* 184(1974): 1176–1179.

Lofroth, Goran. "Pesticides and Catastrophe." *New Scientist* 40(1968): 567–568.

Mayr, Ernst. "Geographical Character Gradients and Climatic Adaptation." *Evolution* 9(1955): 105–108.

McDermott, Walsh. "Air Pollution and Public Health." *Scientific American* 205(1961): 49–57.

McNeil, Mary. "Lateritic Soils." *Scientific American* 211(1964): 96–106.

Meyer, Mary B., and James A. Tonascia. "Possible Effects of X-ray Exposure During Fetal Life on the Subsequent Reproductive Performance of Human Females." *American Journal of Epidemiology* 98(1973): 151–160.

Miller, Robert W. "Delayed Radiation Effects in Atomic-bomb Survivors." *Science* 166(1969): 569–574.

Mitchell, J. M., Jr. "A Preliminary Evaluation of Atmospheric Pollution as a Cause of Global Temperature Fluctuations." In *Global Effects of Environmental Pollution*, edited by S. F. Singer. New York: Springer-Verlag, 1970.

Patterson, H. Wade, and Ralph H. Thomas. *Accelerator Health Physics.* New York: Academic Press, 1973.

Rapoport, Roger. "Catch 24,400 (or Plutonium Is My Favorite Element)." In *Eco-Catastrophe* by the editors of *Ramparts*. San Francisco: Canfield Press (Division of Harper and Row), 1970.

Revelle, R., and H. E. Suess. "Carbon Dioxide Between Atmosphere and Ocean and the Question of an Increase of Atmospheric CO_2 During the Past Decades." *Tellus* 9(1967): 18–27.

Ruzicka, J. H. A., and J. O. Tatton. "Organochlorine Pesticides in Antarctica." *Nature* 215(1967): 246–248.

Sanni A. O. "Seasonal Variation of Atmospheric Radioactivity at Ibadan." *Tellus* 25(1973): 80–85.

Sax, Karl, and Hally J. Sax. "Possible Mutagenic Hazards of Some Food Additives, Beverages, and Insecticides." *Japan Journal of Genetics* 43 (1968): 89–94.

Schaeffer, Vincent J. "The Inadvertent Modification of the Atmosphere by Air Pollution." *Bulletin of the American Meteorological Society* 50 (1969): 199–206.

Scholander, P. F. "Evolution of Climatic Adaptation in Homoiotherms." *Evolution* 9(1955): 15–26.

Schreider, Eugene. "Ecological Rules, Body-heat Regulation, and Human Evolution." *Evolution* 18(1964): 1–9.

Silverman, Charlotte. "Nervous and Behavioral Effects of Microwave Radiation in Humans." *American Journal of Epidemiology* 97(1973): 219–224.

Smith, J. C., Henry J. Steck, and Gerald Surette. *Our Ecological Crisis.* New York: Macmillan Publishing Co., Inc., 1974.

Wagner, Richard H. *Environment and Man.* 2nd ed. New York: W. W. Norton Publishing Co., 1974.

Walker, Martin. "Drought." *The New York Times Magazine*, 9 June 1974, pp. 11–13, 42–46.

Warner, J. "A Reduction in Rainfall Associated with Smoke from Sugar Cane Fires—An Inadvertent Weather Modification." *Journal of Applied Meteorology* 7(1968): 247–251.

Whipple, W., J. V. Hunter, and S. L. Yu. "Unrecorded Pollution from Urban Runoff." *Journal of the Water Pollution Control Federation* 46 (1974): 873–885.

chapter
5

INFECTIOUS DISEASES AS A STRESS FACTOR ON CONTEMPORARY HUMAN POPULATIONS

Infectious disease has existed as a stress factor in the evolutionary progress of man from his most incipient stage. Whether caused by viruses, bacteria or protozoan and metazoan parasites, disease has wielded a powerful selective force on human populations, although a number of infectious diseases were absent from primitive societies (Black 1975). The development of culture, which as it evolved bound men together into larger aggregates, has been a vital factor in the relationship of man

113

to disease. Not only did culture condense human numbers, but through the development of agriculture, it placed man in proximity to certain diseases with which he previously had minimal contact.

There are three primary variables in the study of infectious disease: the host, the pathogen, and the environment. A study of disease in man or in any other animal necessitates a consideration of the interrelationships of these variables, as the transmission of disease concerns all three. Man's environment incorporates all aspects of his culture; also, man's culture is responsible for his ability to effect great changes in the natural environment. These in turn affect his relationship to disease vectors— sometimes to his advantage and at other times to his detriment. For example, flooding areas for agriculture may cause the proliferation of disease, as by mosquitoes that transmit malaria and the snails that harbor schistosomiasis. The latter has currently replaced malaria as the number one health problem resulting from increased agricultural technology throughout the world.

The Coevolution of Man and Disease

Five stages in the culture-disease history of man have been suggested (Polgar 1964): hunting and gathering, settled villages, preindustrial cities, industrial cities, and the ameboid urban aggregates of the present. Each of these levels of interaction between man and his environment presents its own benefits and liabilities. Among the hunters and gatherers, a low population density and group size restricted the spread of infectious diseases. They can be divided roughly into two types: those already specifically adapted to prehominids, such as external lice, pinworms and yaws; and those not specifically adapted but transmitted accidentally, as from insect bites, wounds, or through eating parasite-contaminated food. Diseases accidentally transmitted to man, without specifically coevolving with man as a host, include trichinosis, sleeping sickness, schistosomiasis, and tetanus. By the time of *Homo erectus*, some meat was being cooked and some clothing had been innovated, cultural practices that undoubtedly served to reduce parasite infestation.

The sedentary villages that began to appear as man increasingly adopted agriculture added new dimensions to disease possibilities. Population density increased, allowing disease pathogens to be disseminated more easily. Also, animal domestication in the Neolithic brought man into closer contact with pigs, cattle, goats, dogs, and other animals carrying particular pathogens. *Salmonella*, a bacterium, and *Ascaris*, a nema-

114

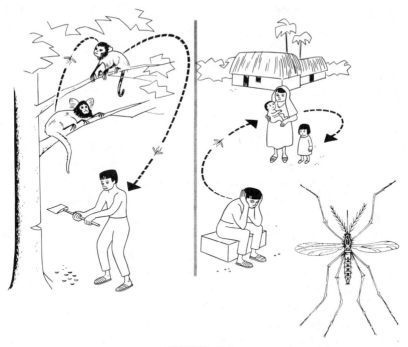

FIGURE 5–1

The transmission of yellow fever to man. The virus is primarily maintained in monkeys and mosquitoes. However, an individual infected may return to an urban area, where the disease will then be transmitted from one human to another by the domestic *Aedes* mosquito. Numerous diseases may be passed on to man in such incidental fashion.

(Marston Bates, *Man in Nature*, 2nd ed., © 1964. Reprinted by permission of Prentice-Hall, Inc., Englewood Cliffs, New Jersey.)

tode parasite, are transmitted by animals bringing their pathogens into intimate contact with man. As well, certain products of these domesticated animals—milk, meat, skin, and hair—allowed the transmission of tuberculosis, brucellosis and anthrax.

The plant agriculture of these early sedentary societies exposed men to additional health hazards. When new ground is broken for crop planting, the incidence of scrub typhus increases. It has also been demonstrated that the spread of agriculture in tropical Africa may be associated directly with malaria and sickle-cell anemia. When early West Africans pushed farther into the forests, clearing trees for agriculture, they encroached on the habitat of the pongids, a kind of ape, which were killed or driven deeper into the bush. The pongids had been a primary host

115

for the causative organism of malaria, *Plasmodium falciparum*, carried by a mosquito, *Anopheles gambiae*. But as the pongids were displaced by man, the mosquitoes readily transferred from their primate hosts to humans, passing on the malaria in the process. As malaria increased, so did sickle-cell anemia, that otherwise deleterious trait conferring a relative immunity to malarial infection (Livingstone 1958).

Preindustrial cities were the next stage for the coevolution of man and disease. Water supplies polluted with human waste resulted in the transmission of typhoid and cholera. Unsanitary conditions fostered the well-being of rats harboring lice, which transmitted typhus and, of greater consequence, plague. Social changes accompanying the crowding of humans affected the expression of some diseases. Previously, syphilis had not been a venereal disease, but with the crowded conditions in cities, changes in family structures, and sexual promiscuity, it became one (Hudson 1965). Concentrated populations in these cities also gave rise to the perpetuation of certain diseases in endemic form. It has been demonstrated that measles needs a human host population of about one million to exist as an endemic disease, so it could not have been an indigenous problem among early groups of men whose interconnecting settlements never approximated that size. Even by 1800 A.D., only 2.2 per cent of the population of Europe lived in cities of 100,000 or more (Armelagos and Dewey 1970).

The industrialization of urban areas accentuated existing problems as well as producing new ones. Industrial wastes increased air and water pollution. The growth of urban slums, an ever-expanding problem in human culture, resulted in unsanitary conditions ideal for the spread of infectious disease. During this same period, increasing explorations and colonial expansion spread previously localized diseases to human populations having no experience with or immunity to them. In Hawaii, neither venereal diseases nor measles was known until their introduction by Europeans. The spread of epidemic diseases during this period, locally and globally, was more pronounced than it had ever been in the entire course of human evolution. Epidemics were especially prevalent in industrial cities; typhus, typhoid, smallpox, and diptheria raged during the late eighteenth and early nineteenth centuries.

Perhaps the most devastating epidemic disease ever to have scourged mankind was the Black Death or plague, caused by *Bacillus pestis*, which swept through Europe and parts of Asia from the times of the Greek and Roman Empires. The best known epidemic in prerenaissance Europe lasted for three years, from 1348 to 1350, eliminating about a fourth of the entire population. Outbreaks occurred throughout Europe in the years following this first major epidemic. In 1665, plague killed about a tenth of London's population of 460,000. People fled, consequently carrying the disease to other locales. In 1830, 60,000 people fled from Moscow during an epidemic, and in 1832, about 55,000 terrified New Yorkers sought refuge elsewhere when plague was reported, leaving in stagecoaches, steamboats, carts and wheelbarrows (Langer 1964). It is now known that the disease is transmitted to man by fleas, carried chiefly by black rats, ground squirrels, and some other rodents. Unsanitary conditions gave an impetus to the plague epidemics, as flea-infested rats swarmed in the refuse of the cities. Plague is not historical; it still lurks, even in the United States, where a few cases are diagnosed and reported annually, waiting for a formula of rats, lice, and accommodating circumstances to unfold once more.

Less obvious cultural factors may be responsible for the selective value of disease and its transmission in human populations. In Vietnam there are two major geomorphological features: fertile deltas and fertile hills. In the low deltas, houses are built on the ground, next to the stables; in the hill country, houses are constructed on stilts eight to ten feet above the ground, and domesticated animals are quartered below the house. For the last few decades, delta people have been moving into the hill country, as a result of overpopulation in the deltas. They have, however, not adopted the culture of the hill people, but have continued to build their houses on the ground. These newcomers often contract malaria, whereas the hill people contract it infrequently. The explanation lies in the culturally-rooted differences in house construction. The flight ceiling of the malaria mosquito (*Anopheles minimus*) is eight or nine feet, placing the vector below the elevated houses of the original hill dwellers. Also, the hill people cook in their living area, providing a smoky, noxious atmosphere for those mosquitoes that do wander in. Migrants from the deltas not only live within the flight range of the mosquitoes, but they build separate kitchens; their living quarters are smoke-free and therefore more inviting to the malaria mosquitoes. Delta people have become fearful of moving into the hills, believing that the incidence of malaria is the work of evil spirits inimical to their presence (May 1960).

Increased infectious disease may also be a concomitant of projects undertaken for a culture's benefit. The Aswan High Dam in Egypt, which is a disaster in several ecological respects, has made possible perennial irrigation in areas where this practice was previously impossible. Irrigation in subtropical and tropical regions provides an excellent habitat for the growth of snails serving as hosts for a blood fluke that causes *bilharzia*, a disease characterized by serious anemia. In Egypt, as in some other countries, bilharzia has replaced malaria as the primary health problem. Perennial irrigation, however, also provides a successful breeding ground for disease-carrying mosquitoes. Habitat modification for irrigation, especially for the extension of rice fields, results in an alteration of the species composition of mosquitoes, and accordingly the variety of vectors to which man is exposed (Surtees 1970).

The control of infectious diseases, particularly those transmitted by contact, is made more difficult with rapid, global transportation. Within hours, a vector may be transferred distances that would have taken weeks a century ago. Now, more and more people are able to travel, increasing the possibility that diseases will be carried from one locale to another. The potential dangers in expanding population mobility are accepted and dealt with to the best of our present medical knowledge by required immunization. Of course, viruses are essentially exempt from treatment and probably constitute the major international hazard. If ever a fatal and easily transmitted disease develops, one resistant to medical technology, the ease with which it could be spread throughout the world is a grim reality. This eventuality is neither impossible nor improbable. Much as we do not savor contemplating the rapid spread of virulent epidemics, worldwide conditions are moving in directions quite favorable to the dissemination of new strains of viral and bacterial pathogens. The human population explosion is an accommodating situation. The predicted masses of humanity that will be teeming on earth within the next forty to fifty years will create an even more conducive medium for the coevolution of man and disease. Along with gross overpopulation will come malnutrition for large numbers of the world's peoples. As man exhausts his resources, there will simply not be enough food to go around. Malnourished individuals are more susceptible to almost any infectious disease. Given these circumstances, it is no mere fantasy to suppose that a drug-resistant and highly virulent pathogen might diffuse through the human population at some future time, travelling swiftly from continent to continent, as indeed influenza viruses do today, until most of humanity has been infected and possibly exterminated by it. As human population increases greatly, so do the resources for the evolution and transmission of infectious disease.

If the foregoing assumption seems an exaggeration of possibilities, consider the difficulties experienced in the United States in recent years in coping with flu epidemics. In 1968, an epidemic of Asian flu caused four times the number of deaths from influenza reported in 1967. This is a relatively mild situation compared with that which could result from the release of a truly virulent disease into the human environment, yet it was a serious health hazard, taking a total of 618 lives in the United States alone and taxing society both in extra medical care and in the loss of working hours suffered by those thousands who contracted the flu and survived.

Genetics and Disease

Infectious diseases provide a good case for the value of genetic heterogeneity in human populations. The resistance of prior genotypes to existing diseases is not necessarily of any value against new strains of pathogens, but the more diverse the population in its genetic base, the greater the probability of a substantial number of immune individuals. If, to speculate on an extreme example, a virus were to decimate the majority of humanity, those individuals possessing a natural immunity or resistance could maintain the species. In a microcosm, such was true of island populations decimated by smallpox and measles during the eighteenth and nineteenth centuries. It cannot be overemphasized that in terms of population genetics, diversity is ultimately beneficial.

Although it is difficult to demonstrate in man, there is evidence that the ability to produce antibodies as a response to stimulation by a foreign antigen has a genetic basis, which may have played a dominant role in man's evolutionary response to infectious disease. For example, when measles was imported into the Hawaiian Islands by missionaries and whaling ships, a large number of the native population contracted the disease and died. In contrast, mortality from the disease among European stock was relatively low. Among the Hawaiians, those with genetic characteristics affording some resistance tended to survive the disease, so that in subsequent epidemics the mortality rate was lower and the course of the disease less severe. As most of the population lacking a degree of natural immunity had died, the frequency of resistance in the gene pool soared in a single generation.

The evidence for specific genetic factors is even more convincing in the case of metabolic polymorphisms that have evolved in response to disease. With sickle-cell anemia, which developed as an adaptive response to malaria, we know that the appearance and widespread incidence of a trait that is lethal in the homozygous condition provides resistance to malaria when heterozygous. There are other pathologies

119

that would seem to carry a selective advantage by virtue of their frequency in the population, but the nature of the advantage is yet unknown. One of these is cystic fibrosis of the pancreas for which the recessive gene shows a high frequency among Caucasian populations (Knudson, *et al.* 1967). Several studies in separate areas of the world have shown that carriers of cystic fibrosis tend to have large families, but the meaning of this finding is unclear. Although many cystic fibrosis children die before reaching reproductive age, the great number of offspring born to these families compensates for this loss. The possibility seems to be that the gene frequency for this disease is increasing somewhat, although the physiological basis for an advantage remains a mystery. It could well be that afflicted parents are compensating for perinatal loss.

In considering the genetic response to disease, it must be remembered that opposing advantages may be at work; one characteristic, which is disadvantageous in relation to a given disease, may harbor qualities

TABLE 5–1

Smallpox Mortality in Relation to ABO Blood Groups

		Blood Group					
		A				AB	
Mortality	N (% Died)	A_1	A_2	B	O	A_1B	A_2B
1965 Fresh Cases Survived	97 (48.5%)	43		30	22	2	
Died	103 (51.5%)	63		18	15	7	
1966 Fresh Cases (unvaccinated) Survived	116 (54.0%)	29	13	36	19	17	2
Died	99 (46.0%)	54	5	10	4	23	3
1966 Fresh Cases (vaccinated) Survived	14 (63.6%)	1	0	7	6	0	0
Died	8 (36.4%)	8	0	0	0	0	0

After F. Vogel, and M. R. Chakravartti, *Humangenetik* 3 (1966): 166–180.

beneficial under other circumstances, so it does not disappear from the population. In India, individuals having blood groups A and AB are at a considerable disadvantage during smallpox epidemics in contrast to those having groups B and O. Studies were carried out in an area remote from modern hospitals with particular attention to the mechanics of natural selection (Vogel and Chakravartti 1966). It was found that survivors of smallpox were predominantly of blood groups B and O, and that they were also less severely scarred than the smaller number of survivors in blood groups A and AB. Efforts were made to study *all* smallpox patients within the prescribed area in order to make the conclusions valid statistically. Smallpox has been endemic in India for a very long time, so during these epidemics, a relatively small percentage of the population is affected, the others having either a genetic or acquired immunity. If there were not some advantage in having A and AB blood that offsets the heightened vulnerability to smallpox, these groups should have been eliminated from these local populations. The advantage is as yet unknown. What *is* known is that there is blood type correlation with various diseases and also some infections, and that blood grouping in a given population is associated with other selective factors. Minimal progress has been made in separating and defining these effects, or in explaining the actual gene frequencies in populations.

Disease Today and in the Future

It is ironic, and a fact that will be surprising to many, that diseases are likely to become more of a stress factor on the natural selection of human populations in years ahead. Disease is an unfortunate determinant as it has undoubtedly caused the spread of many genes that were rare among the populations of our less crowded ancestors. The fact that these genes were rare indicates that they may lower fitness, or be neutral, and incorporation of such genes into contemporary populations undoubtedly may do the same except in specific cases where the benefit— as with sickle-cell anemia—outweighs the cost. Infectious disease is extremely compatible with dense populations—the human condition of the future.

The question has been raised as to whether some of the degenerative diseases of older age, such as cancer and cardiovascular failure, may act to confer fitness on a population. The genetic basis could stem from a time when there was a population advantage in the elimination of adults past their period of sexual reproductivity (Nye 1966). Proponents of this idea suggest that a selective value existed in the "built-in obsolescence" of societal members who had passed their height of social usefulness. Under the stressful living conditions of primitive societies, shorter generations provide a more rapid turnover of the gene pool and, consequently, allow more rapid evolution in response to altering circumstances. Individuals past their peak performance sexually and in terms of societal, cooperative activities, such as food production, might place strains on the overall population by competing with younger and possibly more genetically fit individuals for mates, material resources, and social dominance. The selective mechanism of degenerative conditions would theoretically aid in reducing these burdens on more primitive societies, especially in times of food shortages, migrations, and other periods of duress.

As the advocates of this idea will concede, however, the facts of contemporary primitive societies do not support the thesis. The South African Bantus suffer less from heart disease than do affluent Caucasians. It is suggested that the selective mechanisms began in very early populations of primarily carnivorous men, who in consuming large amounts of animal fats subjected themselves to arteriosclerosis and heart disease. The essence of this argument is quite tenuous. It seems far more likely that man's contemporary diet is responsible for the cardiovascular disease occurring in populations that are affluent enough to afford meat. Today in countries where food is plentiful, overweight is a common problem. A majority of adults in the developed countries of the world lead relatively sedentary lives and consume diets inappropriate to their levels of physical activity. A high incidence of cardiovascular disease is what might be anticipated as a result of current lifestyles, rather than as the result of hypothetical selective pressures of thousands of years past.

The precarious future of the coevolution of man and disease may be seen as a less obscure reality when one ponders a case from the near past. In 1967, a shipment of African vervet monkeys brought into laboratories in Marburg, Germany and Yugoslavia were found to harbor an unknown virus (Smith, et al. 1967). An outbreak of the virus occurred among twenty-five laboratory workers, seven of whom died from severe hemorrhagic symptoms. Five more were infected after coming into contact with blood from the original patients. The Marburg virus, as it is now termed, was resistant to all medical treatment and was overcome only by the natural resistance of infected individuals who survived. By a stroke of good luck, the disease appeared within the confines of laboratories and was therein contained. But what would have happened had this contagious, lethal pathogen been released accidentally on the population at large? The rapidity and ease of mobility that we enjoy could have caused its easy dispersal to diverse areas of the world, affecting large segments of the human population with a disease that medical technology could not hinder. If the virus retained its strength, millions could have died in its wake. There are no means for predicting the ultimate effects of such a disease; one could only score the survivors against the victims. How long it will be before man may be plagued with a catastrophe of this nature is anyone's guess. Viruses and the bacteria with which they coevolve—and both coevolve with human populations—adapt thousands of times more rapidly to environmental stress factors than can human populations.

In reference to bacteria alone, as viruses are insensitive to antibiotics and demand their own medical technology for treatment, we are in danger of exhausting our stores of effective antibiotics as a result of infectious drug resistance. Furthermore, it is doubtful that enough new antibiotics will be discovered to combat familiar as well as unfamiliar strains of disease. As discussed previously, we may now be on the threshold of a "preantibiotic" age in modern medicine.

The contemporary situation should not be likened precisely to the period in human medical history before antibiotics were discovered. The world is now as it has never been in terms of human population, mobility, and demographic shifts. The conditions for the evolution of pathogens are markedly different. There has never been a human population equal in numbers to the present, and that number will double in only a few more years. The rates of evolution of disease organisms are probably more rapid now than at any previous time. As the vectors for bacteria and viruses, we provide them with endless opportunities for their evolution.

The continuing development of biological warfare organisms adds an additional threat as man is now not only faced with natural pathogens, but also with those cultivated for the very purpose of destroying man, his domestic animals, and his plant crops. More than 2,700 workers in virus laboratories have become infected inadvertently with insect-carried viruses, and of these, 107 have died (Hersh 1969). Man's contempt for his environment and for his own species, adequately reflected in most aspects of warfare, is especially evident in the creation of pathological horrors meant to be released on his own kind. It is also possible that man-created disease might adapt readily to other species for which they were not intended, creating far-reaching ecological chaos. But as Paul Ehrlich has suggested, the virus laboratories may result in an accidental solution to the population problem.

From long before primates assumed an erect posture, diseases have been a powerful natural selective force on human populations that have continuously eliminated individuals lacking the appropriate resistance. Evolutionary responses to disease have been primarily physiological rather than morphological, at times incorporating detrimental traits that confer resistance to a specific disease. Some beneficial genetic characters may have been lost in the compromise resulting from the selective stress of disease. In the past diseases have decimated populations periodically in Europe, India, and elsewhere. Our contemporary civilizations are so constructed that disease will not be contained by geographical boundaries. This situation shadows our swelling numbers with an ominous threat. With the exception of limiting the human population in an attempt to balance the coevolutionary mechanisms at work, there is little that can be done. If the medical resources for combatting disease become ineffectual as a result of the increasingly rapid evolution of human pathogens, and as humanity floods the earth, disease is destined to play an increasingly significant role in future natural selection. Rather than a disease-free world, as was once the promise of medical science, future decades may find disease as a more potent selective force on man than it has ever been in the past.

Suggested Readings

Armelagos, George J., and John R. Dewey. "Evolutionary Response to Human Infectious Diseases." *Bioscience* 20(1970): 271–275.

Black, Francis L. "Infectious Diseases in Primitive Societies." *Science* 187 (1975): 515–518.

Dixon, Bernard. "Antibiotics on the Farm—Major Threat to Human Health." *New Scientist* 36(1967): 33–35.

Ehrlich, Paul R., and Anne H. Ehrlich. *Population, Resources, Environment*, 2nd ed. San Francisco: W. H. Freeman and Co., Inc., 1972.

Hanson, R. P., S. E. Sulkin, E. L. Buescher, W. McD. Hammon, R. W. McKinney, and T. H. Work. "Arbovirus Infections of Laboratory Workers." *Science* 158(1967): 1283–1286.

Hersh, Seymour M. *Chemical and Biological Warfare*. New York: Doubleday and Co., Inc., Anchor, 1969.

Hudson, E. H. "Treponematosis and Man's Social Evolution." *American Anthropologist* 60(1965): 885–902.

Knudson, A., L. Wayne, and W. Hallet. "On the Selective Advantage of

Cystic Fibrosis Heterozygotes." *American Journal of Human Genetics* 19 (1967): 388–392.

Langer, William L. "The Black Death." *Scientific American* 210(1964): 114–121.

Livingstone, F. B. "Anthropological Implication of Sickle-Cell Gene Distribution in West Africa." *American Anthropologist* 60(1958): 533–562.

May, J. M. "The Ecology of Human Disease." *Annual of the New York Academy of Sciences* 84(1960): 789–794.

Nye, E. R. "Natural Selection and Degenerative Cardiovascular Disease." *Eugenics Quarterly* 14(1966): 127–131.

Polgar, S. "Evolution and the Ills of Mankind." In *Horizons of Anthropology*, edited by S. Tax. Chicago: Aldine Publishing Co., 1964.

Reed, T. Edward, and James Neel. "Huntington's Chorea in Michigan. 2. Selection and Mutation." *American Journal of Human Genetics* 11 (1959).

Smith, C. E. G., D. I. H. Simpson, E. T. W. Bowen, and I. Zlotnik. "Fatal Human Disease from Vervet Monkeys." *Lancet* 2(1967): 1119–1121.

Surtees, Gordon. "Effects of Irrigation on Mosquito Populations and Mosquito-borne Diseases in Man, with Particular Reference to Ricefield Extension." *International Journal of Environmental Studies* 1(1970): 35–42.

Vogel, F., and M. R. Chakravartti. "ABO Blood Groups and Smallpox in a Rural Population of West Bengal and Bihar (India)." *Humangenetik* 3(1966): 166–180.

chapter
6

DEMOGRAPHY AND NATURAL
SELECTION IN HUMAN
POPULATIONS

In terms of both man's survival and the direction of natural selection, population phenomena are becoming increasingly important. Before examining specific effects of demography, we should consider some of the ramifications of the population explosion and its effects on human survival. Overpopulation is a phenomenon gauged by criteria that vary according to different situations. It is not, as is often supposed, judged solely by the number of people per unit of land. Overpopulation occurs when the number of individuals exceeds limiting resources, and these limits may be land, food, water, or any of a number of other factors. There may be thousands of acres of open space available to a given population, but if resources are insufficient, then there is the condition of overpopulation.

Overpopulation

The state of Colorado may be taken as a currently appropriate model for understanding overpopulation and conceptualizing a contemporary "Tragedy of the Commons," as first described by Hardin (1968). During the past few years, Colorado has become popular as the new Mecca, advertised as a land of pure mountain streams and endless open spaces. Fickle humanity, having trampled, overdeveloped, and subdivided the California pastures in the last three decades, is anxious to find new pleasure grounds with less development and a degree of peace and quiet. The population of Colorado is swelling, and still there seems to be no end to space. So it appears. The space is there, but already the state is overpopulated in terms of limiting factors, whereas the emigration has just begun. Denver, the hub of Colorado's population, has grown to be one of the most polluted cities in the country, having a higher carbon monoxide level in its smog than Los Angeles. The smog hangs over the entire metropolitan area, often covering Boulder, thirty miles to the northwest. But the real limiting factor in Colorado is water, which is destined to become a critical problem in the very near future. One would never guess that, however, on the basis of official propaganda meant to entice more residents and industry to move into the state. A member of the Denver Water Board recently declared that there was no reason Denver could not sustain a population five times its present level; Denver is one million now and struggling to maintain its per capita reserves of water. In 1973, Denver voters passed a water bond issue that will appropriate money for piping water to the city, which lies on the eastern slope of the Rocky Mountains, from the western slope. Problems associated with water rights in the old as well as the new West are something more believable and rational in the context of a cowboy movie, and, needless to add, inhabitants of the western slope were not consulted in the bargain as to their water needs. To make this contemporary Tragedy of the Commons complete, there was even a proposal to defoliate aspen trees on the western slope by means of chemical plant hormones so that the water transpired by these trees could be brought across the Continental Divide to the service of Denver. This, the increase of human numbers to the point that resources are limiting, causing the quality of life for all to diminish to a greater or lesser degree, is overpopulation. Promoters of growth in Colorado point to the open spaces, which are surely there, and say that there is no overpopulation. But there is, and in the years to come, the problem will become more serious. If population is not balanced with, or less than, the resources needed to sustain it, degradation of the environment and the quality of life for the inhabitants will be the inevitable result. In the bush of Australia, two cows per acre may be overpopulation; it is an exceedingly relative concept, subject to a myriad of variables.

How is overpopulation per se related to natural selection in human populations? Primarily, it results in an exaggeration of existing forces, amplifying the effects of disease and creating severe competition for limiting resources. There is a point in any society, since all are closed and limited systems functioning at greater or lesser degrees of efficiency, at which population increase begins to have diminishing returns. This point has been reached in nearly all the world community; the threats of epidemic disease and the draining of irreplaceable resources are approaching critical levels. Unless the tide of humanity recedes—an exceedingly doubtful possibility—modern civilization may be flooded in a tidal wave of its own making.

With the passing of each year, the doubling time for earth's human population is shortened. Presently, it is about *thirty-five years*, contrasting with an *average* time of 70,000 years over the whole of human history. To comprehend the speed of our contemporary population increase, consider an analogous example on a smaller scale. If one's salary for a month were to begin at one cent per day, then merely doubled each day for the remainder of the month, the last day's pay would be more than $10,000,000! For population increase to continue unchecked at its present rate—although in reality the rate itself would increase in time—in about 1,000 years there would be 1,700 people per square meter on the earth's total surface. Or, to project an even more incredible example, several thousand years at the existing rate of increase would convert the visible universe into humanity, whose mass would be expanding at the speed of light.

Needless to say, human population will never get so out of hand but will be halted, either through the intelligent action of human intervention or by natural controls such as disease and starvation, both of which

TABLE 6–1

Doubling Time for the Human Population

Per Cent Growth Rate per Year	Doubling Time in Years
0.1	700
0.5	140
1.0	70
2.0	35
4.0	18
5.0	14
7.0	10
10.0	7

At the present per cent growth rate per year, the doubling time for the human population is thirty-five years.

are contemporary regulators of man's numbers. But it is discouraging that even some authorities, who should have a more rational perspective, have suggested that the earth could sustain a population of 50–100 billion people. The present world population is approaching 4 billion, and millions of people starve to death annually. Conjecturing on the earth's capacity to support twenty to thirty times more people than it does today is akin to wondering how far a ship will sail before it sinks if there is a large hole in the hull and more passengers are added daily. Unrealistic, armchair speculations about the projected billions that earth might support are irrelevant and irresponsible to our imminent reality.

Aside from a shortage of food, which is perhaps the most pressing crisis associated with too many people, there are additional problems inherent in an overabundance of people. Psychological factors are not to be dismissed. Population pressures resulting in behavioral differences can have effects on man's well-being and on his gene pool. Overcrowded rats exhibit neurotic behavior, as may people in densely overpopulated conditions. Depletion of nonrenewable resources will certainly lower the quality of material life for us all. Various means for containing or reducing the population, which would most benefit the family of man, as universal birth control would do, are hindered by social, religious, political, and intellectual obstacles. There is no facile solution to human overpopulation; perhaps the answer will come only through man-precipitated catastrophe.

Birth and Death

Demographic factors are relevant to human natural selection on a more specific level of population genetics, differential natality and mortality, and population shifts. In developed countries, particularly the United States and those of Western Europe, the ratio of deaths to births has changed greatly over a relatively short period. Far more individuals attain reproductive age—which is dictated by social custom as well as biology—than did so a hundred years past, the increase being somewhat greater for women than for men. In 1880, 71.5 per cent of males and 73.1 per cent of females reached the age of fifteen years; whereas in 1960, 96.6 per cent of males and 97.5 per cent of females lived to this age. Most fifteen-year-olds have reached sexual maturity, but this age group is not very significant to the following generation as custom often prevents most individuals from reproducing at that age. The increase in survival is equally impressive for older groups. Only 65.7 per cent of males and 67.4 per cent of females lived to thirty years of age in 1880; whereas in 1960, 95.1 per cent of males and 96.9 per cent of females attained that age (Jacobson 1964). The latter is a profound increase; improved nutrition coupled with more advanced medical care is the basis for the marked changes.

Deaths and births are *largely controlled* in developed countries in the sense that birth control practices are statistically significant and individual lives have been prolonged so that most of the population lives to a reproductive age. Of course death is not actually controlled, but life is only prolonged. This, however, is of utmost consequence in regard to natural selection, as the person who reproduces has achieved genetic immortality, at least for the next generation. In 1840, children were produced by half the women born, and presently about 85 per cent of all women reproduce—a greater number than even reached sexual maturity 120 years ago.

The influences of natural selection are most often directed toward stabilization, eliminating individuals who have overextended the species' ability to adapt to the environment. The impressive increase in children surviving to a reproductive age is primarily the result of medical assistance in maintaining those who would have died otherwise. Does this fact imply that the genetic fitness of the population has been decreased? In a strict sense, probably it has, but the development of a medical technology that allows many genetically maladapted individuals to lead normal lives must have had a compensating cultural effect.

Deaths from genetically-inherited defects have not been reduced relatively as much as the total of deaths per se. Two thirds of females and 60 per cent of males in the United States who die before the age of thirty still die from genetic defects. This is well past the mean reproductive age, but many of the more serious defects are removed by death postnatally or prior to puberty. Gross malformations and other genetic anomalies are still frequent, but many are eliminated through fetal wastage and stillbirths. However, many live and a great number reproduce.

The Founder Effect

Given that a much greater number of those born are reaching reproductive maturity, it is reasonable to assume that there is increased potential for the accumulation of deleterious genes in populations, and that genetically weaker constitutions are being retained as well through medical technology. With lethal and deleterious genes on the increase, we may expect to see more examples of the *founder effect* in isolated areas where breeding populations are restricted in their choice of partners. The founder effect refers to the genetic influence of a small number of parents on a larger population of descendents. Diseases having an unusually high frequency within a specific population are often the result of this phenomenon. In South Africa, 8,000 carriers of the gene for *porphyra variegata*, the inability to metabolize porphyrin, are descendents of one couple married in 1688. A high frequency for sickle-cell anemia exists among a white population of southeast Maryland, the so-called Brandywine Isolate. Whether the gene is present in this population in response to endemic malaria is unknown, and it is interesting that blacks in the same area do not possess the gene in as high a frequency. The high frequency among whites is believed to have been initiated by a few interracial marriages during the early eighteenth century (Witkop, et al. 1966).

Cultural differences may cause the isolation of certain genes, creating a founder effect. It has been demonstrated that inherited diseases among Ashkenazic and non-Ashkenazic Jews are quite distinct (Sheba 1970). Ashkenazic Jews are those now living in Europe and the United States who came from the central and eastern European ghettos of the middle ages and still speak Yiddish. For generations they have tended to marry within their own religious-ethnic group, thereby accumulating distinct gene frequencies. The non-Ashkenazic Jews came from diverse areas including India, Yemen, Arabia, and the Mediterranean. Genetic diseases found among Ashkenazim but not in other groups of Jews are pentosauria, Tay-Sachs, Gaucher's Buerger's and dysautonomia. Other genetic diseases among Jews are almost exclusive to non-Ashkenazim: pituitary dwarfism, glycogen storage disease, vitamin B_{12} malabsorption and Wolman's disease. These data suggest that population structure is significant in the acquisition of inherited disease; genetic diversity is beneficial.

Demographic factors are inseparable from the distribution of gene frequencies. Changes in demography affect natural selection through differential fertility, manifest in mating and marriage, childlessness, the number of offspring, the age at childbearing, and the mean length of a generation.

Patterns in mating and marriage have been shifting. Until the mid-1960s, an increasing number of women were marrying, and at an earlier age, extending the number of reproductive years spent in marriage. Presently, at least in the United States and Western Europe, the trend may be reversing because many individuals are choosing not to marry. It is also a more socially accepted alternative for a woman to bear a child in the absence of marriage and the conventional family structure. A number of women are doing so by choice—a lifestyle few would have been tempted to undertake until very recently.

Childlessness is significant to a consideration of demographic changes. Whether by choice through birth control methods or abortion, or through infecundity, the result is the same for the individual: genetic death. Currently only 7 per cent of married women and 12 per cent of all U.S. women are childless at the age of thirty-five. It is easier today than formerly to remain childless by choice or to regulate the time and number of desired births through improved technology, and improved medical treatment for sterility of those individuals desiring children has countered somewhat the net effects of childlessness in the developed countries.

The average number of offspring has decreased notably—this trend being most noticeable in the developed countries—to an average of three per couple from seven during the mid-1800s. In terms of natural selection intensity, the range of variance is more significant than the average. And while there are fewer children per couple, still more chil-

TABLE 6–2

Inherited Disorders and Their Correlation with
Racial and Ethnic Groups

Ethnic Group	Relatively High Frequency	Relatively Low Frequency
Ashkenazic Jews	Abetalipoproteinemia Bloom's disease Dystonia musculorum deformans Factor XI (PTA) deficiency Familial dysautonomia Gaucher's disease Niemann-Pick disease Pentosuria Spongy degeneration of brain Stub thumbs Tay-Sachs disease	Phenylketonuria

Mediterranean peoples
  (Greeks, Italians,
  Sephardic Jews)
	Familial Mediterranean fever
	G-6-PD deficiency,
	  Mediterranean type
	Thalassemia (mainly β)
		Cystic fibrosis

Africans	G-6-PD deficiency, African
	  type
	Hemoglobinopathies, esp.
	  Hb S, Hb C, α and β thal,
	  persistent Hb F
		Cystic fibrosis
		Hemophilia
		Phenylketonuria
		Wilson's disease

Japanese (Koreans)	Acatalasia Dyschromatosis universalis hereditaria Oguchi's disease	
Chinese	α thalassemia G-6-PD deficiency, Chinese type	
Armenians	Familial Mediterranean fever	

From *The Biological and Social Meaning of Race* edited by Richard H. Osborne,
W. H. Freeman and Company. Copyright © 1971.

dren are being born than ever before, as the exponential rise in world population attests.

The rate of natural increase is established not only by the number of children produced but also by the length of generations. If average generations are thirty years, there will be only two thirds as many children born over a given period than would be born if the average were twenty years, all other things being equal. Marriages in the United States are occurring somewhat earlier, and the first child is born sooner after marriage. The current generation time for females is about twenty-six years, two years shorter than it was in the 1930s. A median American woman is married at twenty years of age, has her first child when she is twenty-one and her final child at age twenty-seven.

Births occurring to younger mothers and lessened numbers of births have a genetic influence, as the frequency of certain hereditary diseases may be correlated directly to the age of the mother, the order of birth, and the number of children in the family. Genetic factors linked with environmental causes—such as congenital malformations of the nervous and circulatory systems, Rh-erythroblastosis and cerebral palsy—are about twice as common among older mothers with many children than among younger mothers who bear fewer children. There is, then, a distinct genetic advantage to having children at a young age. Close inbreeding was commonly practiced among white plantation families in the antebellum South. In isolated cultural pockets, almost everyone is related in some way to everyone else and genetic aberrations are common under these conditions. The royal families of Europe, extremely inbred, had a high frequency of the gene for hemophilia, originating with a mutation in Queen Victoria of England, but the demise of royalty and the habit of marrying commoners among the remaining royal families have diluted its effect.

Within the total population of the United States and any other country there is a significant differential fertility among social, economic, religious, ethnic, and racial groups. Historically there have been broad gaps between the family sizes of college professors and rural farmers, or of Catholics and Unitarians. Within the white populations of the developed countries, these gaps are being narrowed as mates elect to have fewer children for social and economic reasons. As the cost of living rises, more couples are reluctant to have more than two children if for no reason other than that the expense of rearing them leads to a cramped lifestyle for all. This rationale alone has been responsible, probably more than any single factor, for stabilization of the birth rate in Japan, Western Europe, and the United States. In most rural areas where farm families once valued a large progeny as desirable for working the land, the small family farm is becoming Americana as large-scale agribusiness replaces it, reducing the socioeconomic worth of having numerous children. And Catholics, who have traditionally produced larger families than non-Catholics, are merging into the mean as various methods of birth control are practiced extensively despite papal decrees against anything other than the rhythm method.

Differential fertility is much greater among differing socioeconomic groups of nonwhites, represented in the United States primarily by blacks. Within the U.S. black population, twice as many individuals die before the age of fifteen as do in the white population. Death through the reproductive period is also higher for blacks (Kirk 1968). The reproductive rate of blacks is much higher among the poor than among the socioeconomic middle and upper classes. Whereas overall fertility is higher, there are more childless black women proportionately than white. These differences may be pertinent factors in the outcome of the process of natural selection in the U.S. human population.

Demographic considerations in the United States are becoming less important in contemporary natural selection as social and cultural changes tend to offset their effects, but these ameliorating factors, and those of medical technology as well, are being countered by heightened or newly arisen "artificial" selective forces previously discussed. Demographic factors assume a role in determining the evolutionary directions of populations, but they are only a part of the total thrust. It is frequently stated in academic and popular publications that natural selection is decreasing within human populations, its effects being lessened by cultural compensations, when it may well be that natural selection is overcoming the benefits of man's cultural buffers as a result of the specific bio-cultural factors discussed in this book. Also, in preventing the deaths of individuals having congenital defects that will increase in relative frequency in succeeding generations, medical technology may be fostering the genetic weakening of our species.

The impact of most factors of contemporary human evolution is felt to differing intensities in the developed and underdeveloped countries of the world. A demographic aspect of wealthier nations is that individual mobility has increased greatly. In the United States, the search for better opportunities or a job moves individuals and families from city to city. Marriages with the "hometown girl" are increasingly a thing of the past. Many Americans of marriageable age enroll in a college or university for at least a few years, and thereby come into contact with potential mates from a broader spectrum of geographies, backgrounds, and gene pools. While it is true that increased genetic vigor, on a population basis, should arise from genetic diversity, there is also convincing evidence that a relationship exists between fetal loss and the number of countries, or relatively discrete gene pools, represented in a person's background. The absolute geographical distance between the parents' and grandparents' birthplaces also has an effect. This strongly suggests that our relatively recent increased mobility has intensified natural selection on the unborn.

In introducing the nature of this phenomenon, it is profitable to consider the conclusion of a study undertaken by J. A. Moore on the North American leopard frog, *Rana pipiens*, a species with an extensive range that is similar in its distribution and variation to human populations (Moore 1942, 1946, 1950). These frogs, all races of the same species, are found in diverse habitats throughout North America. Some of the populations are geographically and genetically isolated while others interbreed not only among their own groups, but with others on the fringes of their respective ranges.

Moore found definite correlations between the frog's reproductive success and the geographical distance between parents. While hybrids of frogs from adjacent areas were normal in development and appearance, increasing the distance between parental localities resulted in retarded development time, a greater number of morphological aberrations, and fewer normal individuals. Leopard frogs are all of the same species and theoretically should be able to breed freely, but spatial separation of gene pools is an inverse factor in reproductive success.

A study on humans made by examination of records from the Providence, Rhode Island, Lying-in Hospital indicates a relationship between ethnic heterogeneity, geographical distance between parental origins, and fetal loss (Bresler 1970). The latter was found to increase dramatically with the addition of countries (substitute gene pools) in a person's background. With only a single country in the parental background, fetal loss was 8.6 per cent. With six countries fetal loss was up to 50 per cent! The progression from one to six countries showed an incremental increase for each additional country. According to J. B. Bresler, who conducted the study, the probability of more Mendelian gene pools being brought together increases with the number of countries in one's ancestry. This causes some lack of pairing of chromosomes at specific loci and results in fetal loss. The data on two white populations show that the fetal loss of the parental generation increased 2.5–3.0 per cent with each additional country in the great-grandparental generation, and that distance between parents' birthplaces increased fetal wastage.

Fetal loss accelerates as genetic backgrounds diverge, but reproductive differentials still occur in subcultures in the same area, fertility being lower among subcultures having limited ancestry. The inhabitants of Wales in the British Isles are culturally very much alike, but the true Welsh may be distinguished from the non-Welsh on the basis of their ability to speak Welsh and on the possession of Welsh surnames. Using these bases for segregating out the relatively pure genetic racial stock of Wales, it has been found that women of Welsh descent have lower fertility than their non-Welsh neighbors (Ashley 1969). Information from the Registrar General for England and Wales was used to calculate the number of live and stillbirths per 1,000 women from the age group 15 to 44 years. In areas where the Welsh speaking fraction of the population is high, the mean fertility index (the percentage producing offspring) was 79; in areas of intermediate Welsh speaking, it was 89; and where little Welsh was spoken, it was 96. Variables, such as differential reproduction between cities and rural areas, were considered. It is not impossible that the differences observed are a result of some aspect of the Welsh subculture; women may, for example, practice more efficient birth control from one subcultural group to another. But the differences

---

TABLE 6–3

Relation of Number of Countries in the Great-Grandparental
Generation (P3) to Fetal Loss in Birth of Their
Great-Grandchildren (F1)

Number of Countries	Number of Families	Pregnancies	Live Born	Per Cent of Fetal Loss	Per Cent of Families Ever F.L.
1	224	736	680	7.6	19.6
2	273	901	807	10.3	22.0
3	161	471	419	11.0	22.4
4	40	114	99	13.2	30.0
5	9	28	23	17.9	55.6
6	1	2	1	50.0	100.0
Total	708	2,252	2,029	9.9	22.3

After J. B. Bresler, *Social Biology* 17 (1970): 17–25.

are probably at least partially genetic, for the following reasons. The Welsh, who have retained their cultural integrity, are the last fringes of the earliest inhabitants of the British Isles. Their language has been retained, and they show a high inclination to marry within their sub-cultural group, semi-isolating their gene pool. Since the fertility difference exists not only among Welsh and non-Welsh from different areas, but also among those who are neighbors, it is probably genetic in origin. A relationship between cultural isolation and genetically-originated differences of a major or minor nature is inferred, although not proven, by this example.

There is evidence that altitude is a significant stress factor on perinatal mortality, so persons living in mountainous regions will subject their progeny to different selective pressures than those living at sea level (Grahn, et al. 1963). At higher altitudes, a person is exposed to more cosmic rays, less oxygen partial pressure, increased ultraviolet radiation, and generally lower humidity and temperature. All of these factors are *direct functions* of increasing altitude.

Reduced oxygen is a selective factor both on adults and neonatants, particularly in regard to birth weight. A comparison of birth weight records from Illinois, Indiana, and Colorado showed an average neonatal weight of 190 grams less for babies born in Colorado than for those born in the lower states. Although this does not prove a cause-and-effect relationship, the data suggest that a lower survival rate is a function of the altitude. As the probability of neonatal death increases exponentially with a drop in birth weight below 3,500 grams, altitude is apparently a significant natural selective factor. In a study by the U.S. Department of Health, Education and Welfare, it was found that the mortality

TABLE 6–4
Fertility Index in Wales

Welsh Speaking	Female Population 15–44	Live and Stillbirths	Fertility Index	Per Cent of Women Married
High	78,872	37,509	79	64
Intermediate	288,341	153,434	89	69
Low	142,020	80,327	96	69

After D. J. B. Ashley, *Journal of Medical Genetics* 6 (1969): 180–184.

rate for newborns was 175.8 per 1,000 births for those weighing 2,500 grams or less as compared with only 7.1 per 1,000 births for those weighing 2,501 grams or more (U.S. Department of Health, Education and Welfare 1954). From these data it may be concluded that the higher number of neonatal deaths that occur in the mountain states of Colorado and Wyoming are due, at least in part, to lower birth weights caused by high altitude. Apparently the lower oxygen levels effect a depression on the rate of fetal growth. Since a higher neonatal death rate is directly correlative to altitude increase, by anywhere from 2 per cent to 137 per cent depending on the cause of death, altitude as a selec-

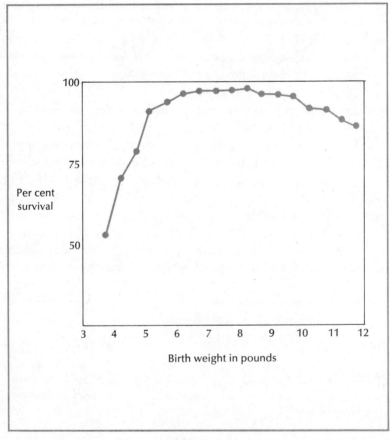

FIGURE 6-1

Relation between birth weight and survival in human neonatants.

(After M. N. Karn and L. S. Penrose, *Annuals of Eugenics*, London, 16 (1951), 147–164.)

tive factor in human populations should not be ignored. An expectant mother in Denver whose family history indicates low birth weight might have a statistically better chance of a successful delivery were she to move to a coastal area during her pregnancy. On a world basis, patterns

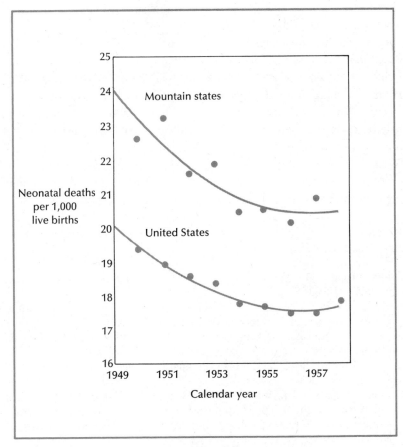

FIGURE 6–2

Regression of neonatal death rate over time for the mountain states of the United States compared with the rest of the country. Lower oxygen tension at higher altitudes affects birth weight and may be a factor in the slightly higher number of neonatal deaths in these regions. Decreasing birth weight results in higher neonatal mortality as an independent variable. (See Figure 6–1 in this chapter.) The decline in mortality from 1949 to 1957 in both areas correlates with improved socioeconomic conditions. Only Caucasians were included in this study.

(Adapted from D. Grahn and J. Kratchman, *American Journal of Human Genetics*, 15 (1963), 329–352.)

of population distribution in relation to altitude create a subtle but meaningful influence on the human gene pool. In the Spanish colonization of Peru, it became necessary to move the capital from the high Inca center of Cuzco in the Andes down to Lima on the coastal plain because it was forty years before a baby of Spanish parentage was born alive in the rarified atmosphere. Furthermore, most of the Spanish livestock experienced similar difficulties!

Demographic considerations are relevant to the disposition of human gene pools and correspondingly to human evolution, although their influences may not be as dramatic or as easily demonstrated as are other factors. Population numbers, geographical mobility, and inter- and intra-cultural barriers, discussed more fully in the following chapter, contribute to man's genetic resources, and affect natality, the distribution of inherited diseases, and a variety of other genetically-based characteristics. A rapid increase of the world's population is certain to accentuate the effects of demography in human genetics, as the interactions of human populations become more intense and complex.

Suggested Readings

Ashley, David J. B. "Welshness and Fertility." *Journal of Medical Genetics* 6(1969): 180–182.

Bresler, Jack B. "The Relation of Population Fertility Levels to Ethnic Group Backgrounds." *Eugenics Quarterly* 8(1961): 12–22.

——— "Outcrossings in Caucasians and Fetal Loss." *Social Biology* 17 (1970): 17–25.

Deevey, Edward S. "The Human Population." *Scientific American* 203 (1960): 194–204.

Grahn, Douglas, and Jack Kratchman. "Variation in Neonatal Death Rate and Birth Weight in the United States and Possible Relations to Environmental Radiation, Geology, and Altitude." *American Journal of Human Genetics* 15(1963): 329–352.

Hardin, Garrett. "The Tragedy of the Commons." *Science* 162(1968): 1243–1248.

Jacobson, Paul H. "Cohort Survival for Generations Since 1840." *Milbank Memorial Fund Quarterly* 42(1964): 36–53.

Kirk, D. "Patterns of Survival and Reproduction in the United States: Implications for Selection." *Proceedings of the National Academy of Sciences* 59(1968): 662–670.

Lerner, I. Michael. *Heredity, Evolution, and Society.* San Francisco: W. H. Freeman and Co., Inc., 1968.

Livingstone, Frank B. "The Founder Effect and Deleterious Genes." *American Journal of Physical Anthropology* 30(1969): 55–59.

Moore, John A. "Study of Embryonic Temperature Tolerance and Rate of Development in *Rana pipiens* from Different Latitudes." *Yearbook of The American Philosophical Association* 1942: 175–178.

———— "Further Studies on *Rana pipiens* Racial Hybrids." *American Naturalist* 84(1950): 247–254.

Osborne, Richard H., ed. *The Biological and Social Meaning of Race.* San Francisco: W. H. Freeman and Co., Inc., 1971.

Sheba, Chaim. "Gene Frequencies in Jews." *The Lancet* 6 June 1970, pp. 1230–1231.

U. S. Department of Health, Education, and Welfare. "Weight at Birth and Its Effect on Survival of the Newborn in the United States, Early 1950." *Vital Statistics—Special Reports, Selected Studies* 39(1954).

Witkop, C. J., C. J. MacLean, P. J. Schmidt, and J. L. Henry. "Medical and Dental Findings in the Brandywine Isolate." *Alabama Journal of Medical Science* 3(1966): 382–403.

chapter
7

SOCIOCULTURAL FACTORS
IN THE NATURAL SELECTION
OF HUMAN POPULATIONS

Sociocultural factors, some of which are interwoven with demographic elements, influence the outcome of natural selection on human populations. Culture can be as important in isolating or otherwise affecting gene pools as any physical factor. Human mating patterns, for example, are always assortative rather than random, so culture, by influencing who breeds with whom, has an effect on the constitution of a population's gene pool. Religious groupings, social stratifications, language, and many other facets of culture exert their effects on human genetics. Were we not cultural beings, our mating probably would occur at random. There would be no selection for particular facial or body types along with the other subjective standards of beauty and sexuality, which vary so extensively among cultures and subcultures. The perpetuation of genetic variety is aided partially by a great degree of intracultural differences in these standards. If all men were attracted only to a physical type resembling the late Marilyn Monroe and would mate only with someone in that category, there would be a dramatic population decline and increasing homogeneity. To equalize the situation, if females were inclined toward only a narrow range of physical types in males, there would be correspondingly less variety. But this is not man's nature, and there are probably as many perceptions of beauty and sexuality as there are individuals. Defined restrictions, such as those imposed by religion and class structure, are more limiting than standards open to subjective realities.

Sociocultural factors in natural selection range from the obvious to the very subtle. The caste system, still adhered to in India although it has been outlawed, is restraining the gene flow within the population, but other restrictive cultural patterns are not as easily discerned. In the United States, college graduates are more likely to marry other college graduates because the couples tend to have more in common than two people with broadly different educational backgrounds. Institutions of higher education foster genetic heterogeneity by bringing together individuals from distant geographical areas and diverse cultural backgrounds, serving as a major cultural factor in gene mixing among certain segments of the U.S. population. Subcultural pressures undoubtedly still serve to reinforce homogeneity to some degree. Parental disapproval, personal misgivings, and other culturally induced reasons for not marrying outside one's cultural and subcultural boundaries are still of importance in determining mating patterns. On the whole, cultural factors enhance genetic diversity in a population rather than restrict its expression. If genetic diversity were not advantageous, it is probable that genetic fixity would have become an evolutionary tactic.

Populations and Races

The concept of race is relevant in a discussion of sociocultural selective factors, as racial groups are characterized by cultural differences that are manifest among themselves and other races. A population is a group of individuals that shares a common frequency of genes; races of man, as races of mice, are simply Mendelian populations that differ from others in the frequencies of some genes. As these populations have much genetic information in common, their environmental strategies as expressed by their phenotypes will also have much in common under similar as well as changing environmental circumstances. Altering differentials in the environment of a population will lead to a change in the differential expression of the phenotype. But elements of culture in human populations modify these principles so that man's phenotypic modifications to an evolving environment involve more time than do changes in a noncultural animal. As discussed in Chapters 3 and 4, physiological change, or natural selection as a result of a rapidly changing physical environment, may be accelerated or, at least, markedly accentuated by man's cultural activity.

Races of the taxon *Homo sapiens* undeniably exist despite the efforts of some physical anthropologists to negate this as a biological fact. The biological reality of these subspecies, or races, is a result of the isolation by geographical and cultural barriers of different gene pools with differential responses to varying environmental selective factors. Even within groups of the same basic racial stock, definable distinctions in differential gene frequencies may be seen after only a few generations of relative genetic isolation. The inhabitants of small Swiss communities, in which most individuals find marriage partners within their own village, have some distinct physical features (Hulse 1957). People of Moghengo, for example, tend to have big noses. These phenotypic expressions result from the repeated intermixing of a small gene pool. Such villages average 400 people or less, and although sanctions condemn unions between related individuals, the small choice of partners makes them unavoidable, and most of the people in these towns have been interrelated for generations. As variations in relative gene frequency and subsequent phenotypic expression may be discerned among separated population units of the same race and subculture in relatively short periods of time, the extent of human variation arising out of marked and extended genetic and cultural isolation should not perplex the rational observer. Subspecies or racial differences in the human population are a result of morphological adaptations and are not correlative with intelligence, creativity, or any other innately expressed capacity.

Gene frequency differences among human populations may also be due to the phenomenon known as genetic drift, the loss of variability in a population over several generations by pure chance. It has been suggested by some students of human evolutionary genetics that most racial variation is the result of genetic drift rather than of the environmental adaptations of natural selection. This view, however, represents an historical misunderstanding of the environmental adaptiveness of morphological variation.

For many years, no particular selective advantage was recognized for blondness in northern climates, where the incidence of light during long winter months is very low, until the importance of light for vitamin D biosynthesis was demonstrated. The postnatal selection of rickets, a vitamin D deficiency of childhood, on black children living at high latitudes would be very high without the culturally acquired knowledge of diet supplementation. To determine the functionality of genetic drift, a population having distinct physiological and/or morphological characteristics must be singled out from a larger population subject to identical environmental stress pressures, and the genetic origin of the study group must be known. This is not a facile set of requirements to fulfill as the origins of most subcultural social units among human populations are not traced easily. Such a study was conducted somewhat more than twenty years ago on a small and socioreligiously isolated group known as the Dunkers, or German Baptist Brethren (Glass 1953). This sect was founded in 1708 in the province of Hesse, in what is now Germany. Between 1719 and 1729 the sect was transplanted to the British colonies, settling in the vicinity of Germantown, Pennsylvania. The population doubled in size during the next century with almost all members being descendants of the original fifty immigrant families. Tradition imposed social ostracism on anyone choosing to marry outside the group. Within this orthodox subculture, divisiveness eventually resulted in three subgroups: one retained the old customs, another modified them, and the third espoused liberal and progressive ideas. The study group was composed of a population of individuals remaining in the Old Order now living in Franklin County, Pennsylvania. The traditionalists numbered only about 3,000, being spread out over 55 small communities throughout the country. These Dunkers are visibly distinguishable from their neighbors mainly by their plain and traditional dress. Most are farmers, own cars, use farm machinery, and in many respects lead the lives of typical Americans. Their children attend public school, and the group is not averse to modern medical care. The principal difference is in their faithful adherence to the customs of the founding Dunkers. While there have been a small number of marriages outside descendants of the original founding nucleus, a substantial number married partners from other Old Order communities.

The incidence of several clearly genetic characteristics was examined in this population. Complete comparisons were possible for the four ABO blood groups (O, A, B, and AB) and the three MN types (M, MN, and N). Four additional traits that could be used to compare the Dunkers with their neighboring Americans were the presence or absence of mid-digital hair on one or more fingers, the ability to bend back the thumb's tip to a 50° angle or more from the basal segment, the incidence of attached ear lobes, and right- or left-handedness. These latter four characters were relevant particularly to the question of genetic drift because their natural selective value is nonexistent, or at any rate unknown, making them random characters in the absence of drift. Blood types, however, are not random but assortative to various degrees among populations. Big noses in a Swiss village or digital hair among Dunkers cannot be supposed to reflect adaptations, but they do serve as excellent examples of small differences that accumulate in frequency through genetic isolation.

Among the Dunkers it was found that the chosen characters occurred in frequencies unlike those present in non-Dunker populations. Of the blood groups, about 60 per cent of Dunkers were found to be in group A as compared with 40 per cent of the U.S. non-Dunker population and 45 per cent of modern West Germans. The frequency of groups B and AB was significantly less—5 per cent among the Dunkers as compared with 15 per cent among North Americans and West Germans. There is not as low a frequency of these types in any other population of western European origin. Studies indicated that the B blood type had been inherited from converts, except in one instance, so the B blood factor must have been all but extinct in this population before its reintroduction through marriage to individuals outside the original genetic lineage. MN types, another serological grouping, showed an even greater divergence. On the average their frequencies are the same for the general populations of the United States and West Germany: 30 per cent for type M, 50 per cent for MN, and 20 per cent for N. In the Dunkers, MN had lessened in frequency only slightly, but M had risen to 44.5 per cent and N had fallen to 13.5 per cent.

Genetic drift is supported also by comparisons made on the population frequency of the four additional measured characters. Dunkers had fewer members with mid-digital hair, fewer hyperextensible thumbs, and fewer attached earlobes. In right- and left-handedness, Dunkers concurred statistically with the U.S. population. But the statistically significant differences in most characteristics underscore the function and importance of genetic drift in small, genetically isolated populations.

Genetic drift operates most significantly in small populations, perhaps of 100 or fewer individuals. In such populations, as long as certain characters are either beneficial or superfluous, there is nothing to hinder their reoccurrence. As demonstrated with the Dunkers, genetic isolation of small groups may occur within the midst of a much larger population through socioreligious mechanisms. It is probable that some racial characteristics in man, particularly those existing before mobility served to dilute the gene pool homogeneity of so many races, owe their inception to small bands of men in which marriage outside the tribal group was seldom or never practiced. Natural selective pressures and nonadaptive but nondeleterious genetic drift caused physical differences to arise within separated groups. These distinctions grew more marked through many generations. Although it is impossible to reconstruct the racial composition of prehistoric man, one may assume, given rates of human evolution, that marked racial differences, which were at least as profound as those existing among modern men, may have existed among isolated populations of *Homo erectus*.

Variation is a phenomenon of all biological populations, and race is no mystery, but a product of genetic isolation of variable populations, an intermediate stage in the process of speciation. Man was arrested in his biological divergence by his cultural evolution. From the fact that all human populations can interbreed freely, we know that no single group has diverged to the degree of becoming a separate species. And as present trends in mobility and cultural amalgamation increase, one may hope that benefits will be accrued from intermarriage in the form of decreasing social tensions and a reunion of the family of man. These are sure to result in genetic influences on contemporary evolution. Another cultural factor to ponder on considering races is that through cultural innovations we have extinguished some of the selective pressures originally responsible for racial formations.

Between and among major racial groups, subcultural units may become isolated breeding populations, as with the Dunkers, causing statistically significant variations resulting from genetic drift. Physical differences having pertinent genetic consequences may sometimes be characteristic of subcultural groups scarcely deserving that distinction. For example, a study on maternal height and stillbirth revealed that the inability to deliver a child through the vagina was about four times greater in women under 5'1" than for those over 5'4" (Bresler 1962). The results also showed that, on the average, Roman Catholic women are shorter than Protestant women in the United States and are, therefore, more likely to be among those who do not give birth easily. The study found that 64.4 per cent of the Catholic women had had at least one stillbirth, and all of these mothers were under 5'6", whereas only 28.4 per cent of Protestants in the same study had experienced a stillbirth. The remaining 7.3 per cent were neither Catholic nor Protestant. The study suggests that Catholic women are much more likely to require Caesarean deliveries, reducing somewhat their reproductive potential. Since Catholics are highly likely to marry other Catholics, although the barriers to extrareligious marriage are not as stringent as they were historically and certainly not as strong as in some other religious groups, assortative mating will tend to keep the average height of Catholic women lower and accompanying parturition problems will

TABLE 7–1

Religion of Women Ever Experiencing a Stillbirth

Religion of Women	Number	Total	Ever Stillbirth	Expected Stillbirths Based upon Per Cent of Total
		%		
Catholic	132	64.4	8	7.7
Protestant	58	28.4	3	3.4

After J. B. Bresler, *American Journal of Physical Anthropology* 20 (1962): 515–517.

TABLE 7–2

Height Distribution for Catholic and Protestant Women

Religion of Women	Under 5'6"		5'6" and Over		
	Number	Per Cent	Number	Per Cent	Total
Catholic	132	69.5	32	50.0	164
Protestant	58	30.5	32	50.0	90

After J. B. Bresler, *American Journal of Physical Anthropology* 20 (1962): 515–517.

151

remain high. In comparing these two religious groups, we are concerned with percentages, but it should be emphasized that a similar difficulty exists among small women of any group, as it is primarily a function of pelvic size. Needless to say, religion has nothing per se to do with pelvic size except that selective mating resulting from religious preference will maintain the higher frequency of smaller women among Catholics.

A minor experiment conducted on a University of California campus illustrates how cultural factors—in this case social and racial discrimination—can effect the genetic composition of human populations as a result of assortative mating (Turner 1970). A sample of introductory physical anthropology students, representing various races but predominantly Caucasian, were given the PTC (phenylthiocarbamide) tasting test, which easily demonstrates the simple Mendelian-inherited ability either to taste or not to taste the substance. The same test was given to members of a Greek-letter social fraternity and sorority. Among the physical anthropology students there was a ratio of one nontaster to three tasters (24.2:75.8 per cent). Among the fraternity-sorority group, the ratio was 37.8:62.2 per cent tasters to nontasters. Between the fraternity and sorority the frequency of nontasters was 38.7 per cent and 37.2 per cent respectively, indicating that sex difference had little to do with the results obtained from the random sampling. The reason for the significant difference in nontasters between the physical anthropology class and the fraternity-sorority group was the practice of overt or de facto racial discrimination, so that the fraternity-sorority sample came from an all-white group.

The relevance of the above experiment issues not from the importance of the ability or inability to taste PTC—a relatively useless genetic trait—but from the clear illustration of the genetic effects of assortative mating in human populations. Social class and status barriers are just as real in their genetic effects as are racial ones; the effects of the former are simply not as conspicuous. If social and cultural precepts had no bearing on mate selection, then gene frequencies would not be affected. But these factors are relevant, and the many-faceted effects of sociocultural dynamics are reflected in population genetics.

There is no better evidence of the influences of cultural values in affecting the composition of a gene pool than the medical preservation of genetically maladapted individuals who live to reproductive age and pass their genes on to subsequent generations. Our society considers it illegal and immoral to terminate the lives of these individuals in infancy,

TABLE 7-3

The Distribution of a Simple Inherited Character (the ability to taste or not to taste PTC—phenylthiocarbamide) in Two Social Groups

Group	Non-taster	Taster	Total
Random students	24.2%	75.8%	161
Fraternity and so-rority members	37.8	62.2	82

After J. Turner II, *Social Biology* 17, No. 2 (1970): 142.

but in some cultures infanticide of newborn children with gross inherited defects is commonly practiced. With preservation of these individuals and their genes, the overall incidence of any maladaptive trait increases in succeeding generations, concomitantly increasing the medical and social costs of maintaining such individuals.

One of the better studied examples of cultural dynamics involving a persistant and generally deleterious mutation is that of albinism among the Cuna Indians of the San Blas Province of Panama (Keeler 1964). Among the Cuna there is an extremely high incidence of albinism, estimated at more than 60 per 10,000 births. These children, called "Moon children" from a belief that albinism is caused by a parent staring for too long at the moon during pregnancy, appear at the rate of 398 mutations per 18-year generation per 10,000 population. Nele Kantule, a Cuna chief who died in 1944, condemned the common practice of infanticide of albinos, believing that they sinned less than other Indians,

TABLE 7-4

Estimates of Cuna Indian Population and Albinism

Date	Population	Number of Albinos	Albinos per 10,000 Population
1925	20,100	138	69
1940	20,831	98	47
1950	22,822	152	67
1962	23,743	144	61

After C. Keeler, *Journal of Heredity* 55 (1964): 115–120.

and accordingly should be kept to teach their brethren more about the ways of god. During his reign, the incidence of albinism rose, but after his death there was a resumption of infanticide, again lowering the frequency of albinos in the Cuna population.

Although the average number of albinos is 60 per 10,000 population, the figure is low when considered by village. In the larger towns, infanticide is not favored and the frequency of albinos is 144 per 10,000. Nargana, the most modern of Cuna towns, had a rate of 475 per 10,-000! In the more remote villages, the rate drops to 31 per 10,000, an indication that infanticide must be practiced to a much greater degree.

In the tropical home of the Cuna, where the sun's intensity is high and reflected by the Caribbean, albinism is incontestably a disadvantageous quality. Statistically, neither albino males nor females live as long as normally pigmented individuals. This reduced viability is expected in an environment harsh even on darkly pigmented skin. Few albinos marry, but the rate of spontaneous mutations in the population for the recessive gene is constant and high enough to keep the percentage at a predictable level. If, as seems to be occurring, the acculturation of the Cuna into the modern world progresses, resulting in less infanticide, the rates of albinism should rise. A greater social acceptance of the condition should facilitate marriage, leading to an additional spread of the gene among the population.

Genetics and the Unborn

A factor that may bear significantly on the genetics and subsequent development of the unborn is the internal environment of the mother.

TABLE 7–5

Incidence of Albinism in Towns Selected as Civilized,
Less Civilized, and Uncivilized

Community	Number of Moon Children	Population	Moon Children per 10,000 Population
Civilized	92	6,365	144
Less civilized	14	2,594	54
Uncivilized	33	10,411	32

After C. Keeler, *Journal of Heredity* 55 (1964): 115–120.

At one time it was thought that the fetus was protected effectively from the external environment by the biological buffer of the mother. However, many substances are absorbed from the environment by the mother and the fetus. A number of culturally produced substances enter the pregnant woman's body, altering her internal biochemical environment and, consequently, that of the fetus (Monie 1963). Some of these agents are neutral, some are teratogenic (causing developmental abnormalities, as with thalidomide), while the potential effects of a multitude are unknown. Diseases of the mother, such as rubella and gonorrhea, during critical periods of pregnancy also act to alter the fetal environment. An additional problem in the bioassay of potentially dangerous environmental substances is that when abnormalities are induced, they are in no way distinct from those that are congenital and genetic in basis. Thus, it is not always possible to define a causal agent. What is of ultimate importance in terms of natural selection, apart from the misery and suffering of individuals having developmental defects, is that foreign substances present during fetal development may affect both somatic and gametic genes in the child. There is potential both for subsequent breakdown in the cell division regulation of the postnatally developing child and for environmentally induced genetic defects to be passed on to another generation should the individual live to reproductive maturity. In contemporary pharmacology, there is a wide spectrum of drugs with contraindications for the pregnant woman, but there is scant information on their short-run or long-run potential for inducing developmental or genetic defects. There is also a personal skepticism regarding official reports on the effects of drugs, especially among the young, which leads to a casual attitude toward experimentation. At one time it was propagandized that LSD-25 caused chromosome damage, although there is no conclusive proof that such is the case with moderately ingested amounts. Yet the fact remains that significant numbers of people in various cultures and subcultures are ingesting both prescribed and unprescribed drugs during pregnancy that may be potentially mutagenic to the fetus. The impact of such changes on the internal developmental environment of man is yet to be ascertained, so for the time being all drugs should be avoided by pregnant women if they fall under suspicion of being teratogenic or mutagenic. Research necessary for indicating a substance as mutagenic or teratogenic beyond doubt is time-consuming, and there are more drugs being developed than there is research on their long-term effects. In this sense, human evolution is truly an experiment in progress.

Where a person lives may well have an effect on his genetics and reproductive capacity. Few people would choose to live by a high radiation source or in an area where the risk of an unsuccessful pregnancy was increased if they were aware of these potential dangers. In Chapter 6, we discussed the effects of altitude on fetal development, yet developing metropolitan centers such as Denver, at 5,280 feet, will continue to attract large numbers of child-bearing couples.

Clearly, if an individual has all knowledge and choice, there are genetically high risk areas that one should avoid. Certain regions of the United States contain unusually large quantities of naturally occurring radioactive materials that raise the incidence of mutations and developmental defects (Gentry, et al. 1959). The initial clue, leading to a study showing that a high level of radiation in naturally-occurring rocks may cause excessive congenital malformations, was the observation that an abnormally high number of cleft palate patients were from a single county in northern New York State. Further, data from the Office of Vital Statistics of the New York State Department of Health revealed that there was a high incidence of other congenital malformations from certain townships within the same county. The late Atomic Energy Commission supplied data confirming that igneous bedrock outcroppings in the area had high levels of radioactivity. All rocks contained at least minute amounts of radioactive elements—primarily C^{14}, K^{40}, Ra^{226}, Th^{232}, and U^{238}.

It was shown by examining records on children born in New York State that the areas containing the more highly radioactive materials had an average of 17.5 congenital malformations per 1,000 live births. Also, data was collected on sources of drinking water, and for those areas where water was contaminated by contact with radioactive subsurface rock, the rate of malformations per 1,000 live births was 16.9 as contrasted with 12.4 for communities using uncontaminated water. Demographic factors were also considered in the study, and no significant differences were found. Parental ages, rank among siblings, parental occupation, and infant mortality after the first month did not vary statistically from one part of the study area to another.

The above study is significant, particularly when one considers the problems of disposal of radioactive waste and long-term, low-level radioactive emission from atomic power plants, both of which will become more conspicuous in the ensuing decades. Radioactive wastes from a nuclear reactor plant in Idaho have been buried directly above the Snake River aquifer, the largest remaining supply of fresh water in the United

States. Contamination of water supplies with radioactive wastes, particularly tritium, will become increasingly critical. One might do well to check the radioactivity maps of the Atomic Energy Commission before planning another move. Proponents of nuclear power argue that the isotope emissions from the power plants will produce a negligible effect, but this claim would appear to be overly optimistic (see Chapter 4).

There is also evidence that the choice—or more appropriately, perhaps, the circumstance—of where one lives has an effect on mortality. Using data obtained from Britain's National Health Service, a study determined the standardized mortality ratio (SMR) for different areas of Britain; that is, the mortality for individuals of a particular area as contrasted with that of the country as a whole (Howe 1968). Geographical patterns of death were found, although explanations were not as readily forthcoming. The SMR for chronic bronchitis in London, for example, is about 35 per cent above that for Britain as a whole, and marked differences were found from one area to another within London. In this instance one may assume that the greater air pollution of London accounts for the increased number of deaths from bronchitis, but why is there so broad a variation within the city itself? Certainly there is a variable distribution of polluted air from one part of the city to another, and there may be sociocultural variants such as a larger percentage of smokers in some areas than in others. In studies of this type it is extremely difficult, if not impossible, to isolate single variables, principally because the net effect is due to multivariables—demographic, sociocultural, environmental—rather than to a single determinant. Variations in the SMR for cardiovascular diseases were also wide, from 117 per cent in Hampstead to 85 per cent in Holborn. These differential rates are certainly the result of a combination of physical and cultural factors in living situations, some of which are more obvious than others. If one lives in an urban area with high smog levels, the possibility for illness or death from associated diseases is increased. These risks are intrinsic in any given cultural living situation, to greater or lesser degrees, although most individuals are unaware of the high differentials. As cultural and social conditions affect the total genome of a population, we cannot afford any longer to dismiss their importance.

The genetic constitution of a population is the summation of a legion of determinants, some of which may be defined easily, and others not. An examination of some genetic effects of antebellum plantation slavery illustrates how genetic composition may affect one's cultural status

(Weyl 1970). This is still true to an unsettling degree, and the social ramifications of today are more complex and less easily confronted. With slaves, their status, occupation, residence, and freedom before emancipation were closely correlative with the degree of racial admixture shown by an individual. Interbreeding began soon after slavery became established in the New World; it is estimated that all Americans classified as black now have from 2 to 50 per cent white genes. Slaves exhibiting Caucasian characteristics usually received more favorable treatment as they were more likely to be employed as household slaves or artisans than as field workers. Because the mortality rate was quite high for field workers, particularly in the sugar plantations of the West Indies and the South, there was unavoidably a culturally induced selective advantage in having a discernable degree of Caucasian genes. On the other hand, freed slaves before emancipation had a shorter life span than high-status retained slaves because the freed men had little access to the quality of medical care provided—out of property self-interest—by slave owners. Accordingly, on plantations, culturally induced selection operated in favor of individuals with white genes and cooperative behavior. Noncooperative or independent personalities were seldom tolerated, and such individuals engendered the risk of being sold to sugar plantations, where life was hard and usually short. The social circumstances of slavery clearly constituted an important factor on the genetic makeup of slaves in the New World. Whether or not selective breeding ever was practiced intentionally, it was practiced de facto through the social structure of that time.

As a result of emotional associations, there has been a tendency to ignore the issue of genetic influence on both behavior and intelligence, with a few notable and rather sensational exceptions. To suggest that behavior and intelligence are determined partially by one's genes is in many minds equivalent to supporting a "Brave New World" or providing fuel for the cause of racial discrimination. Neither fear is justified; genetic determination of a degree of intelligence and behavior is not synonymous with engineered genetic control. As for racial discrimination, the inheritance of intellectual capacity is not a function of race; perhaps that notion will someday be laid to rest. However, in terms of present knowledge, no biologist can maintain that genetics are irrelevant to behavioral traits or intelligence. Arguments center on the degree of relevancy. Genetically, all men are not created equal; in fact, no two men are, and no degree of wishful thinking or genetic engineering will make that so. Human equality as an ethical precept is not related to the nature of biological endowments. Unfortunately, it can be difficult to make this point without engendering misunderstanding, principally because there are always individuals who use the evidence for the inheritance of these qualities to promote the concept of the inequality of human races. Equality is not a matter of races but of individuals. Some are more or less intelligent, athletic, artistic, musical, or creative. It is highly probable that as individuals we carry in our genes the determinants for more personal qualities than most people—including many scientists—have been willing to examine.

Inherited behavioral characteristics are especially difficult to demonstrate in man, due to methodological problems and the predilection most human behaviorists have for attributing behavior entirely to environmental conditioning. However significant the environment may be in allowing expression or repression of behavior, there is an individual genetic component that cannot be negated. There may even exist population differences in the genetic determinants of behavior. A comparison of Chinese-American and European-American infants lends support to this supposition (Freedman and Freedman 1969). Twenty-four children of each racial descent were examined while still in the nursery, taking into account potentially important covariables which might affect the study. Twenty-five general behavioral characters of neonatants and fifteen standard neurological indicators were used in comparing the two groups. A multivariate analysis of the data indicated that the two groups were significantly different, especially in terms of temperament. The European-American infants were more inclined to alternate between states of contentment and upset, and exhibited more facial and body reddening as a result of the wider range of excitability. The Chinese-American infants tended to be calmer and more relaxed, and habituated more readily to a light shone into the eyes and to having a cloth placed over the face. Whereas there was no significant difference in the amount of crying between the two groups, the Chinese-Americans were more easily consoled and ceased to cry sooner than the European-Americans when picked up. In the areas of sensory development, central nervous system maturity, motor development, and social responsivity, the two groups were equal.

While behaviorists do not hesitate to accept the genetic basis of behavior in other animals—even very highly developed primates—it has long been taboo in one school of thought to suggest a genetic as well as social determinant in the formulation of human behavior. There is now more than enough evidence to suggest that the determination of behavioral patterns in man is complex, resting on multivariables that include genetically determined components. Environmental influences contribute to the personality structure of a developing child, but the foundations for all biological responses rest in genetics. The same is true of intelligence, which may be either stimulated or subdued by social factors but which in inherited capacity is largely innate. This has been borne out in studies of monozygotic twins reared in divergent home atmospheres, which should have, were environment a critical determining agent, resulted in children of different intellects. In most instances, these twins' intelligences proved to be remarkably alike.

It is now known that severe behavioral disorders, such as schizophrenia, may be inherited (Erlenmeyer-Kimling and Paradowski 1966). Schizophrenia results in a partial to total disability in an individual's effective social functionality. Its frequency in our present U.S. population is about 1 per cent. A variety of reasons have been offered as to why this dysfunctional trait has been retained in the human gene pool, but supportive evidence is lacking for any hypothesis. One suggestion is that schizophrenics have an unknown survival advantage concomitant with the genetic information for the disorder, as is the case with sickle-cell anemia conferring resistance to malaria. It is an appealing hypothesis, but remains unproven. Past social advantages for schizophrenics have been suggested, but none are wholly convincing. For example, it has been proposed that in primitive groups the schizophrenic's hallucinations and delusions might have given them respect as shamans or priests. Whether or not this is true, the fecundity of shamans or priests is not notable, so this explanation would have little effect on the gene pool. The most reasonable contention is that the manifestations of schizophrenia are the product of a genotypically heterogeneous group of conditions. Its frequency of occurrence, about 1 per cent, could not be sustained by mutation alone were it a condition traceable to a single gene. Polygenic origins would allow the possibility of persistently recurring mutations while permitting the explanation of some selective advantage stemming from disease immunity.

Whether the existing frequency of schizophrenia has been constant in the human species over its history cannot be determined. Its manifestations create great personal liabilities for those afflicted; thus, it seems probable that in the past schizophrenia occurred at a lower level than presently, as society has grown more understanding of aberrations.

There has been a relaxation of selective pressures against schizophrenia as a result of eased social sanction and effective medical understanding and treatment. As a defined medical entity, the condition is a relative newcomer. A somewhat restrictive definition of *Dementia praecox* was given by Morel in 1860, and a more modern description was offered by Bleuler in 1911. It has been present in the human population for millenia, however, as *possession* or whatever seemed the explanation of the time. Marriage and reproduction among schizophrenics have been low, at least as far back as records exist. As a result of a more enlightened attitude toward mental illness than previous generations exhibited, much of the social stigma of schizophrenia has been lifted, leading to a higher incidence of marriage among schizophrenics. Somatic therapy and maintenance on drugs that aid the function of the schizophrenic coupled with greater social acceptance increase the likelihood of reproduction. An inspection of records of two similar groups of schizophrenics, one from 1934–36 and the other from 1954–56, indicate that marriage among the males rose from 26.4 per cent to 40.8 per cent. The gain for females was somewhat less. These marriages for that period followed trends representative of the population as a whole; fewer childless marriages and an increase in the number of children. Thus, the reproductive differential between schizophrenics and the total U.S. population is being closed, and there should be more cases of schizophrenia proportionate to population in the future. In this instance, the explanation is sociocultural. Schizophrenia is a lucid example of the importance of social structures in their effects on natural selection. In turn, disabilities that might not be maladaptive to a nonsocial animal may be so in a highly social one such as man.

Culture and Intelligence

Since the advent of human culture, a variety of human traits have been selected for quite arbitrarily. Standards of beauty, personality, and other qualities requiring subjective interpretation may be neutral or even counterproductive from an evolutionary standpoint. If in a given culture a narrow-hipped woman is considered the most desirable, there may be negative selection operating because a narrow pelvis structure correlates with difficulty in childbirth. In the past, cultures calling for human sacrifice sometimes reached the point of biological and cultural counterproductivity. The Carthaginians of Roman times sacrificed their first-born children, perhaps hastening the demise of their culture (Weyl 1968). Most cultural practices are biologically neutral rather than advantageous or deleterious, particularly those relating to appearance.

Large noses, small feet, large lips, straight hair, blue eyes, and a multitude of other culturally preferred traits are irrelevant to evolutionary success. It is only when culture causes a rising percentage of biologically maladaptive traits to accumulate that the virtue of such standards may be questioned. Of course, this accumulation may be the result of a humanitarian value system rather than of an evolutionary value system. In modern countries an ever-increasing percentage of individuals with congenitally nonadaptive traits are able to live and reproduce with the aid of sophisticated medical technology. While no one would suggest that insulin be withheld from diabetics, some pertinent questions arise relative to increasing the percentages of severely disabling characters in the population. An example of the dilemma raised is *retinoblastoma*, a cancer of the eye, which arises by mutation in each generation. Formerly it was self-eliminating, as victims always died during the first few years of life. Now the eyes may be removed surgically, allowing the carriers of the gene to live, marry, reproduce, and pass the gene for retinoblastoma along to 50 per cent of their offspring. This and many other interactions between medical technology and human genetics present us with an increased commitment to more medical technology for more people in the future—a humanitarian and ethical dilemma, as there will be an increased percentage of deleterious genes in future human populations. There are no easy answers to these problems.

Another human characteristic greatly influenced by cultural selection is that of intelligence. It has been said that man did not make tools, but that tools made man. This is still partially true. A complex material culture places strong selective pressures on individuals who can conceptualize, innovate, and operate artifacts and ideas. Previously we stated that intellectual capacity is determined largely by genes. Cultural values determine the expression of those genes and, indeed, their selection. If great selection priority is given to physical attractiveness, or athletic prowess, levels of expressed intelligence may not be as high, and mean intellect may be lessened somewhat in the population. Or there could theoretically be selection for certain types of intelligence, such as verbal ability over mathematical, or vice versa.

A difficulty in dealing with the concept of intelligence from a nonstructural point of view is its definition. The idea of intelligence quotient (IQ) has been widely used, criticized, and misunderstood. Intelligence quotient simply measures the statistical probability or potential for success of an individual in a highly structured, culturally defined educational situation. Its virtue lies in its predictability. Intelligence quotient tests are limited in what they measure, even those purporting to be un-restricted by cultural or subcultural differences. Further, some of the most important aspects of intelligence cannot be quantified or pre-dicted: creativity, productivity, the rationality of the politics of human interaction, and humanitarianism. True genius may become manifest in ways never reflected by societal testing. Charles Darwin was something of a failure and disappointment to his family, who were, perhaps, re-lieved to see him off on the *Beagle*. Where intelligence testing is kept in perspective, it serves a useful but limited role as a predictive measure of innate potential.

However, all potential must be expressed to be realized, and herein lies the role of environmental enhancement or repression of intellect. It is regrettable that the experimental design of studies that supposedly ellucidate the relative importance of heredity versus environment in human intelligence is difficult to actualize; and such experiments are nearly impossible to conduct. All environmental influences would neces-sarily be randomized and accounted for, as would the genetic endowment of each individual considered. As both of these are impossible to realize operationally, the most detailed and conscientious investigation bases much of its conclusions on inference. However, there is evidence that environmental experience does affect developing individuals (Hunt 1969). Chimpanzees reared in total darkness never develop normal eye-sight, and the retinal and optic nerves show abnormal histological growth. Environmental stimulation does, then, play a role in the matur-ing brain and its environmental receptors. Recently a great deal has been made, by a few, of the fact that U.S. blacks score ten to twenty points lower than whites on IQ tests, fifteen IQ points being the mean differ-ence between the two groups (Jensen 1969 a and b; see Dobzhansky 1973, and King 1971, for rebuttals). If indeed only 20 per cent of mani-fest measured intelligence is environmentally regulated, that in itself is enough to account for these mean differences, if one considers the extreme divergence in cultural advantage and perspective between the two groups. Many blacks score above the white mean, and many whites score below the black mean. In this light, a socially rather than a bio-logically intrinsic explanation appears more rational. After more than 200 years of social inequality it is surely tunnel-visioned and racially presumptuous to assume that the effects have been negated in the last decade. Perhaps it would be wiser to suspend such attempted measures until there is true social-environmental equality among Americans.

There is an important distinction between genetic and social inequality. Genetic inequality is a biological fact expressed by individuals, not populations or races of man. Social inequality is a social, cultural, and political phenomenon arising from a variety of sources, and cannot be correlated with one's genetic endowments, ethnic heritage, or racial origin. In a meritocracy, where individual worth is valued, social equality merely allows each person an opportunity according to his or her abilities.

There are no guarantees that everyone comes out on the top of the ladder. Biological and social equality are not the same, and equating them is a disservice. As Theodosius Dobzhansky, the eminent geneticist, stated in his John Dewey lecture of 1972 (see Dobzhansky 1973): "Diversity is an observable fact of nature, while equality is an ethical commandment." It is probably one of the hardest to keep.

A final factor of human culture that affects expressed genetic intelligence is nutrition. In both the underdeveloped and developed countries nutritional deprivation may be caused by the inheritance of a recessive allele that if homozygous will cause galactosemia, the inability to metabolize galactose, a milk sugar. In nursing infants, if unchecked, it leads to cataracts, an enlarged liver, and severe mental retardation. If discovered within a few days of birth, a galactose-free diet can be prescribed, and normal development ensues. Other congenital diseases in which abnormal levels of metabolites occur may also cause mental retardation or slight impairment. Many of these effects are subtle, rather than so striking as mental retardation, but their result is a lower mental capacity than might have been. There is accumulating evidence that protein deficiency in prenatal and postnatal development of human infants results in smaller, underdeveloped brains. The damage, sadly, is irreparable once effected. This tragedy has always been a part of human history. The colonialist of the nineteenth century viewed the natives of his coopted country as dull, indolent, and dependent while, in reality, many may have been victims of malnutrition. Presently, this biological and social disaster is common in India, Africa, Indonesia, and many underdeveloped—and probably never-to-be-developed—countries. It is an aspect of world starvation for which the victims and many others pay the price. The starving children seen in photographs permanently carry the scars of malnourishment in a reduced mental capacity, a condition that can only proliferate in an overpopulated and protein-scarce world.

Suggested Readings

Brace, C. Loring. "A Nonracial Approach Toward the Understanding of Human Diversity." In *The Concept of Race*, edited by Ashley Montagu, London: Collier-Macmillan, 1969.

Bresler, Jack B. "Maternal Height and the Prevalence of Stillbirths." *American Journal of Physical Anthropology* 20(1962): 515–517.

Burch, P. R. J. "Schizophrenia: Some New Aetiological Considerations." *British Journal of Psychiatry* 110(1964): 818–824.

Damon, A., and Thomas, R. "Fertility and Physique—Height, Weight, and Ponderal Index." *Human Biology* 39(1967): 5–13.

Dobzhansky, Theodosius. *Genetic Diversity and Human Equality*. New York: Basic Books, Inc., 1973.

Eichenwald, H. F., and P. C. Fry. "Nutrition and Learning." *Science* 163 (1969): 644–648.

Erlenmeyer-Kimling, L., and W. Paradowski. "Selection and Schizophrenia." *American Naturalist* 100(1966): 651–665.

Freedman, D. G., and Nina Chinn Freedman. "Behavioral Differences Between Chinese-American and European-American Newborns." *Nature* 224(1969): 1227.

Gentry, John L., Elizabeth Parkhurst, and George V. Bulin, Jr. "An Epidemiological Study of Congenital Malformations in New York State." *American Journal of Public Health* 49(1959): 1–22.

Glass, H. Bentley. "The Genetics of the Dunkers." *Scientific American* 189(1953): 176–181.

Hamilton, W. J., and F. Heppner. "Radiant Solar Energy and the Function of Black Homeotherm Pigmentation: An Hypothesis." *Science* 155 (1967): 196–197.

Howe, G. Melvyn. "The Geography of Death." *New Scientist* 40(1968): 612–614.

Hulse, Frederick S. "Some Factors Influencing the Relative Proportions of Human Racial Stocks." *Cold Spring Harbor Symposia On Quantitative Biology* 22(1957): 3–45.

Hunt, Joseph M. *Intelligence And Experience*. New York: The Ronald Press, 1969.

Jensen, Arthur R. "How Much Can We Boost IQ and Scholastic Achievement?" *Harvard Educational Review* 39(1969a): 1–123.

——— "Reducing the Heredity-Environment Uncertainty." *Harvard Educcational Review* 39(1969b): 209–243.

Keeler, Clyde. "The Incidence of Cuna Moon-child Albinos." *Journal of Heredity* 55(1964): 115–120.

King, James C. *The Biology of Race*. New York: Harcourt Brace Jovanovich, Inc., 1971.

Monie, Ian W. "Influence of the Environment on the Unborn." *California Medicine* 99(1963): 323–327.

Record, R. G., Thomas McKeown, and J. H. Edwards. "An Investigation of the Difference in Measured Intelligence Between Twins and Single Births." *Annals of Human Genetics* 34(1970): 11–20.

Shields, J. *Monozygotic Twins Brought up Apart and Brought up Together.* London: Oxford University Press, 1962.

Turner, Christy G., II. "PTC Tasting in Two Social Groups." *Social Biology* 17(1970): 142.

Van Valen, L., and G. Mellin. "Selection in Natural Populations. New York Babies." *Annals of Human Genetics* 31(1967): 109–127.

Weyl, Nathaniel. "Some Possible Genetic Implications of Carthaginian Child Sacrifice." *Perspectives in Biology and Medicine* 12(1968): 69–78.

————"Some Genetic Aspects of Plantation Slavery." *Perspectives in Biology and Medicine* 13(1970): 618–625.

section
II

chapter

8

A SURVIVAL OVERVIEW

In previous chapters we have reviewed factors of natural selection on human populations in the past and present, but what of the future? Will natural selection become less important in determining the human makeup, or will it, as intimated in some examples already described, become even more acute? The reality is that each line of thought has support, since natural selection is being reduced in some aspects, as through medical technology, and intensified in others, as through pollution, diseases, and other man-created hazards that permeate the fragile

FIGURE 8–1

and abused ecosphere. Any new stresses imposed on the human genome, whether due to man or to some other cause, will act as natural selection forces. It is unfortunate that the exploration of space has diverted attention from our own planet's depreciating condition and engendered the false notion that solutions to imminent problems may be found through migration from Earth. Anyone but the most naive optimist must know that entertaining such ideas may provide interesting material for theoretical problems, but they have no relevance whatsoever to the critical

170

morass of issues on survival confronting our species and many others, albeit the latter have no voice in the outcome.

Natural Selection

We have stressed the fact that natural selection continues to be a force on human populations. It is inaccurate to infer, as many have done, that the altering character of natural selection shows its reduced importance in the evolution of man. Natural selection, to reiterate, refers to a selection for the survival of individuals best able to cope with environmental stresses as reflected by genetic constitutions. If there were no pressures of any kind remaining on the human population, then natural selection would not be an aspect of human evolution. The total absence of biological stress, however, is a hypothetical projection that will never merge with fact (see Hardy-Weinberg law, Chapter 1), so natural selection will always be directing the course of evolution on humans and on all other organisms. The elimination of mortalities resulting from congenital defects, changes in differential reproduction, and any other modifications of past circumstances will fail to cause an end to the process of natural selection. Surely the stresses of overpopulation, severe pollution of the environment, evolution of new strains of viruses and bacteria, and additional factors concomitant with technological and cultural activities are causing intense selection, but with differing criteria than in pre-1970s man. In a similar fashion, the development of rudimentary human culture added new modes for the operation of natural selection while deleting others among pre-cultural men. To maintain that natural selection is becoming inoperative creates too simplistic an impression of the role of culture and of the current human condition. It is more nearly a situation of *quid pro quo* in which certain selective pressures have been reduced or eliminated, but others substituted.

Many of the ideas set forth regarding the relationships among man-culture-natural selection are rooted more deeply in speculative philosophy than in operable biological reality. Conjecture often conveys unrealistic impressions of man's capacities and limitations. *Homo sapiens*, versatile and intriguing being that he is, dimensionally unique, is not a demigod, and his culture is not capable of divesting him of his heritage; he remains a biological organism. Although he is capable of altering his environment, both internal and external, in ways and degrees

171

unknown to other species, man is still far from transcending environmental influences and has, in fact, generated many new ones. Creativity and a vast intellectual capacity characterize man, but whether or not *sapiens* is a deserved adjective is open to question.

Would the elimination or severe reduction of mutations in man comprise a biological danger to his survival, or would cultural flexibility provide more than enough compensation? Mutations in man, as in any other organism, are spontaneous and occur at predictable rates. Even among laboratory organisms, such as mice or protozoa, it is impossible to erase spontaneous genetic change. Although mainly deleterious, mutation still remains the creative springboard for the evolutionary process. There is little reason to believe that even the most sophisticated scientific technology could erase mutation as an uncontrolled aspect of human evolution. The wisdom of eliminating this spontaneous force of the evolutionary process is wholly open to question. Yet man in foreseeing his own survival and genetic evolution would like to remove this randomness, this lack of predictability from his course. This, in essence, is the contemporary eugenic perspective.

If the capacity for spontaneous mutation were to be weeded out of the human genome and limitless degrees of genetic flexibility discarded for a predictable and supposedly desirable few traits, man would become wholly dependent on a homogeneous culture, technology, and environment designed to support his new self-limited and self-regulated genetic freedom. Any plant that is a product of artificial selection by a plant breeder is genetically engineered *for* an environment, a technology, and a culture to assure its survival and reproduction. Man's assumption of what is random in nature entails tremendous custodial knowledge to insure survival. Few roses of today would survive a cultural collapse, and would become the weeds of tomorrow. Man is potentially no different. If he rejects the conditions of the natural world and ceases to be molded by random chance, electing instead to secure his survival by his own wisdom, he will then have shifted his evolutionary course toward his own predictive survival strategy. Predictive value is gained, but it is inevitable that some random survival value is lost. If man attempts to bring his evolution more under the control of his cultural directives and less under the influence of random natural selection, he contracts another bargain in the process. For the absence of mutation to be irrelevant to man, for example, he would first have to construct a flawlessly functioning and permanently regulated Utopian environment and society. An important aspect of the nature of biological organisms is their

172

biofeedback with the environment. Reduction of randomness in the organism is only profitable if it is accompanied by corresponding reduction of randomness in its environment. Thus, we see the dilemma of man's assumption of control of his own genetic destiny, and the insurance of his survival by his own means. Although it is a fine armchair prospect, the grim realities of balancing ourselves with Earth's ecosystems on a global scale must be achieved before there will be wisdom in attempts to completely manipulate our own genetics.

A major aspect in which selection on the human population has changed is achievement, not in the sense of social accomplishments but in survival. Prior to the development of cultural interactions, many individuals who did not cope effectively with the environment did not survive. Cultural development allowed those who might have failed in precultural times to live by virtue of new values placed on qualities and abilities that were irrelevant outside of a cultural reference. A skilled artisan, for example, may have been a poor hunter, but the imposition of cultural criteria elevated his social worth and survival potential, whereas in a hunting band his selective value was hardly positive. Long before modern medicine and better nutrition lessened the influence of natural selection in certain situations, culture was allowing the survival of individuals who would not have fared well on the basis of their own physical merits. As cultural interactions develop, there is lessened differential mortality between the physically fit and the less fit, a condition more true today than ever before. Unfortunately, man has imposed a greater number of culturally engendered stresses on his population during the past three decades than during all his prior history, a condition counter-pointing the adaptive value of retaining physically maladapted individuals. If, at any given time, the mechanisms for maintaining biologically inferior individuals were to fail, natural selection pressures would be exerted rapidly and decisively. From a biological standpoint, there is no direct correlation between physiological fitness and qualities prized by most human societies. Creativity, intelligence, compassion, and most other characteristics in which the essence of civilization is harbored may be present in individuals who, deprived of cultural protection, would not survive to transmit their genes. An optimistic aim of positive eugenics, discussed at length in the following chapter, is to select actively for the most desirable physical and mental qualities through controlled genetic determination. Those attributes considered most desirable at a given time are subject to change. Standards of beauty, competitiveness, and cooperativeness are not static even within the same culture. A quality that may have been selected for quite intensively 3,000 years ago may not have value in any contemporary culture. Adaptive standards are dynamic—both biologically and culturally—and if man is able to manipulate his genetic evolution, he will be wise not to eliminate the capacity for variability, not only for the obvious reasons of biological plasticity, but in anticipation of changing perceptions of desirable human qualities.

In modern societies, individual choice serves as an important facet of selection. Various means of birth control are now so effective that in most developed nations selection operates through controlled births rather than uncontrolled deaths. The contemporary situation has been inverted from that operating only several decades ago. Were effective birth control to become a genuinely universal practice, its impact on the world population would be significant, but that point—if it is attainable at all—lies some years in the future.

As illustrated earlier in the text, differential reproduction is a significant factor in determining gene frequencies in human populations. Wide-spread birth control will markedly affect differential reproduction if its practice is employed among all world populations. It has already done so in the United States, although a wide gap between its potential and employment still remains. Couples practicing birth control tend to base the number of children on their income. It is practiced more widely by the more highly educated and economically advantaged members of society, resulting in fewer children for that group than for the less educated and economically disadvantaged. There is some concern when viewing this as a problem of population genetics. If the more obviously intelligent and creative members of society choose to have fewer children, there will be a genetic decline in these qualities in succeeding generations. This anxiety is rooted in spurious reasoning, as we have indicated in Chapter 7. Hopefully, the concepts of the two-child family and zero population growth will spread to all socioeconomic groups, nullifying this concern. It is unfortunate that the practice of universal birth control is not simply a matter of education. There are religious and cultural dicta against it which, until they are eased, will remain as obstacles affecting both population control and differential reproduction.

As modern societies become more complex and man becomes more dependent on the products of a sophisticated technology, the individual in his understanding becomes further removed from the processes which shape him and on which he depends for his survival. How many individuals can repair a computer, operate a laser, or comprehend their own genetic assets and liabilities? Only a few generations ago most of the skills and knowledge underpinning society could be learned by most people of average intelligence. But today, and increasingly so in the future, the mechanisms underlying a variety of critical functions can be mastered effectively only by relatively bright individuals. This is significant to our present discussion in that culture itself is a strong selective determinant. In increasingly technological societies of the future, what will the genetic reflection be? We may surmise that technological maintenance of many deleterious genetic traits will be a commitment, and that the percentage of maladaptive genes in many human populations will rise. There may be strong cultural selection for particular kinds of intelligence, particularly technological expertise. Whatever the future does hold, the proliferation of an increasingly sophisticated and technological world cannot be dissociated from human genetics.

Many of the natural selection-survival stressors of today are going to be increased with time, at least until man achieves a balanced population and ecosystem. As long as the human population expands at its present rate, pressures related to pollution and overpopulation may be expected to exert themselves with even more severity than in the present. Globally, malnutrition, disease, and pollution will continue to degrade human potential—a seeming paradox in the context of existing technological advances.

Technology itself may fade, at least temporarily, into the shadows of relevance in insuring man's survival and providing solutions for our most pressing contemporary dilemmas. Indeed, existing genetic technology is somewhat irrelevant to man's survival as long as environmental change and degradation progress at present rates. An engineered genotype needs an engineered environment in which it can predictably function. As Paul Ehrlich suggested several years ago, whatever man's concern may be, overpopulation and its concomitant problems should be the primary concern. This is rationally true in regard to man's genetic survival and future design.

Previously, we considered some evolutionary stress factors having effects on human genetics per se. However, if evolutionary success is survival, it is necessary to include in the succeeding test those factors threatening man's survival as a species. Some of these factors have unknown or indirect effects on the human genome. We are currently in an epoch wherein our survival is a sociopolitical and biological issue with imaginative but often ineffectual technological solutions offered us. It is unlikely that man as a species will soon become extinct, but the imminent possibility of elimination of vast numbers of people as a result of the increasing selective pressures operating on the world population could totally alter the course of man's future. History is not cyclic in regard to the critical problems of population versus resources now facing man. As a result of our technology and inflated numbers, we are in a place we have never been before.

Overpopulation and Social Pathologies

Human overpopulation is accompanied by a variety of social pathologies that have biofeedback on reproductive capacity. Unfortunately, precise data on such effects in human populations is not as complete as we might wish. There are many variables, including the fact that overcrowding seems to have fewer adverse effects among certain cultural groups than others, an indication that future selection may favor those persons better able to lead successfully productive—and reproductive—lives under crowded conditions (Dubos 1968). In some mammals, such as rats, behavioral pathologies from overcrowding become rampant, including a lessened reproductive capacity, a high infant mortality rate, increased hostility, and even cannibalism of the young (Lorenz 1967).

In a crowded human world, there will certainly be a need for increased social cooperation and a stable social order, but these are the very qualities that tend to disintegrate under the pressures of overpopulation. If grim prophecies become reality and the Earth's land surface is covered only with masses of men and the agriculture necessary to sustain them, what reproductive patterns will emerge? Certainly if this point is ever reached, regulated birth control would be imperative. We may, however, safely surmise that our resources will have been exhausted long before this hypothetical world view becomes fact. Social pathologies resulting from overcrowding will have an effect on all of the variables inherent in reproduction. No data—from man or any other animal—indicate that there are any advantages to be gained from too numerous a population, and no rational person would advocate that humans continue their population increase at this point. But advocated or not, the human flood will surge on for at least the next several decades. Our only grace is that our present awareness of the anticipated biological and social problems may help us to alleviate them.

As René Dubos suggested in *So Human an Animal,* even a temporal adjustment to the conditions of overcrowding will not necessarily prove

TABLE 8-1

Demographic Estimates of Human Population Size and Density

Years Ago	Density per Square Kilometer	Total Population (millions)
1,000,000	.00425	.125
300,000	.012	1.0
25,000	.04	3.34
10,000	.04	5.32
6,000	1.0	86.5
2,000	1.0	133.0
320	3.7	545
220	4.9	728
170	6.2	906
70	11.0	1,610
20	16.4	2,400
A.D. 2000	46.0	6,270

beneficial in the long-run. Humans are gregarious and many enjoy crowded, stimulating urban situations. Also, people tend to adjust better to conditions they have known since birth, so in time man may be better suited to crowding as more of the world becomes carpeted with his civilizations. But does this have survival value for the species; is it adaptive? People may become habituated to eating dirt or drinking excessive quantities of alcohol, but in both instances the cumulative results are undesirable. If man becomes accustomed to overpopulation, accepting it as a neutral fact rather than as a potentially dangerous phenomenon, the result may be increased ease of living in close quarters for a few generations, but the denouement of our acceptance could be biological and social disaster. However, most of the world's population, occupied in its efforts to eke out another day of life from a decreasing and deteriorating environment, is faced presently with more imminent and less theoretical problems, than to be interested in dealing with overpopulation in affluent countries. To them, overpopulation exists today in terms of limited resources or actual overcrowding and is a harsh reality.

What would be the price for an overpopulated species under the best physical conditions possible? Vastly overpopulated Japan can serve in some respects as a world model. All flat land would be taken over by human dwellings, agriculture and perhaps a few parks. There would be no wilderness areas, and all wildlife, save a few species that could cohabit with man, would be eliminated. The surrounding oceans will become increasingly sterile of life and polluted. The aesthetic value formerly placed on nature and wilderness will become a memory of the past.

Perhaps the most uninviting aspect of a world given over to masses of humanity is the loss of personal freedom and choice. George Orwell's *1984* is a liberal sanctuary in comparison with the regulated society that may of necessity exist with intense overpopulation. Those creative individuals who have contributed so much in the past to our visions of literature, art, and humanism could not be tolerated. In the words of the late Alan Watts, "unregulated tripping" would be strictly prohibited. Life would be highly structured, and social selection would be for those individuals able to lead socially-oriented, conformist lives in a rather monotonous world. In time, the capacity for dissent, free-thinking, and personal conviction might be bred out of the human race as nonadaptive; society would be so precariously balanced between resources and numbers that no socially nonconformist behavior could be allowed. It might be a peaceful world—one attractive aspect—but it would be a tediously dull one in which men would exist as subdued groups, blissful perhaps, but inspired by nothing. In a world where the capacity for creative impulses engendered by wilderness, and freedom of expression and variety, have necessarily been deleted from the behavioral repertoire, only a placid existence might suffice to assuage the absurdity.

The one imminent reality that cannot be escaped is that the future *will* see Earth overpopulated by man, even if disastrous levels are never reached. Is there anything that can be done to allay certain foreseeable difficulties arising from man's discordant cultures? We may hope that certain human qualities may be selected for that will enable man to interact more peacefully. During the history of human evolution, there has presumably been selective value in territoriality and aggressive behavior. It may be argued that these characteristics have long been maladaptive; there is surely little support for them as present and future survival tactics in human interaction. They have been negated by our technological innovations. Hermann Muller, the late geneticist who was deeply interested in eugenic possibilities, became committed to the idea that cooperation was most important as a survival characteristic in man's future (Muller 1967). Konrad Lorenz, in *On Aggression*, underscored the need for somehow ridding the human species of its aggressive, territorial impulses, a behavioral artifact not only useless but dangerous in a cultural animal. Even now when environmental crises are truly global, surpassing all boundaries, nationalism stands in the way of solutions more than any other factor. The world is still a pie and Jack must have his piece. Nationalism is culture's answer to territorial behavior, and no more self-defeating social force operates today, co-opting natural resources, the talents of our culture, and manpower into absurdly spiraling national defense.

As a cultural imperative, nationalism may yet result in irreparable biological and material damage to modern civilization, as it has fostered the development of nuclear weapons and the means for biological warfare. These stockpiles represent a potential experiment in negative eugenics, more disastrous for the family of man than Hitler's 6 million. We have examined previously some of the possible outcomes of the use of nuclear weapons. While many people would survive such a holocaust, the aftermath would entail a long struggle to reconstruct civilization. The effects of radiation on the ecosystem and survivors could be even grimmer than predicted, and at best the human species would be plagued for many years with an abundance of undesirable mutations, placing a heavy burden on society. Our genome might be so affected that we could lose our hand in the game of survival.

Overpopulation, although it is a worldwide problem, does tend to be amplified or diminished within national boundaries. In the United States, zero population growth has been reached functionally, whereas in African nations or in Asia, the multiplying masses represent a crucial problem that increases daily in severity. In many areas of the world, population density is far greater than in the United States, relative to land area. This has stimulated a growing awareness in the third world countries to the fact that a large quantity of the world's resources are being usurped by the wealthier nations with lesser populations. The developed countries consume a vastly disproportionate quantity of nonrenewable resources, causing hostility on the part of those seeing their own natural resources being shipped to wealthier countries with benefits for only a few local capitalists and politicians. Ideally, all countries should have high standards of material wealth, were not overpopulation the denominator negating this possibility. Resources are being exhausted on a global level to the point that even those nations already enjoying relative prosperity are destined to experience reductions in their standards of living. Despite the allure of Utopian fantasies, the truth is that many developing countries will never be able to realize their aspirations of a halcyon future, pulled down as they will be by the weight of their

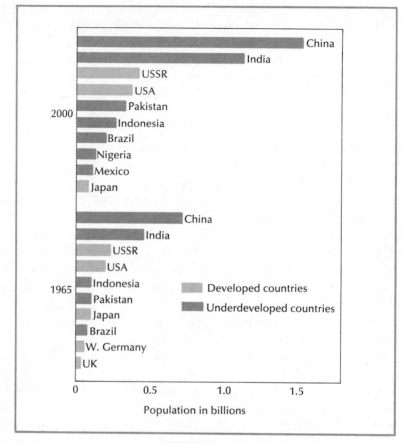

FIGURE 8-2

The demographic shuffle. As the developed countries stabilize population during the coming decades, the top ten nations in population size are increasingly composed of underdeveloped countries that have been less efficient in population stabilization.

(Adapted from P. R. Ehrlich and A. H. Ehrlich, *Population, Resources, Environment*, 2nd ed. W. H. Freeman and Company, 1972.)

own populations. Even in the United States, long the leader in materialistic advantage, the demand for resources is rapidly surpassing availability. In 1957 the gross national product of the United States was 453 billion dollars, compared to 728 billion in 1969 (Thant 1970). And in 1973, it was 1,289 billion (Survey of Current Business 1974). The idea that an increase in the gross national product is equivalent to individual benefit is ingrained deeply in the American value system. Corporations are expected to produce more to raise their profits, and in all quarters one sees growth extolled as a virtue. The fallacy of such thinking has become clear during the past few years. There are indeed limits to growth of any kind. The shortages and inflation of today are only mild previews of future conditions. The depletion of resources will not only deprive wealthier countries of luxuries that have been taken for granted for too long, but technological development—including medical tech-

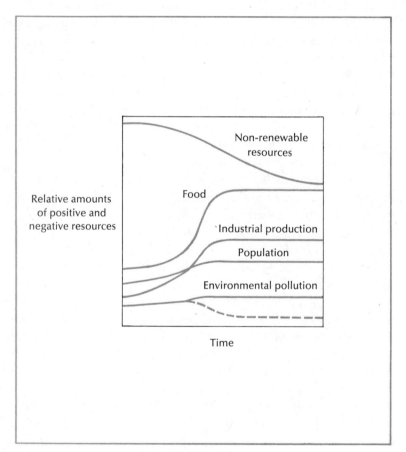

FIGURE 8–3

The interplay between population, resources, and environment. With a stabilized human population and a stabilized consumer lifestyle, food, population, and industrial production do not show continued growth. Depending on social priorities and biotechnological understanding, environmental pollution may remain relatively constant or decrease. Nonrenewable resources by definition decrease as they are utilized in industrial production.

181

nology—will experience deprivations that will affect the ability of a society such as ours to maintain genetically unfit individuals dependent on accessory technology for their very lives.

We have discussed the necessity of complete, high-quality protein for the development and maintenance of optimally functional individuals. Deprivation of protein in the unborn and newborn causes permanent damage (see Chapter 7). Animal protein has always been premium, and the probability is great that in the years ahead such protein will become a scarce food. As animal protein is energetically a less efficient product than plant material, there will be less produced, a fact carrying much relevance when there are many people and less land available for agriculture. When a cow consumes its diet of plants, only 10 per cent of the sun's energy captured by those plants is retained by the cow. When the cow is eaten, again only 10 per cent of its total captured energy is utilized. Clearly a diet of plant matter is economically and energetically more conservative, despite the fact that man fares better on animal protein. A world in which energy expenditures must be weighed will be forced to turn more to plants for food.

Many of the materials and contrivances necessary for the maintenance of a single genetically disadvantaged individual are extremely consumptive of resources. If we are moving, as seems inevitable, into a time of greater scarcities and material limitations imposed by the excessive proliferation of the human race, how will it then be possible to enter at the same time into a period of increased incidences of manifest genetic conditions where a large number of individuals are dependent on accessory technology for life support? A "reverence for life," as Schweitzer put it, is a necessary component of man's philosophy if we are to evolve toward the unique cultural levels of which man is capable. But does the definition of reverence include the support of all individuals, however unable they may be to survive without artificial aids or extensive care? Perhaps man must equate all genetic disorders and resolve to alleviate what suffering he can. But we know that such disorders will increase in the human population in time, given our technological perpetuation of afflicted individuals to reproductive age. And obviously the social and financials cost will increase also. In the realm of severely incapacitating conditions, especially those involving the functioning of the mind, the issues become more complex and, perhaps, from a moral standpoint, insoluble. The science of eugenics offers some possible solutions to these dilemmas, but there are inherent technological and moral difficulties in this approach, as will be considered in detail in Chapter 9.

Beset with an increasing array of problems, how can man insure his survival as a species and as a cultural entity? One possibility, offered by the study of evolution and greatly overlooked in current analyses, is that fostering diversity both in man and in his environment may be the simplest and wisest means for allowing man's genetic future a hopeful prospect. But here again we are confronted by the fact of overpopulation and its corollaries. There will be less natural diversity due to an increasing amount of land being usurped by urbanization, agriculture, and other priorities. With a decreased variety of environments, genetic variability will become more dependent on nonadaptive genetic drift and environmental stresses imposed by poisons, radiation, and other byproducts of cultural activity.

Henry David Thoreau penned the now well-known phrase, "In wildness is the preservation of the world." There is more within this sentiment than the subjective expression of a love of nature, as biological systems may be considered sensitive indicators of the state of the ecosphere. The malaise and death of numerous ecosystems should be taken as signs that man has something immediate to worry about in terms of insuring his own survival. Man is an animal inhabiting nearly all terrestrial habitats, but even so his culture has not freed him from his biological requirements. These needs are psychological as well as physiological. The future of man might be relatively predictable in technologically controlled, closed-system environments, but it would not be rich.

For these reasons the conservation of wildlife and wilderness is not irrelevant to man's survival. One could argue that the extinction of any particular form of life or the destruction of an ecosystem has a negative impact on man, apart from aesthetics; we do not know where we stand in the total scheme of things. It could also be argued that the destruction of Da Vinci's Mona Lisa would have less impact on man than the destruction of the apparently most insignificant form of life. We have a tradition of valuing a great many things, not because we presume an objective worth, but because we place subjective value on them. Perhaps the only reason for conserving owls is to hear them sing in the night, or hummingbirds, to watch them glint in the sun. But man risks a long step backwards in denying the worth of species that apparently carry no direct survival or monetary value. Expanding from the particular to the general, habitat conservation is a similar matter. As varied habitats are destroyed, covered with asphalt, replaced by endless rows of wheat and corn, or whatever, diversity lessens, and we cannot know the ultimate

183

impact. There are those who will argue that as long as the earth can support man—which is scarcely the case even now—our own habitat is obviously adequate. This is specious logic, implying that man is capable of predicting the survival value and outcome of a homogeneous world; he is not. Once ecological and species diversity have been reduced as drastically as seems inevitable, it will be impossible to recreate, literally, what has been lost, even if man's very survival were thus dependent.

FIGURE 8–4

Man is a part of the global ecosystem, however apart from it he may seem at times. Environmental diversity will be to our long-term benefit.

The future of man hinges on a great many qualifications and uncertainties. Where there might have been the opportunity for the whole family of man to live in a world released from hunger, disease, and material want, allowing man's further transcendence, as Teilhard de Chardin suggested, into the *noösphere*, or world of the mind, we now seem to be on the brink of a rather dismal future. Biological stress factors are increasing at an alarming rate, and we must live under the threat of nuclear warfare and epidemic disease capable of ravaging the human species. The sacred cow of technological optimism is growing rather thin, for it is plain that not only has science been unable to solve most of our growing problems, but technological abuses and the unwise and unecological administration of humanitarian projects have resulted only in further crises. The application of technology alone to the solution of current problems in biology is being doubted by many, including a growing number of scientists. "I spend my days in the midst of noise, dirt, ugliness and absurdity," wrote the scientist René Dubos, "in order to have easier access to well-equipped laboratories, libraries, museums, and to a few sophisticated colleagues whose material existence is as absurd as mine" (Dubos 1968).

We have become estranged from the only world we have, alienated from the environment on which our existence depends, all before we really came to know it. The Judeo-Christian ethic, embraced by most technologically advanced countries, has fostered the idea of man as a controller-conqueror-master of nature rather than man as an integral part of the natural world. Controlling the environment, in the ways presently practiced by man, is on a par with cutting off one's head in order to master one's body. The more man has done to exercise authority over the ecosphere, the more selective forces he has engendered against himself. Hopefully our current dilemma will pass—in about fifty years— and we can get down to the business of rectifying some old mistakes. Science does hold the key to solutions for many of our more pressing problems, but whether or not these solutions can be implemented in time to avert the ecosystem collapse that many foresee as unavoidable in the near future is doubtful. At best, technology is being asked to undo situations for which it was originally responsible. It is probably not unduly pessimistic to assume that technology will prove unable, and that individuals in authority will prove unwilling, to confront effectively the burgeoning environmental crises bearing so heavily on man's biological and cultural potential. Should we, then, extend our technological optimism to the complexity of our own genes?

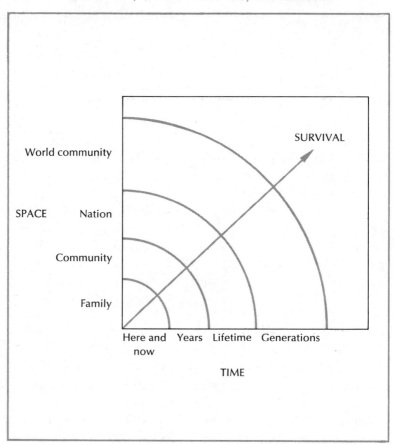

World community

SURVIVAL

SPACE   Nation

Community

Family

Here and   Years   Lifetime   Generations
now

TIME

FIGURE 8–5

Grasping some of the essentials of the human dilemma demands a broader time-space perspective. In terms of survival of the human community, the localized here-and-now perspective must give way to the concept of a global community for our children's children's children.

Suggested Readings

Bajema, Carl J. "The Genetic Implications of American Life Styles in Reproduction and Population Control." In *Natural Selection And Human Populations*, edited by Carl J. Bajema. New York: John Wiley and Sons, 1971.

de Chardin, Teilhard. *The Phenomenon of Man.* New York: Harper & Row, 1959.

Dubos, René. *So Human an Animal.* New York: Charles Scribner's Sons, 1968.

Ehrenfeld, David W. *Biological Conservation.* New York: Holt, Rinehart, and Winston, Inc., 1970.

Lorenz, Konrad. *On Aggression.* Translated by Marjorie Latzke. London: Methuen and Co., Ltd., 1967.

Muller, Hermann. "What Genetic Course Will Man Steer?" *Proceedings of the Third International Congress of Human Genetics* 1967: 521–543.

Ornstein, Leonard. "The Population Explosion, Conservative Eugenics, and Human Evolution." *Bioscience* 17(1967): 461–464.

Orwell, George. *1984.* New York: Harcourt Brace Jovanovich, 1949.

Osborn, Frederick. "A Return to the Principles of Natural Selection." *Eugenics Quarterly* 7(1960): 204–211.

Thant, U. "Human Environment and World Order." *International Journal of Environmental Studies* 1(1970): 13–17.

United States Department of Commerce. *Survey of Current Business* 54 (1974): S-1.

chapter

9

IMPROVING THE QUALITY
OF MAN

The Development of Eugenics

Eugenics, that science dealing with the improvement of man through the control of hereditary factors, has received renewed attention in recent years as scientists search for ways to eliminate congenital defects and to subdue overpopulation. Eugenics has acquired undesirable connotations as a result of the attempts of the Nazis to create a "superrace" by means of enforced selective breeding and the elimination of "undesirables," and by the continuing fears of minority groups that such techniques would be employed to commit racial, ethnic, or ideological genocide. On an informed, voluntary basis, eugenics may result in positive benefits, but it is not, as proponents are at times wont to surmise, a cure-all for genetic and related social problems.

Eugenic measures may be either positive or negative. Negative eugenics employs such techniques as abortion, birth control, and sterilization to effect a reduction in the spread of deleterious genes. As a means of improving the quality of man, however, negative practices are ineffective. Positive eugenics, which includes artificial insemination, microsurgical operations on the genetic material itself, and genetic counseling, is rooted in a sounder biological basis. Most negative procedures have long been a part of human culture, whereas positive proposals, which will be far more effective, have never been widespread in any society.

The term eugenics was coined by the English scientist, Francis Galton, in 1883. One of its better known and most rational advocates was H. J. Muller, who received the Nobel Prize in 1947 for his work on the effects of radiation on hereditary materials, an event focusing attention on his work and on the subject of eugenics itself. In Muller's mind the scientific and social aspects of eugenics were unavoidably threads in the same fabric, a true supposition if eugenic measures are ever to be widely and consciously used to influence the genetic destiny of man.

Eugenic methods encompass several diverse techniques for improving, in theory at any rate, the genetic fate of future generations. Some of these methods, such as abortion and infanticide employed in keeping populations at stable levels or in eliminating undesirable individuals, have been a part of human social practice since long before the term was originated by Galton. In some instances the rationale for infanticide is wholly cultural. In feudal Japan, it was considered animal for a woman to give birth to more than one infant at a time, and multiple births generally resulted in infanticide of all except one infant. Other methods, such as widespread birth control and artificial insemination, are relatively recent. Some types of birth control have been used with varying degrees of success even in the most primitive of cultures. Genetic microsurgery, the deletion, addition, or substitution of genes or gene complexes on the chromosomes, is currently only a projected aim of eugenics, as the techniques for its implementation have not been perfected. Put into practice, genetic microsurgery would be the ultimate means for selection in favor of desirable qualities and the elimination of deleterious ones. Present knowledge of human genetics is such that microsurgery remains in the future as a viable and universal tool for engineering the genetic makeup of man.

A brief recounting of the development of eugenic thought gives perspective to its myths and realities. The eugenics movement was founded by Galton in England in 1870, but its most fertile ground was in the United States (Hofstadter 1955). Some of the social attitudes resulting from the notions of early eugenics supporters are completely unacceptable in the light of contemporary concepts of biology and social psychology, and their advocacy helped to foster suspicion of eugenics among egalitarians. Galton, Charles Darwin's cousin, and a man of avid interests, was intrigued by the ideas set forth in Darwin's *The Origin of Species*. Galton's interests in humanity were versatile—he once published a paper on the inefficacy of prayer—and he spent much of his life collecting data on human variation. Convinced that unless remedial steps were taken to correct the situation of "inferior" human types breeding faster than the supposedly superior stock, he founded the National Eugenics Laboratory in England and spent the latter years of his life promoting the value of eugenics.

In *Social Darwinism in America,* Richard Hofstadter divides the eugenics movement into three periods. From 1870 to 1905, hereditarian attitudes became pronounced. Poverty, insanity, and other socially disadvantageous aspects were considered the result of genetic inheritance. From 1905–1930, there was a surge in the ideology that all human weakness was due to poor heredity, and in a typically chauvinistic fashion, immigration of foreign groups was denounced as endangering the "superior" American stock. One might wonder what Americans considered themselves to be. From 1930 onward, eugenics lost much of its appeal. Sociology, psychiatry, anthropology, and biology were providing information to suggest that the issue of inheritance was not as simple as once believed. The tactics of Hitler and his followers added a stigma to eugenics from which it has not yet recovered.

During its first period, eugenics became very popular in the United States. In 1907, the state of Indiana passed legislation requiring sterilization of the feebleminded and inveterate criminals. By 1915, twelve other states had followed suit (Laughlin 1926). The altering social conditions of that time were also significant in the acceptance of eugenics. The rapid urbanization following the Civil War resulted in the proliferation of slums, which housed the infirm and the poor. At this time Social Darwinism was a popular rationale for social ills. A non sequitur derived from Darwin's biological and evolutionary theories, social Darwinism maintained that a man's station in life was essentially inherited, as those who were "fit" would survive in capitalistic competition. In reality, this idea bore no relationship to Darwin's theories, but America was ripe for the spread of such a doctrine. In a setting where capitalists were exploiting masses of the poor consciencelessly, it provided a righteous rationalization. The rich were rich due not to luck, avarice, or cutthroat competition but as a result of their own inherited superiority. Eugenicists of this period followed a similar line of thought, believing that the way to prevent slums and other social ills would be to prevent "inferior" individuals from being born. Even controls on the breeding of immigrant groups were suggested, as it was thought that they must surely be inferior, having so poor a command of English! The primary divergence in thought between the Social Darwinists and these early eugenicists was that the former believed in a laissez-faire approach, insisting that interference with existing conditions would be unnatural, while the latter, however misguided, sought active change. But the eugenicists too, albeit less vociferously than businessmen and politicians, accepted the assumption of the superiority of the upper class. David Starr Jordan, a foremost biologist and president of Stanford University, stated, "it is not the strength of the strong but the weakness of the weak which engenders exploitation and tyranny" (Jordan 1911). Attitudes such as these, although they have not yet disappeared from American society, are now recognized as irresponsible as well as invalid. While there is evidence that behavioral traits may well be inherited, social conditioning and physical environment also play their parts. And of most importance, eugenics as a weapon of discrimination, whether by class against class or race against race, must never be tolerated.

Hermann J. Muller stands out as a leading figure among those interested in the potential of eugenics in improving the quality of the human race on all levels (Allen 1970; Carlson 1967). Graduating from Columbia College in 1910, Muller thereafter went to work with the famous geneticist Thomas H. Morgan, participating in research that laid the foundations for the knowledge of the chromosomal basis of heredity. Since his earliest years, Muller had been interested in the possibility of man exerting an influence on his biological future by exercising a control over his own evolution through the manipulation of hereditary factors. It was his desire to improve humanity that led him to the study of the rediscovered science of Mendelian genetics. As early as 1910, Muller raised the question of accumulation of inherited defects in the human population in a paper given at a meeting of a student club at Columbia College. In his paper he considered both the negative eugenics of sterilization and the more positive approach of artificial insemination.

In 1916, Muller began work on the effects of X-radiation—more easily quantified than that from radium—on *Drosophila*, the fruit fly. It is still widely used in genetic studies, due to its rapid rate of reproduction, easily identified genetically-based characters, and the ease of maintenance under laboratory conditions. Although he had no evidence at that time for correlating his findings on *Drosophila* to humans, Muller observed a great capacity for the accumulation of deleterious genes in his fruit fly populations. Were it not for natural selection eliminating the mutants, there would be enough lethal factors within a few generations to extinguish the whole population. Later in this work, Muller devised a stock of fruit flys having three known markers on the X chromosome that allowed him to identify immediately by phenotypic observation the percentage of offspring possessing mutations induced by a given dose of radiation (Muller 1927). From these studies he concluded that most mutations are lethal, that artificially induced ones are qualitatively the same as naturally occurring mutations, and that the transmission of nonlethal mutations from one generation to the next followed a Mendelian pattern. Muller was especially interested in the relation between radiation dosage and mutation rate. He deduced that anything generating an increase in the mutation rate of man would be pushing the human species precariously close to extinction, a cogent and unsettling observation in light of currently augmenting levels of radiation. As underscored in Chapter 4, man's haphazard abuse of radioactivity, particularly through the use of nuclear power plants even more than through nuclear test explosions, is leading him unobtrusively down a path toward increasing mutation.

By the early 1930s, Muller knew that background radiation from the atmosphere and biosphere caused the occurrence of mutations in every generation, that most mutations are harmful, and a small percentage beneficial and utilized in natural selection and evolution of populations. Man, as the only animal capable of perceiving these facts, is the only one able to use them advantageously by reducing the frequency of harmful genes and attempting to increase desirable ones. Muller felt that eugenic control of human biology could "further the interests, the happiness, the glory of the God-like being whose meager foreshadowings we the present ailing creatures are" (Sonneborn 1968). At the time of this optimism there was less reason to harbor doubts about these flowering hopes, as human society was not yet plagued by its present stresses, or the prospect of so grim a human future as may be now unfolding.

Certain eugenic practices, such as abortion and infanticide, have long been present in human societies. Perhaps the most basic of eugenic controls are taboos and laws prohibiting consanguineous marriages. Few societies sanction sibling unions, and usually matings with other close kin are discouraged. In the state of Georgia in the United States, a man is not prohibited from marrying his daughter or his grandmother. In all other states, marriage between any person and a parent, grandparent, child, or sibling is not legal (Farrow and Juberg 1969). Most knowledge of genetics is less than a century old, but there has long been an awareness in man that matings between closely related individuals are likely to result in aberrant offspring. So stated Noah Webster in 1790: "It iz no crime for brothers and sisters to intermarry, except the fatal consequences to society; for were it generally practised, men would become a race of pigmies" (Webster 1790). In the United States, laws regarding the marriages of kin were not penned until the late nineteenth and early twentieth centuries, at which time individual states drew up their own policies. Except for those restrictions mentioned above, there are no standardized laws even in the United States as to who may or may not marry with whom. Uncle-niece marriages are not prohibited in Georgia, nor among Jews in Rhode Island. Less than half the states in the United States have any laws against marriages between affinous relatives. In many rural areas there are probably a greater number of consanguineous marriages than one might infer from laws prohibiting them. Genetically, the reality is one of consequence, not of law.

Laws against consanguineous marriages are given merit by the statistics of population genetics. The coefficient for a deleterious recessive gene appearing in the offspring of an uncle-niece mating is 0.125, in a union between first cousins it is 0.062 and it is 0.015 in a second cousin marriage. Clearly, marriages between closely related individuals result in a greater likelihood of producing defective offspring. The royal families of Europe, who tended to be inbred, suffered from such genetic defects as mental retardation, hemophilia, and certain types of insanity.

General disapproval of consanguineous marriages, despite the existence of exceptions, has served as a kind of eugenic control over the quality of the human species. Another eugenic measure which has been a part of human culture since long before written history is abortion, currently the center of heated debate in many countries. Ethnological

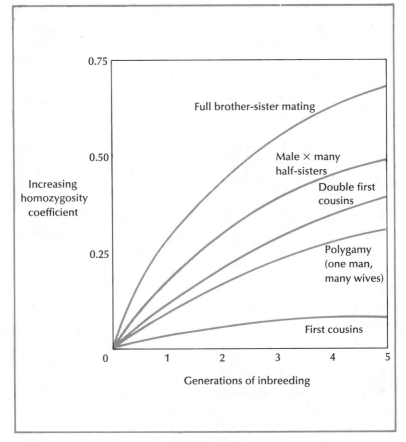

FIGURE 9–1

Increasing homozygosity with generational inbreeding. A coefficient of 1.0 would indicate genetic identity.

(From *Heredity, Evolution and Society* by I. Michael Lerner. W.H. Freeman and Company. Copyright © 1968.)

studies of socially primitive groups have found that abortions are practiced among them for many of the same reasons given in modern societies. Illness, advanced age, economic considerations, the desire to avoid the social sanctions accompanying an illegitimate child, personal choice, and a gamut of other social and biological factors determine a woman's decision to abort. Overpopulation and liberalization of cultural attitudes have combined to present the choice of abortion to many women in a more favorable light, but it remains as a focal point of legal, ethical, humanitarian, and religious conflict.

References to abortion may be found far back in written literature (Tietze and Lewit 1969). A writing said to be by the Chinese emperor Shen Nung of about 4,600 years ago includes a method for inducing abortion by the ingestion of mercury. Hippocrates, a physician of classical Greece, advised that violent exercise was an effective abortion technique. Aristotle and Plato advocated abortion as a means for controlling the size of a population, to maintain an economically healthy society. This rationale would carry even more validity today. The rise of Christianity caused a great condemnation of abortion in Europe, an ethic still influencing attitudes today. Even so, in England abortion was not classified as a statutory offense until 1803, and in the United States not until 1830.

While few if any knowledgeable individuals would argue for abortion over birth control practices, it is nonetheless an effective measure in controlling population growth, as evidenced in Japan, and in preventing the personal and social hardships accompanying unwanted children. It relieves the burdens imposed on low income families, which given a greater accessibility to birth control information might prophylactically limit family size. Arguments revolving around birth control range from the reasoned to the emotional and vitriolic. The majority of those opposing birth control by abortion derive their arguments from religious philosophies or dicta. According to official Roman Catholic dogma, for example, the developing fetus is believed to have acquired a soul at the moment of the union between the sperm and egg, and therefore abortion is tantamount to murder.

From a biological point of view, the above and similar reasoning can be dismissed as having no foundation. A fetus is no more a conscious human being in the socioethical sense than a set of oil paints and canvas is the Mona Lisa. There is no evidence that a fetus has conscious awareness of any kind until the time of birth. Biologically, the *soul* of man may be considered an expression of genetic factors and the cumulation of cultural-ethical experience. Whether or not there is a spiritual soul must remain within the realm of speculation. Suffering due to unwanted children and general overpopulation is not theoretical, however, but dismally real. In arguing so steadfastly against abortion, opponents are maintaining that the continued existence of an organism which is as yet little more than an appendage of the mother, at least in the first trimester of pregnancy when most legal abortions are performed, is of greater value than the existing conscious life and well-being of the mother, other familial members, and human society as a whole. Many opponents believe that the social acceptance and legalization of abortion will degrade society, placing it only a step away from approval of euthanasia, infanticide, and other practices violating man's reverence for life. This is a non sequitur, however, as may be inferred from the examples of countries wherein abortion has been legal for several decades with no such dire consequences. Biologically and legally, until the fetus can survive independently of the mother, stopping its growth should not be considered, even in the broadest possible sense, an act of murder. Obviously these dicta are products of cultural and subcultural relativism. Fetal growth apart from the maternal environment, a biological reality at present, stretches the definitions of the nature of human life even further, and for these reasons has met with opposition, although the technique has been used mainly to enhance the fertility of women unable to ovulate or implant successfully, creating rather than destroying life.

In about two thirds of the world, abortion is either entirely illegal or severely restricted, being limited to those instances involving rape or the health of the mother. Until recently legal abortion was proscribed for most reasons in the United States, but during the past few years laws have been relaxed considerably. Legal sanctions against abortion, rather than preventing it, have caused the widespread practice of illegal methods, which due to technique, septic conditions, or both, entail a high degree of risk. In the United States, it was estimated that until recently several hundred thousand illegal abortions were performed annually, many by physicians in ethical dissent of local laws. Many women left the country seeking illegal services, or took advantage of more liberal laws in Japan and Europe. With changing abortion laws in the United States, it will become a more pronounced eugenic practice; women may obtain safe abortions, and, most importantly, they may exercise personal choice determined by their own ethic and experience. More reliable statistics on the eugenics of abortion in the United States should become available, although illegal practice will no doubt continue to some extent, as it has in Japan.

Several European countries, particularly Denmark and Sweden, have a relatively liberalized history of abortion. The criteria for allowing abortions were open to broad interpretation, taking into account the physical and mental well-being of the mother and family. In Mao's China, legal abortion is reportedly a widespread practice. Statistical data are, however, lacking. In Japan the Eugenics Protection Law has been interpreted so liberally that legal abortion is also open there to any woman. In

1949, the year of the law's passage, there were 246,000 abortions contrasted with 1,170,000 in 1955. By 1967, the number had declined to 748,000 (Tietze and Lewit 1969). But official statistics on abortion are almost always an understatement of the real number, as many practitioners do not report all abortions performed to minimize personal embarrassment—and income taxes. These reasons may explain why, in 1966, "The Year of the Fiery Horse" on the Buddhist calendar, the birth rate dropped markedly, as did the number of abortions! By tradition, girls born during that year possess unseemly temperaments and have difficulty in finding marital partners.

Where abortion is practiced with proficiency as in Japan and the socialized European countries, there is a very low maternal mortality rate among women, ranging from 1–4:100,000. The low rate is due in part to legal restrictions on abortion beyond the twelfth week of pregnancy. During the first three months, abortion is a relatively safe procedure, but the risks to the mother become greater as she approaches parturition. This is probably the greatest supporting bit of evidence for legalized abortion, as the mother is required to solicit services early, avoid procrastination in her decision, and consequently avoid the time-lag between contact and performance inevitable in an illegal abortion arrangement. Legal abortions are much safer medically and consequently less traumatic to the mother, who may choose to have another pregnancy at a later date, and are more conducive to earlier action as the woman is aware of the choice available to her.

Clandestine operations are performed and unreported in those countries where abortion is legal as well in many parts of the world where the practice remains illegal. Under existing population conditions, abortion may be assumed to be more beneficial than otherwise. It becomes a social pathology under situations where the technology, information, and distribution of birth control information is lacking or prohibited. It is a disease of underinformed societies. From a humanistic and logical perspective, the ethical arguments against abortion seem rather weak in contrast with the certain outcomes of overpopulation: disease, poverty, and a continuous reduction in the quality of material and nonmaterial life for all.

In the scope of voluntary measures intended to improve the human species, assortative mating may produce a desirable eugenic effect, as has always been true of human populations. Village idiots and sociopathic personalities have never been nor are they now deemed the most desirable partners. Cultural values always have and will continue to influence mate selection. If one accepts the assumption that intelligence and other individual characteristics are to varying degrees the results of inheritance, cultural mating patterns uniting individuals of superior capacities should lead toward an encompassing improvement in the genome. If the options of choice valued in a free society are to be maintained, it will not be possible to dictate anyone's selection of a mate. But as the nature of the social structure exerts a profound influence on assortative mating patterns, even now, it is certainly *possible* to direct the gene flow in a population, as these patterns are products of cultural precepts. In most societies, even in relatively egalitarian ones such as the United States, mating occurs more by pattern than is realized. Educated individuals tend to marry others of similar educational backgrounds, and countercultural individuals marry mates of similar ethical and material values. If society reinforced "desirable" matings—whatever they might be deemed to be—then theoretically there would be an increasing percentage of individuals showing those desirable characters, all other differential reproduction being equal. The widespread use of artificial insemination would make this an even greater likelihood, since a desirable biological father could be selected for with more precision.

Muller was a leading advocate of the eugenic technique of artificial insemination, or *eutelogenesis*, as it has been termed to avoid an association with the misunderstandings centered around eugenics. His proposal was that frozen sperm from males selected as genetically superior might be stored in sperm banks throughout the country and, eventually, the world. He noted that artificial insemination already was sanctioned socially and was a viable solution for couples if the male was sterile or impotent. That being so, Muller reasoned, why not attempt to insure the superior quality of the genes of the offspring? And why not use the method as well to secure a genetic improvement in the whole race by encouraging people to provide their children with the genes of one superior parent? A major obstacle in the realization of artificial insemination as a wide-spread practice among fertile couples is the human ego, which seeks to renew itself in its progeny—"a chip off the old block." Many people have deep-seated feelings about children of their own blood-line and an understandable reluctance in admitting that while they may be able to provide their children with an excellent environment, someone else might provide better genes. And many individuals wish to bear the biological child of the mate they love. There are, however, two kinds of parents, as individuals who adopt children are well aware. There is the traditional biological parent, and there is the parent of the family of man. Clearly, artificial insemination is not a desirable choice for everyone at this time. As *parent* comes to indicate the person or persons who rear the child, the technical point of the origin of egg and sperm will assume less importance. Currently there are approximately 10,000 children born each year as a result of artificial insemination. The practice is a reality and constitutes a clear and rational choice for some.

Presently artificial insemination is effected within a few hours of receipt of sperm from the donor to the recipient. Cryogenic techniques, where sperm are frozen at ultralow temperatures and stored subsequent to thawing, could be immensely useful in fostering the widespread practice of artificial insemination. The process would then be independent of time and space, facilitating the ubiquitous distribution of selected sperm samples. Freeze preservation of cattle sperm has been perfected to a high degree, but such is not the case with that of humans. As there have been no social, religious, or ethical grounds to hinder research on bovine artificial insemination, more progress has been made in that area than in investigations on human sperm. One might assume that the treatment of all mammalian sperm would have similar physiological properties, but unfortunately, this is not the case. There are significant differences in the response to freezing between sperm of cattle and humans, requiring further research on the specific properties of the human male gamete before sperm banks would be operable even in an atmosphere of complete social acceptance. Techniques will have to be developed for the freezing and thawing of human sperm in a manner consistently conducive to high fertility.

Indications are that human sperm may be frozen for relatively long periods (Behrman and Ackerman 1969). In controlled experiments, women were given frozen sperm obtained from donors who were young and in good reproductive and general physiological health as well as from husbands of childless couples whose sperm samples proved to be oligospermatic (a low sperm count per unit volume) or contained a high number of immature cells. In these latter cases, sperm samples were concentrated and thereby resembled the samples obtained from normal couples. A control group was given fresh nonfrozen sperm via artificial insemination. Samples were frozen at $-80°$ C, thawed, and used within 30 minutes of thawing. The resultant conception rate proved to be lower for the group receiving frozen sperm (42.6 per cent) than for the one receiving fresh sperm (69 per cent), but the percentage for frozen samples is high enough to justify research and refinement of the procedure.

Once the technique of artificial insemination has transcended the impediments of prejudice and the clinical difficulties of storage, new avenues will be open to human eugenics. The reluctance of many men to obtain vasectomies, although the number is increasing annually, is based in part on the fear that should children be desired at some later time or circumstance, a pregnancy would no longer be possible. Other reservations regarding vasectomies, relating to ignorance or virility can be overcome through education. But doubts about future fatherhood potential would be laid to rest by freezing a quantity of the individual's sperm that could be used later via artificial insemination. It has been suggested that sperm could be stored in radiation-proof banks as genetic insurance against the effects of nuclear war on human genes. Such protected sperm would have escaped mutagenic damage, insuring a source for women desiring children in the aftermath of the holocaust. The proponents of this plan do not suggest what fail-safe technology would maintain the sperm bank in such an event.

There is evidence that spermatozoa respond differentially to cryogenic techniques. This fact indicates that under the conditions of artificial selection there will be selection in favor of those more viable sperm and accordingly on the differential fertility of certain donors over others. In time a gradually increasing differential would arise in the number of offspring attributable to the various donors. Although this would make a technical difference in the anticipated ratios, as the system of widespread artificial insemination would under any circumstance effect a radical change in gene frequencies, and donors would have been selected on the basis of subjectively valued qualities, the results of this differential would be irrelevant to future generations.

In terms of existing possibilities for improving the genetic potential of the human race, eutelogenesis offers some hopeful prospects. Negative eugenic techniques such as abortion and birth control may reduce the frequency of certain genes in a population and are certainly of use in our struggles with overpopulation, but their practice is employed for a great variety of reasons, few of which have anything to do with conscious attempts to improve the quality of the gene pool.

Even extreme selective pressures against lethal or undesirable alleles would result in minimal change, as most are carried in the heterozygous condition by normal individuals in the population. Because mutations arise *de novo* in each generation and because detection of heterozygotes is impossible in many instances at this point in our understanding of human genetics, any negative eugenics program would effect at best an unnoticeable change in gene frequencies.

More information on mutation rates, gene mapping and recombination, and the consequences of linkages of certain alleles in the human genome would be needed to make any program dealing with man's genes truly eugenic. There are no intrinsic guarantees of immediate benefit of any eugenics program. The sperm of an Einstein will not predictably produce a theoretical genius, nor will that of a Solzhenitsyn necessarily produce a humanitarian and writer. The only promise in theory is that given a long-term program with clear and unchanging goals, there might be a statistical increase in the frequencies of certain traits in the population. Under such a program a directional selection would operate, resulting in a statistical shifting of the population's mean for a given character.

While most attention has been directed to the possibilities inherent in sperm preservation and artificial insemination, in the future women will probably be able to give birth to children whose genetic endowment is independent of the mother or father. It is already possible to initiate the growth of a human embryo outside the female's body under laboratory conditions. In those instances where a woman carries deleterious genes and desires the fulfillment of pregnancy and birth, implantation of a foreign embryo in her body may be possible. Rather than evoking images of a sterile, technological process, this kind of test-tube baby, being a product of desire and conscious choice, is more likely to receive its share of affection and care then many normally-conceived infants born to parents who neither want nor can afford them. Such a technology is ideal for many types of infertility problems in women. There should be no more psychological or social stigma to this practice than to that of artificial insemination, although the technology and logistic difficulties are sufficiently complicated to restrict the procedure much more than the artificial injection of male sperm. Were genetic microsurgery or biochemical euphenic (improvement of the phenotype) engineering widely possible, their ramifications to the human genome could be far-reaching. The practice of medicine has concentrated on saving human life whenever possible, a premise with which no humanitarian could argue in principle. Much of the thrust of future medical treatment may be concerned with euphenic engineering on a biochemical level by correcting gene-enzyme deficiencies, and metabolic blocks or dysfunctions. One cannot ignore, ethically or practically, the problems associated with the perpetuation of dysfunctional, deleterious genes. The social and personal costs would be minimized in the instances of prospective parents who are aware of the high probability of perpetuating a damaging genetic code in their children, and who are at the same time determined to have a family of their own, were they to make the conscious choice of a genetic heritage having the probability of freedom from aberrations and continuous biomedical support. However, a mentally, physically, or morally perfect race of men will not thereby appear as mutations are spontaneous in each generation.

Whether or not an individual who will probably bequeath deleterious genes to his or her progeny should reproduce constitutes a relatively unexamined subject in a world where most individuals assume the right to have children. Although a sociopolitical turmoil would surely ensue, making the issues of birth control and abortion appear so much idle chatter, our society should openly examine the possibilities for further eugenic control. Such an inquiry is not antilibertarian, antihumanitarian, or antilife. The individual and social costs of the status quo will increase markedly in the next few generations. Many people now accept the ethic that it is personally and socially irresponsible for couples to have more than two children given the state of world population, resources, and environment. It is irresponsible both to the present and to the future. Is perpetuation of a genetic constitution demanding more than its share of social and economic resources both now and in the future not irresponsible as well? Such bioethical questions will become more pertinent in following decades.

Knowing the limiting factors on human growth and what our genetic liabilities and potentials constitute, we should opt for choices that will best insure our social and genetic integrity. Many believe and much evidence indicates that as a global community, man harbors no intention of limiting his numbers or his defects by his own volition. Many also find the concept of diminished personal freedom and assertion of control over population quantity and quality abhorrent. How is the anticipated future any more desirable? We have for too long ignored the gap between our ethics and our technology. Population and resource limitations of the future are going to force the closure of that gap.

A minor eugenic technique that has been practiced somewhat in the past few decades and which could be of wider significance in the future is genetic counseling (Lynch, *et al.* 1970). Physicians aware of congenital problems in the family history of a patient should counsel the patient on the risks of his or her reproductive potential and, if there exists a high statistical probability of giving birth to an afflicted child, strongly suggest a eugenic solution—artificial insemination or steriliza- tion if applicable—or perhaps adoption. A problem inherent in even the most basic genetic counseling is communication—to the physician and the patient. Most physicians are not well trained in human genetics, and most patients have difficulty grasping the concept of the statistical probability of risk inherent in their decision to have children. The establishment of genetic clinics with trained counselors concerned with diagnosis, dissemination of information to patients, and related activities regarding public information would provide a much needed service. Al- though in accord with social concepts of individual freedom and choice as currently understood in most societies, it seems contradictory to the finer aims of medical science that many more resources are committed to the care of congenitally deficient individuals than are given to the prevention of the aberrations. All efforts should be made in assisting persons suffering from congenital defects, but if such defects could be prevented from occurring, the social and economic benefit to society would be immense.

In considering the capacity for human improvement inherent in eugenics, some proponents—including geneticists—are swept up in their enthusiasm into claiming results that cannot be anticipated realistically in the foreseeable future. The most sophisticated of eugenic measures is only an attempt to direct man in what is deemed at the time to be the most desirable direction. On the brink of a global crisis of population, environment, and resources, one could not expect to see eugenic po- tentials fulfilled. In fact, if eugenics were to accomplish nothing more at present than to prevent the decline of the human genome and to reduce detrimental genes, its contribution to mankind would be great. The more realistic goals of eugenics involving changes in ethics, values, and choice are not impossible, but others relying on vast technological development will be necessarily delayed until such a time as the present human crises are solved.

A eugenic measure looming as a technological possibility which would entail more diverse sociopsychological ramifications than any other is *cloning,* the reproduction or replication of an individual from a single cell. By this technique, genotypically and phenotypically identical indi- viduals, barring mutation in development, could be cultured from de- sirable individuals. Societies might choose to duplicate men and women who excell in any given quality or combination of qualities. As other geneticists who have considered the implication of cloning suggest, the political nature of the society would have much to do with its choices. "Desirable" clones would be determined by those in power, for various personally and politically motivated reasons. In a democracy, choice might be left to a public vote with various interests campaigning for the candidates. For a number of genetic and social reasons, it would probably be just as well were cloning never to become an accepted method of reproduction. In all political climates, cloning would invariably serve other than universal and humanitarian ends. And biologically, the proliferation of many individuals from a few sources would diminish genetic variety which, given time, could downgrade the survival potential of humanity.

If eugenics becomes more widely solicited and practiced in the future, it does not necessarily represent a Pandora's box or a panacea. There is no good or evil knowledge; it is man's utilization of knowledge that directs creativity or destruction, depending on prevalent ethics and values. An intriguing question, and one that will occupy future thought as evidence accumulates that behavioral traits are hereditable to a degree, is which qualities entail the greatest potential for man's survival. Many ethologists believe that aggression in man is an archaic character, having lost its adaptive or survival value. As the ethologist Konrad Lorenz suggested in *On Aggression*, and as Hermann Muller believed, existing aggression in man is a counterproductive phenomenon. Aggression in vertebrates, as analyzed by the Nobel Prize winner Lorenz, is a manifestation of territoriality. Among men the territorial impulse assumes the character of nationalism and regionalism, now blocking the solutions to many of our global problems and crises. Syllogistic reasoning suggests, accordingly, that man might benefit greatly as a species were it possible to eliminate or sublimate any territorial motive. At least, it might be transferred from its materialistic and geographic horizons to those of the mind. The ethic of every man, interest, or state for itself is certainly dysfunctional in contemporary society at both the local and global levels. Human culture began through interpersonal and group cooperation, flowered because of it, and presently needs it more than at any time in our history. It has become an adaptive survival tactic. In his last public address Hermann Muller placed cooperation alongside intelligence as the characteristic needed for human survival. If behavior in man also has a genetic basis, as evidence implies, it should be possible to select for individuals having not only mental and physical superiority but congenial, nonaggressive behavior as well.

Unfortunately, the fabric of behavioral selection is not simple in man. Aggressiveness is not a universally distasteful quality intra- or interculturally. Reference to a "bright, aggressive person" constitutes more of a compliment than a social condemnation, and the linking of those two adjectives suggests that in many minds intelligence and aggression are correlative. This may be due to the overly competitive structure of many societies, but there is also the possibility that other advantages are obtained from aggressive behavior. That is, if aggression is bred out of human nature, the selective process should be one restricted to certain kinds of aggression. Cooperativeness and nonhostile qualities are going to be at great premium as ecocrises become more intense, yet humanity would be disadvantaged by the acquisition of submissive behavior that might subject it to the domination of demagogues. A prevalence of non-aggressive individuals is desirable, but will profit us only if the quality of personal independence is retained as a counterpart. In essence what is needed is the deletion of one of the qualities included under aggression —that of interpersonal hostility—but the retention and amplification of another—independent initiative. The confusion of these characteristics is due more to semantics than to real similarities.

In spite of its most optimistic aspirations and projections, eugenics is not likely to be the cure for man's biological and social ills. Eutelogenesis might cause over-all trends where employed, but that is the most that can be expected of it. Each and every male gamete, no matter how superior the individual from which it is obtained, also carries some genes for undesirable traits. Sperm or egg banks cannot insure that every child conceived from selected donors will reflect the biological parent's superiority. Random assortment and regression toward the mean negate this assumption. Apart from a few physical and biochemical characters—and intelligence—we know very little about human inheritance and the correlation of qualities. Musical, artistic, and other abilities have an unknown but assumed genetic foundation, but there is no unequivocal evidence of positive correlation with parental abilities.

The Future of Eugenics

What is the realistic future potential for *genetic engineering*, the alteration of the genetic code by adding, deleting, or changing the information contained in the genes? Currently the prospects are still speculative, but as the practice has been applied successfully to bacteria and *Drosophila*, it may not be too distant in man's future. If applied to somatic cells, the condition under treatment would be cured in the individual at hand, but defective genes would still be passed on to succeeding generations. Microsurgery effected on germ cells, however, would permit elimination of deleterious genes, causing the transmission of normal ones to the following generations, at least until new mutations resulted in aberrant genes. At present, such application is futuristic, but genetic microsurgery could well become integrated into our medical technology with far-reaching eugenic effects.

There is much to be said for retaining a balanced perspective on the subject of eugenics. When employed in a free society, it constitutes no threat to the dignity of man but instead offers to elevate him. However, its possibilities are limited in insuring man's survival, and we should view it as a single, potentially beneficial component. Eugenics is no more unnatural than a great many practices devised to eradicate human suffering. It may be considered unnatural to interfere with natural selection by taking antibiotics to avoid death from infectious bacterial disease, but few people would choose to ignore this option. Such may someday be the rationale for eugenic practices. What is natural or unnatural derives not from any objective reality but from the relative perceptions of society. In following the course of cultural evolution, there is ample substantiation that these standards have undergone a continuous evolution in themselves.

A key point, as we have previously mentioned, one often overlooked or underplayed by proponents, is that eugenics can be employed to its full potential only in the circumstances of stable, long-term cultural goals and, most importantly, under stable environmental conditions. These issues reveal some of the dangers inherent in the full-scale use of eugenics, because they assume that qualities selected in the present will always be desirable and advantageous to human survival. A counterpoint may be made that higher intelligence, greater physical fitness, social cooperation, and the absence of congenital defects would be considered beneficial in any society. But this argument carries with it the assumption that genetic diversity will be retained while man is at the same time, in essence, becoming more specialized. Two of man's most valuable biological attributes are his generality and diversity, principal reasons he has been so remarkably successful as a species.

In striving for the betterment of man, eugenics advocates should keep in mind that the loss of any diversity for the gain of apparent physical benefits would be an unwise course. Not only do we lack assurance that the world environment will improve and stabilize or that human societies will become more integrated, but the reverse seems more likely. Overpopulation, environmental deterioration, and international conflict do not support contentions that advanced eugenic measures can be initiated to better man on a global scale. The pervasive influence of positive eugenics lies yet in the realm of hopeful speculation. The only eugenic activities currently in widespread use are negative, such as abortion and birth control. Even these are not accepted to as great an extent as would be desirable. As overcoming the religious and cultural objections to such basic methods has been only partially successful, even under the threat of massive starvation and other increased human suffering due to overpopulation, it does not seem unduly pessimistic to surmise that the eugenic improvement of man will be possible only when solutions have been found to more urgent crises, if indeed such solutions exist. In the meantime, eugenics may be employed on a limited basis to relieve what it can of man's ills. In affluent countries there are, no doubt, greater immediate potentials for positive eugenics than among underdeveloped nations struggling to survive. For the moment it is, more than a reality, a hope offering some alternatives for the genetic improvement of man.

Euphenics

In consideration of the many generations and long-term social goals necessary to accomplish the majority of eugenic ends, *euphenics*, the biological improvement of the existing phenotype, has been preferred as a more pragmatic solution to the problem of human improvement. Euphenic improvement has been operating for some time under the guise of biomedical engineering and biochemical alteration of the genetic constitution. Furthering euphenic practices is mainly a question of scope and degree, rather than a newly created reality. Artificial organs and the synthesis of hormones, enzymes, antigens, and other proteins have been and can be increasingly utilized in persons afflicted with metabolic malfunctioning of a genetic origin. These techniques may be applied at almost any stage of human development, from a prenatal state to old age.

Euphenics also gives the promise of providing means for changing the human brain. Correlations between intelligence and brain size are not substantial, but it is of interest that experiments with rats have produced larger brains as a result of environmental manipulation, causing variations in learning experiences. Also, a relationship between birth weight

208

and subsequent intelligence of human children has been demonstrated. Among California infants included in a study, only 2 per cent weighed ten or more pounds at birth, whereas 17 per cent of the children with I.Q.s of genius came into that category (see Lerner 1968). It has been suggested that the limitations of pelvic structure in the female acts to restrict the potential prenatal size of the human head and brain. If the practice of Caesarean delivery were to be adopted widely, head size would no longer be a limiting factor in prenatal survival, and the human brain would be given freedom to grow to a much larger size. However, breeding a race dependent on Caesarean delivery seems a risky process. If the average human head became too large during fetal development for normal birth, Caesarean operations would be a requisite, or nearly so, for the continuation of the species. Any disaster reducing or eliminating facilities for such delivery would have a correspondingly negative effect on humanity.

The aims and possibilities of euphenics carry more of the seeds of 1984 than eugenics, as the latter requires a very long time to effect its goals, which are interdicted with many unknown variables and lack of predictability. The potentials inherent in euphenics are a different matter; they can be effected rapidly and a number are possible already. For example, the pharmacological manipulation of developing brains could be employed to create a conformist society or to engineer intelligence potentials by controlling brain growth differentially in order to create a society of genetically determined classes. The prospect of unethically employed euphenic techniques, and there is no reason to suppose that this might not occur, is cause for deliberate pondering on the virtues of any measures that may be widely practiced in the future.

The potential benefits, dangers, and social implications of euphenics are poised over us and in all probability will be real facets of future societies. Chemical and electrical brain control would vastly facilitate governmental manipulation of the human mind and personality. Total organ transplants, including the brain, would engender identity crises, from personal and social perspectives. Euphenic advocates cheerfully predict that the introduction of human chromosomes into the genotypes of apes and other primates will be possible, and conversely, if there were some reason to wish it, the chromosomes of other primates could be infused into the human genome!

Whether or not any of the more incredible aspects of euphenics are ever realized—and we should not discredit that possibility—the science is sure to become an integral part of society, particularly in the technologically advanced countries. There are numerous associated potentials for improving the human race and alleviating human suffering, but there are negative potentials that are quite real and worthy of studied consideration. Man is characterized more by his abilities than by his wise use of them. The integration of euphenics into society does not insure that the purposes for which it is employed will be for the benefit of

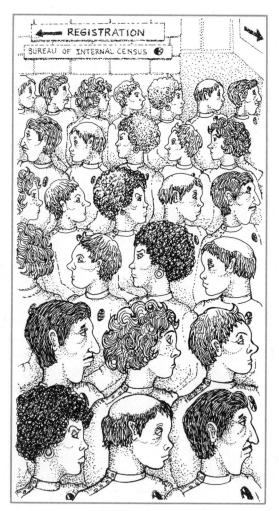

FIGURE 9–2

Decreasing human diversity would not portend future survival advantage for the human species.

man, nor that the scientists possessing technical knowledge of euphenics will be the best qualified to direct its implementation.

Suggested Readings

Allen, Garland E. "Science and Society in the Eugenic Thought of H. J. Muller." *Bioscience* 20(1970): 346–352.

Behrman, S. J., and D. R. Ackerman. "Freeze-Preservatio 1 of Human Sperm." *American Journal of Obstetrics and Gynecology* 103(1969): 654–664.

Carlson, E. A. "The Legacy of Hermann Muller: A Memorial Tribute." *Canadian Journal of Genetics and Cytology* 9(1967): 436–448.

Darwin, Charles. *The Origin of Species by Means of Natural Selection*. 6th ed. New York: D. Appleton, 1931.

Farrow, Michael G., and Richard C. Juberg. "Genetics and Laws Prohibiting Marriage in the United States." *Journal of the American Medical Association* 209(1969): 534–538.

Haller, Mark. *Eugenics: Hereditarian Attitudes in American Thought*. New Brunswick, N. J.: Rutgers University Press, 1963.

Hofstadter, Richard. *Social Darwinism in America*. Boston: The Beacon Press, 1955.

Huisingh, Donald. "Should Man Control His Genetic Future?" *Zygon* 4(1969): 188–199.

Jordan, D. S. *The Heredity of Richard Roe*. Boston, Mass.: American Unitarian Association, 1911.

Laughlin, H. H. *Eugenical Sterilization*. New Haven, Conn.: Yale University Press, 1926.

Lerner, I. Michael. *Heredity, Evolution, and Society*. San Francisco: W. H. Freeman and Co., 1968.

Ludmerer, Kenneth. "American Genetics and the Eugenics Movement: 1905–1935." *Journal of Historical Biology* 2(1969): 337–362.

Lynch, H. T., G. M. Mulcahy, and Anne J. Krush. "Genetic Counseling and the Physician." *Journal of the American Medical Association* 211(1970): 647–651.

Medewar, P. B. "Do Advances in Medicine Lead to Genetic Deterioration?" *Mayo Clinic Proceedings* 40(1965): 23–33.

Muller, Hermann J. "The Effects of X-Radiation on Genes and Chromosomes." *Science* 67(1927): 82–85.

——— "What Genetic Course Will Man Steer?" *Proceedings of The Third International Congress of Human Genetics* 1967: 521–543.

Sonneborn, R. M. "H. J. Muller, Crusader for Human Betterment." *Science* 162(1968): 772–776.

Tietze, Christopher, and Sarah Lewit. "Abortion." *Scientific American* 220(1969): 21–27.

Webster, N. "Explanation of the Reezons Why Marriage Iz Prohibited Between Natural Relations." *Collection of Essays and Fugitive Writings on Moral, Historical, Political, and Religious Subjects.* Boston: Thomas And Andrews, 1790. Referred to in Farrow and Juberg, 1969.

chapter

10

THE NATURE OF INTELLIGENCE

As man's ancestors evolved gradually toward existing human intellectual capacity, physical and mental qualities provided reciprocal feedback. Intelligence becomes man, setting him apart from other animals far more distinctly than any morphological characteristics. When man adopted his material and nonmaterial culture, albeit step by minute step, great impetus was given to the survival value of intelligence. It aided in man's adaptive dispersal throughout the world, conferring on him the cultural plasticity that enabled him to cope successfully with a diversity of habitats. To what degree intelligence has increased since *Homo sapiens* evolved would be impossible to demonstrate, but the increasing demands of his complex material and nonmaterial culture have, no doubt, increased selective pressures favoring a higher capacity.

In human terms, intelligence is not limited to a single definition. Generally it refers to one's ability to conceptualize effectively, whether on the level of man-tool interactions or in more abstract realms of human endeavor and thought. Other animals, with intelligence that differs quantitatively and qualitatively from that of man (Bitterman 1965), cope adequately with their environments or they do not survive. In fact, all evidence leads to the conclusion that for many species intelligence has very little to do with biological survival. For many hundreds of millions of years, life has expressed itself in a great diversity of forms, many of which lack any "purposeful" behavior. Dinosaurs, dominant animals for more than 200 million years, fared well with minimal brains and existed much longer than mammals have yet had the opportunity of doing. And yet, it may have been the rise of the mammals with more successfully competitive behavior that led to the extinction of this large and diverse group.

It is difficult to correlate intelligence and biological survival in many species, perhaps because we do not know enough about intelligence on a descriptive and quantitative level in other species. With man it is tempting to adopt the viewpoint that there is such a correlation, as man's intelligence has been responsible for his invasion of nearly all parts of the world, and his ability to mold a great deal of the environment to his own convenience is a function of his mental prowess. But lower forms of life, evolving for a billion years, did not need intelligence to survive. In terms of species survival, intelligence is most important when there is other intelligent life with which to compete for resources. In the context of man's survival, intelligence is important when there exists a material and nonmaterial culture to transmit. The latter adds survival value beyond the efficient biological design of a species, and is the reason that a particular species became man.

Race and Intelligence

Previously, we presented arguments indicating that man has remained a single species by virtue of his mobility and transmitted culture. Although they are more difficult to define than subspecies (or races) among other biological species, races of *Homo sapiens* do exist, and it would

214

FIGURE 10-1

Is intelligence necessarily a key factor in survival? No, but in terms of competition or adapting to change, it may provide a decided advantage. (The actual proximity of men and dinosaurs is not implied here, as the latter were extinct for millions of years prior to the appearance of *Homo sapiens*.)

be a disservice to scientific fact if the biologist or physical anthropologist were to ignore this reality. Races exist as a physiological-morphological response to differing environmental conditions and have been increasingly blurred and dissipated by transcultural contact. The capacities, however, that define man as man—morphology, brain size, and intelligence—existed among all these populations, being derived from common ancestors at the dawn of man's beginnings.

Some researchers have been attempting to demonstrate that quantifiable differences exist in intelligence levels among the various races of man. While their data are presented undoubtedly with honest intentions, although some are acknowledgedly racist in outlook, there are logical fallacies in the reasoning of all. The notion that there are varying abilities among races is not, however, new but is at least as old as written history. It has been employed to justify a gamut of social ills, from slavery to genocide. But when examined closely, no information demonstrates conclusively the innate intellectual superiority of any race. Difference does not signify inferiority in spite of the fact that most cultures —not just Western ones—have histories of designating one or more groups as inferior on the sole basis of variation in racial origin.

It is a well known and tedious truth that any point of view may be "proven" despite the facts. So it is with any particular outlook on race and intelligence. In 1840, the United States Census provided some extraordinary statistics on the percentages of insane or "idiotic" blacks as opposed to whites, and even more startling data as to regional differences (Litwack 1961; Stanton 1960). There were no particular geographical variations in the percentage of mentally ill whites, but with blacks there was reported to be an incidence of 1:144.5 in the North and only 1:1558 in the South. Of course, the census later was shown to be entirely inaccurate; some of the northern communities were reported to have numbers of insane or "idiotic" blacks exceeding their total black populations. However, weighty propaganda, printed and supplied by none less than the U.S. government, was given to the supporters of slavery who used the misinformation to further their cause. If the incidence of mental illness was so much less in the South, was that not evidence enough that the benign institution of slavery was protecting blacks from the pressures of a society with which they could not cope? As with most such cases, the original incorrect figures must have received far more publicity than their succeeding negation. It has always been that any group of people forced into servility are considered inferior by their overlords. There is no more comforting rationale for justifying social inequalities than that of superiority versus inferiority—whether it involves races, sexes, or social classes.

The possibility that intelligence is largely inherited has also clouded

216

the issue. Recent investigations supposedly substantiating racial differences in intelligence and those of over a hundred years ago have been used incorrectly to support racism. And the high heritability of intelligence is being used presently to create the same kinds of misunderstandings.

Before delving further into the heritability of intelligence, an examination of it in terms of sociocultural relevance may serve to cast a more just perspective. Higher intelligence has been responsible for the creation of culture in every sense of the word. Without art, literature, music, and science, our world would provide us with a much drabber vantage and experience. Without the technology of medicine and science, there would be considerably more suffering in the world than already exists. On all fronts of human culture, men of high intelligence have contributed to the increased quality of life. So it is granted that in man high intelligence is adaptive and preferable to low. When attention is focused on intelligence, it becomes distorted in emphasis only when the necessity for certain other qualities is negated. Philosophers may ruminate on the perfection of a world inhabited only by men of superior intellect, but this in itself is not enough. There appears to be little correlation between superior intelligence and other qualities valued by human cultures. Compassion, reasoned judgment, patience, and cooperation may or may not be found in persons of above-average intellect. A high intelligence does not put one at the pinnacle of humanity, although it may provide one with a heightened capacity for realizing a fuller potential in respect to what it means to be human. Some of the greatest atrocities against man have been perpetrated by the intellectually superior, and the most beneficial contributions come from those in the same category. Loren Eiseley succinctly worded the sentiment in *The Immense Journey:* "The need is not really for more brains, the need is now for a gentler, more tolerant people than those who won for us against the ice, the tiger and the bear."

A preliminary difficulty in determining who is intelligent is the measurement of intelligence itself, a problem discussed in Chapter 8. It is worth reiterating here, as illustrative of the variables inherent in attempts to define what is in many respects an intangible quality, a phenotypic character with a genotypic basis that is mainly unknown. For example, the Weschler Adult Intelligence Test, which is in wide use, includes material that is patently subjective (King 1971). For one to be given full credit on the question, "Why are child labor laws needed?", the respondent must include at least two of these reasons:

"health; education; general welfare; exploitation; avoid cheap labor." Not only is this culturally biased, but the assumption is that unless one's cultural values are similar to those of the originator of the test, one is not intelligent. There are probably many intelligent individuals in New York or Hong Kong who might have difficulty suggesting two items from this list.

The aforementioned factor of nutrition is also important to the question of intelligence, probably more so than is acknowledged generally. As prenatal and postnatal malnutrition can be responsible for a retarded development of the brain, large segments of certain populations probably do have relatively low expressed intelligence, not through lack of genetic endowment but due to impoverished environmental or social conditions. In India, the Sahel of Africa and in many other areas of the world, millions—both adults and children—are suffering from dietary deficiencies so severe that every year large numbers die of starvation. Children born to mothers living in these circumstances cannot receive the nourishment required for full mental or physical maturation. If these children live, they reflect permanently their heritage of poverty. One reason that the culture of poverty is self-perpetuating is that in each generation a large percentage of the world's population is handicapped irreparably by inadequate diet. As a factor in ensuring the full expression of genetically innate intelligence, sufficient nutrition is vital to human welfare.

There are so many variables in the question of human intelligence that it is not possible to define all of them clearly or to rank them in importance. Many vary radically with set and setting, and many attempted correlations are, at best, tenuous. A Scottish study showed that a negative correlation existed between family size and average I.Q. of members, but subsequent data showed that these measured differences were related to environmental factors rather than to the innate capacity of individual siblings. Other studies have indicated positive rather than negative correlations between intelligence of a child and the number of his siblings. The reservations and discrepancies in I.Q. testing arise from variables that cast doubt on the possibility of designing tests free of cultural and other environmental biases.

Additionally, there is the problem of the determination of intelligence in man and the measurement of its genetic and environmental components. The concept of an intelligence quotient, or I.Q., for measurement of individual capacity and predictive value has been widely used over the last few decades in the United States. Intelligence quotient is

TABLE 10-1

Correlation Within Pairs of I.Q. Scores of Monozygotic
Twins Reared Together and Apart

	Newman, Freeman, and Holzinger (modified by Shields)	Shields	Burt
Together			
Correlation	.881	.76	.925
Number of pairs	50	34	95
Apart			
Correlation	.767	.77	.874
Number of pairs	19	37	53
Difference	.114	.01	.051

Adapted from J. C. King, *The Biology of Race*. New York: Harcourt Brace Jovanovich, Inc., 1971.

defined as the ratio multiplied by 100 of an individual's test score to that of the average score for his age group. Thus, an individual having an average score for his age group has a ratio of 1.0 and an I.Q. of 100 (King 1971). Although such measures may have an intracultural, predictive value of an individual's potential for achievement in a defined set of circumstances, such as secondary school or college, there are several reasons that such measures are viewed with reservation by cultural relativists, psychologists, and subcultural groups alike.

Theories of Human Intelligence

There are essentially two polar theories of human intelligence, and which theory one subscribes to largely determines the value placed on I.Q. measures. The first theory, which we shall call genetic determinism, has received much publicity and examination recently because it has been used to support ideas of differential racial intelligence between American blacks and whites. The reader is referred to the paper (Jensen 1969) in the bibliography at the end of this chapter for a further examination of its concepts. The theory supports a static, determined intellectual ability. It is granted that the phenotype results from interactions between the genotype of the individual and his environment, but it is held that the genotype determines the upper limit of intellectual expression of the phenotype and that this limit cannot be exceeded no matter how enriched or privileged the environment. A deprived environment can depress the potential expression of the genotype, but in most instances the upper limit is reached.

The second theory of human intelligence may be called developmental determinism and is well presented by Joseph M. Hunt in his book *Intelligence and Experience.* He holds that sequential and continuous interaction between the growing child and his experience form intelligence, a concept in harmony with developmental genetics, and that while there are genetically determined parameters of intelligence, creative experience can result in overreach of these vague boundaries. Such a model is dynamic rather than fixed.

Because there is no agreement on the nature of intelligence nor on the relative restrictions and enhancements of experience in the development of intellect, there is considerable dissatisfaction with the measurement of intelligence as it is now employed in our culture. Substantial disagreement also exists among psychologists as to what I.Q. scores mean individually as well as in populations. It is now accepted widely that data from one population, given its unique environment and precepts of cultural conditioning, cannot be compared with data from another. Many psychometricians believe it impossible to bypass cultural biases in test design.

Socioeconomic Disadvantage and Intelligence

A vast and little known array of social and cultural factors cause profound differentials in measured intelligence among populations inter- and intraculturally. Because of socioeconomic disadvantage, human nutrition is far from comparable, to say nothing of equitable, even in America. In a study completed in 1956 by Harrell et al., it was found that dietary supplementation with vitamins during the last half of pregnancy had subsequent benefit in the I.Q. scores of the children. Among children of mothers from the lowest socioeconomic level, of whom 80 per cent were black, vitamin supplementation for the pregnant mother and the maturing child resulted in a mean I.Q., measured at three years of age, five points above that of the control group: 103.4 to 98.4. When measured during the fourth year after birth, the difference had expanded eight points: 101.7 to 93.6. It is noteworthy that these researchers did not observe the same effect in a study consisting entirely of rural whites. But apparently the malnutrition that is a concomitant of the culture of proverty for American blacks can perpetuate that culture even before the appearance of the next generation.

There have been numerous studies to indicate that personality and identity problems may modify normal intellectual development among black and white children alike. There is a positive correlation between personality problems and low intelligence scores, particularly among blacks, suggesting that the social role of "Negro" is damaging. That this role can deplete the resources of highly able individuals is documented by personal case histories in *Black Rage* (see bibliography).

There is increasing evidence that improvement in socioeconomic advantage itself leads to a mean rise in intelligence scores among economically disadvantaged populations. Among poor whites in the Tennessee Valley, an eleven point rise in I.Q. was observed in ten years correlative with increased economic resources in the community. Similar observations have been made among racial groups of disadvantaged children in the Honolulu public schools—notorious in the past for poor quality education—and among increasingly affluent groups of American Indians.

It is also clear that when one is a member of a disadvantaged social class, ethnic group, or racial subculture motivational conflicts exist between the cultural group of the family and that of the dominant social group. An example is the lack of value and support for the development of intellectual abilities. In *Five Families*, Oscar Lewis recounts this problem of cultural conflict in a Mexico City family:

Neither Guillermo nor Julia was eager to send the children to school for they were not convinced that two or three years of schooling, which was the most they could hope for for the children, would really help them get better jobs. For that, one needed a certificate of graduation from the sixth grade. Julia, who was illiterate, said that she could earn more money than many who knew how to read and write. This year Herminio (a son) had been kept home because he has a serious illness. His parents did not consider him strong enough for school, but he was permitted to work full-time for two pesos a week.

The intelligence of a given individual, however, is *intrinsically* independent of the social, ethnic, or racial class of which he is incidentally a member. It is paramount to remember that superior, as well as inferior, intelligence comes in all colors. This phenomenon of individual variation is evidenced in any characteristic in any population. Given any two races of man that have been compared, the individual differences in I.Q. greatly exceed the differences between races. It is the phenomenon of individual variation that accounts for the 25 per cent of blacks tested who surpass the performance of half the whites tested in a given I.Q. measurement. The ranges of variation are the same, although the means may be slightly different as a result of sociocultural inequalities.

The recent controversy precipitated by contentions that American

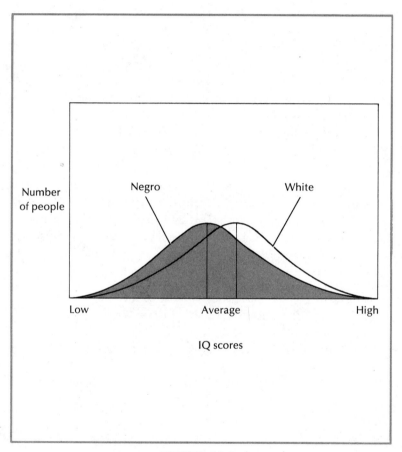

FIGURE 10–2

Typical I.Q. test distributions with the 25 per cent overlap. Lack of congruence between these curves more probably lies in socioeconomic inequality than in inherent genetic differences.

(From *The Biological and Social Meaning of Race* edited by Richard H. Osborne. W.H. Freeman and Company. Copyright © 1971.)

blacks are inferior genetically in intelligence to American whites revolves around the reported fact that the mean I.Q. score of the black
population is one standard deviation below the mean for whites. Those
who wish to read more on this controversy may refer to papers listed in
the bibliography at the end of the chapter, especially the excellent book
by James King, *The Biology of Race* and the polemic of the geneticist
Theodosius Dobzhansky, *Genetic Diversity and Human Equality*.

The most inaccurate and irresponsible assumption on the part of the
proponents of genetic racial inequality is that the figures for heritability
based on data collected from American white populations are applicable
to blacks in America. As James King points out, "What makes the problem almost inaccessible to scientific investigation is that to a very considerable extent the difference in environment between blacks and whites
is determined by whether an individual is classified as black or white"
(King 1971). The same could be said for cultural bias in Hong Kong
or Singapore among Japanese, Chinese, and Malay, where there are
often deep prejudices based on quite arbitrary race classification. What
constitutes racial identity in America is often an equally arbitrary social
definition. In *Counseling in Medical Genetics*, Sheldon Reed lists test
criteria that can be applied to babies of unknown parentage offered for
adoption and help the agencies decide whether the infant, when mature,
will be able to "pass for white" and should, therefore, be offered to
white parents rather than to black.

Blacks and American Indians in the United States comprise an unduly large percentage of the socioeconomically disadvantaged, primarily
because their opportunities have been relatively so poor compared with
those of whites. Only in very recent years have concerted efforts been
applied to the goals of racial equality, an ethical commandment as yet
unfulfilled. Although equal opportunities may be legislated and other
efforts implemented to nullify racial inequality, discrimination, the
price of which is high in terms of lost humanity and human resources,
is not erased unless the socioeconomic values of the society change. In
granting that many severe socioeconomic inequalities still exist between
American blacks and whites, a difference in the mean I.Q. scores between the two groups of some fifteen points has no relevance to inherent
intelligence. Individuals raised in Black ghettos are as much a product
of a distinct subculture as were Jews living in the ghettos of eastern
Europe. Intelligence quotient tests *are* culturally biased. This fact,
coupled with inferior opportunities in school, at home, and on the job,

223

offers a reasonable explanation for the purported difference. At the least, it should be taken as a working hypothesis until true racial equality of opportunity is a reality in America.

Another factor making the question of racially differential intelligence indeterminable in the United States is that nearly all American blacks carry some white genes—between 2 and 50 per cent. This does not imply that the presence of white or black genes has anything to do with intellectual capacity, but simply that it confounds scientific measurement. If most blacks have white genes of an undetermined percentage, the answer to the question of racial origin as a factor in intelligence is not only unanswerable but socially irrelevant. It seems probable that comparison of I.Q.s of upper-middle-class whites with those of extremely disadvantaged whites would yield similar differences.

Many questions concerning the nature of human intelligence remain unanswered, but the controversy revolves around the false complexities of racial difference. A variety of environmental and cultural factors have fueled the flames of the controversy, generating a replete myriad of statistics tailored to any point of view. The "unfacts" are so many that the Wonderland of Alice's inadvertent experiences might be a better place for them. Romans thought the Nordics were inferior barbarians; Latinos believe in the innate inferiority of Ladinos, who, in turn, scorn the Indians of Latin America. So it goes throughout history. Having an inferior around apparently complements the darker side of the human ego, since in nearly all civilizations with which we are familiar, someone, somewhere, is viewed as intrinsically of less worth. Members of a neighboring tribe may suffice, or a particular ethnic or racially distinguishable group within the culture might be designated as inferior. It may be a group within a culture distinguished by no visible stigma but by circumstances of social position or economics. Or it may be a woman. Anyone who looks down on another as an inferior, for whatever reason, is implying, consciously or otherwise, that he is intellectually superior. It is a necessary component of the justification.

India's traditional caste system is a case in point. Dobzhansky termed it, "the grandest genetic experiment ever performed on man" (Dobzhansky 1973). For more than 2,000 years, Indian society maintained a large degree of genetic segregation among the castes, into which men were born and destined to remain. Although there was a certain degree of interbreeding—resulting in a person being designated an outcast—the net effect was a successful erection of genetic barriers. The castes existed for such a long time that if the imagined heritable differences on which they were based held any validity, they should be detectable to some degree in modern populations. Those in various classes should show some genetic specialization as a result of the various selective pressures associated with their stations. There is no indication that this ever developed, since in contemporary India individuals from all castes are capable of filling positions and social roles previously unavailable to them. Despite its present illegalization, social inequalities associated with the old caste system still exist in many forms.

The failure of these segregating systems to achieve genetic differentiation is no surprise. Even under intense selective pressures, it would be impossible to take a randomly designated population and to culminate with one homozygous for many genes. Even hundreds of generations of genetic separation will not effect that end, as illustrated by the biology of race in human populations.

Intelligence and Culture

Man is distinct in the nature of his intelligence, which has given him his culture. Whether or not certain primates and other social animals have some kind of culture is a moot point in relation to that of man. But it is illogical to uphold the belief that man's mental achievements are separate from, rather than continuous with, those evolving in primates and perhaps some other mammals, particularly highly social ones such as wolves and coati mundis. The human mind has expanded vastly in its potentials, as both the creator and creation of culture, but it is nonetheless the product of a physical brain which is in many respects similar to those of hominoid relatives. It is a species-centric assumption that man's mind is a totally original phenomenon unrelated in any degree to the workings of other primate brains.

In *The Phenomenon of Man*, the paleontologist and philosopher Teilhard de Chardin explored the rise of thought. One of the primary steps in mental evolution was that of reflection, or the conscious awareness of self. Man is a particularly self-conscious animal, a quality breeding the eccentricities of conceit, guilt, transcendence and the gamut of related human characteristics that cause both greater personal joys and vexations than other species are capable of experiencing. Self-awareness also has given man the facility for reflecting on his own evolution and his culture.

According to de Chardin, the essence of man is not only that he knows, but that he knows that he knows; and this is reflection. Other

225

FIGURE 10–3
Self-awareness.

animals know their environments, but they are not self-aware, it is suggested, or they quickly would have multiplied their innovations and capabilities. But is this true? Are we concerned with absolutes or degrees? Surely man's brain is far advanced in its power of conscious thought. But is it logical to assume that there are no incipient reflections of our own mental processes among other animals, such as the higher primates, which suggest the prehominid awakenings of conscious

226

thought that must have been present in our own ancestors many hundreds of thousands of years ago? We do not assume Australian Bushmen, who evidence a severely limited material culture, to be mentally inferior to any other representative of *Homo sapiens*. Accordingly, is it not setting man apart with heavy black lines, when they should in fact be vague grey ones, to distinguish him so totally from his mammalian relatives on the basis of his brain? The cultural expression of man's intelligence is surely unique, but it has happened in what is evolutionarily a very short period and fails to negate the possibility that higher primates and other animals are capable of self-awareness to some degree.

The question of the distinctness of human intelligence is related to that of the relationship between thought and language. It has been argued that the evolution of abstract thought would have been impossible without the corresponding development of language. Is an animal without language limited to the *now*, incapable of consciously projecting its awareness into the past or future, or of abstracting realities? This is an open question although it is again a matter of degree, as abstraction and projection are more probably characteristic of man than of any other animal. Within the human experience, users of mind-expanding drugs attest to the frequently nonverbal nature of their experiences, which are marked by profuse conceptualizations, a fact which suggests that language is not *interdependently* correlated with higher thought.

In the future, if human physical-mental evolution is not inhibited in its progress by environmental crises of our own making, it is quite conceivable that the evolution of intelligence will continue to have survival value and proceed with the aid of acceleratory eugenic and euphenic techniques into realms unknown to contemporary man. We will defer on the question of whether man's intelligence has somehow transcended its biological heritage, as this issue is beyond the realm of proof (see de Chardin for stimulating speculation). Even if one considers intellectual capacity as only the expression of the physical brain, it is in its totality a unique and fascinating aspect of our species. As only the product of physical evolution, the organization of the human mind remains exceedingly complex, defying complete analysis. If man should survive the next 100,000 years, our descendants may be as superior in intelligence to existing men as we presently are to chimpanzees. There is no predictable limit on human mental growth, the future of which is subject to circumstance, as any aspect of evolution is, regardless of how explicit the human directive.

FIGURE 10–4

(Courtesy of the American Museum of Natural History)

Suggested Readings

Bitterman, M. E. "The Evolution of Intelligence." *Scientific American* 212(1965): 92–100.

de Chardin, Teilhard. *The Phenomenon of Man*. New York: Harper & Row, 1959.

Dobzhansky, Theodosius. *Genetic Diversity and Human Equality*. New York: Basic Books, Inc., 1973.

Eiseley, Loren. *The Immense Journey*. New York: Random House, 1957.

Grier, William H., and Price M. Cobbs. *Black Rage*. New York: Basic Books, Inc., 1968.

Harrell, R. F., E. R. Woodyard, and A. I. Gates. "Influence of Vitamin Supplement of Diets of Pregnant and Lactating Women on Intelligence of Their Offspring." *Metabolism* 5(1956): 555–562.

Hunt, Joseph M. *Intelligence and Experience*. New York: The Ronald Press, 1961.

Jensen, Arthur R. "How Much Can We Boost I.Q. and Scholastic Achievement?" *Harvard Educational Review* 39(1969a): 1–123.

——— "Reducing the Heredity-Environment Uncertainty." *Harvard Educational Review* 39(1969b): 209–243.

King, James C. *The Biology of Race*. New York: Harcourt Brace Jovanovich, Inc., 1971.

Lewis, Oscar. *Five Families*. New York: New American Library, 1959.

Litwack, L. F. *North of Slavery*. Chicago: University of Chicago Press, 1961.

Pettigrew, Thomas F. "Race, Mental Illness and Intelligence: A Social-Psychological View." In *The Biological and Social Meaning of Race*, edited by Richard H. Osborne. San Francisco: W. H. Freeman and Co., 1971.

Reed, Sheldon. *Counseling in Medical Genetics*. Philadelphia: W. B. Saunders Company, 1963.

229

chapter

11

A FURTHER ARGUMENT
FOR DIVERSITY

Thoreau's often quoted sentiment, "In wildness is the preservation of the world," might accurately be paraphrased, "In diversity is the preservation of the world." It may seem a trite exercise to point out that no two organisms are alike, but therein lies a fact of immense significance to the process of evolution and to the continuation of any particular species. We have emphasized that the species is not a static concept but that all forms of life are continuously changing at rates modified by chance and environmental circumstance. One species may undergo rapid

FIGURE 11-1

evolutionary change, while another may exhibit few alterations in its physiological and morphological design over a period of millions of years. However slowly or rapidly it is effected, evolution progresses, causing both major and minor floristic and faunistic changes that may be observed in the paleontological record and in the world about us. The physical and climatic components of the Earth are dynamic, and today barren deserts baking under the sun once were life-filled seas, and great ice sheets now lie where, millions of years ago, tropical cycads and seed ferns formed forests.

The predominant life on earth evolved from the simplest of self-replicating forms into ever more complex organisms specialized for energy capture and conservancy, and even today, as we perceive around us an apparently static biological world, this process continues. It is a temptation to think of evolution in terms of a past process; it is not, it is ongoing. There is no reason to suppose that evolution is not as dynamic now as ever before, and there are many reasons to suspect it of being more dynamic and accelerated in the present. A varied and largely unknown biotic world has preceded this one. A probable assumption is that our knowledge of extinct plants and animals, known from their preserved imprints, casts, and bones, reflects only a small fraction of all life that has arisen and declined on earth. The variation of life has been profuse, expanding and receding according to the interactions of energy availability, biological design, and environmental parameters. The interactions, or biofeedback, among these parameters must be balanced to ensure a species' survival in evolutionary time. Dinosaurs, which varied in size from only several inches long to others of enormous dimensions, were the predominant animals for many millions of years. Yet today only remote relatives remain; the majority were unable to pass through the eye of the needle of changing circumstance. Supposition attributes various causes to their demise, but no one knows unequivocally the reason, or reasons, for their failure beyond the certainty that in some way they were unable to adapt to changing conditions, whether those of increased competition with other more rapidly evolving and intelligent forms of life, climatic change, or floristic change that resulted in a depletion of their food sources.

Man is a relatively recent product of evolution, but during his brief span he has wrought more changes on Earth than any previously existing organism. He is not an apex, his present state being merely a point on a continuum of change with an unknowable future. Man has no insurance against extinction, despite the eternal human hope that by genetically and rationally controlling his destiny, the survival of our species may be assured. It has been suggested that by the time the Earth has approached the sun closely enough to extinguish life, man will have found new planets to inhabit. The prospect provides some interesting problems in theoretical biology, but unless there is a radical alteration of man's present course, it is unlikely that the natural resources and technology necessary will be available, even if the human species has not by then become extinct.

Man as a species unquestionably has been successful, having occupied a greater variety of niches than any other animal. The development of his culture, a unique product of the biofeedback between his evolving brain and environment, assisted in his dispersal throughout the world. Physically a generalized animal, man has employed culture to remain bio-

233

logically unspecialized. Invading diverse niches resulted in less physical variation than would have been true if cultural aspects had not existed to subdue environmental stressors. Whereas the course of physical evolution usually progresses from generalized biological design to the more specialized, that same progression can also make an organism more vulnerable to extinction. The more specialized an organism becomes, the less capacity it retains for generalized expression, and there is accordingly less flexibility for adaptation to alterations in its external interactions. Extreme degrees of morphological specialization, behaviorally induced and selected for, may maladapt an animal to its present environment. The Irish elks' success in obtaining mates was directly proportional to the size of their antlers. In time, these became enormous, resulting in an essentially overburdened animal that is now extinct, eliminated by the size and weight of its cumbersome adornment.

When viewed objectively, man represents a series of paradoxical qualities combined in the creation of a unique species that has retained the adaptive advantages inherent in physical generalization while achieving extreme specialization via cultural mechanisms. We have no horns, bony plates, or highly particular morphological adaptations, nor do we have any dietary dependence upon certain plants or animals. The human genome is rife with the potential for selection of adaptive variables should cultural defenses fail again, exposing man to the necessity to be wholly adaptive to the environment.

The genetic bases of diversity are those underlying the evolutionary process: mutation, recombination, isolation, and natural selection. Mutations, although more than 99 per cent are eliminated as quickly as they arise by the pressures of stabilizing selection, provide from the less than 1 per cent that are potentially beneficial a continuous pool of individuals that might be better able to accommodate to the conditions of changing environments. Recombination of the genetic material in the formation of gametes permits new combinations as well as assorting new genetic information from mutations that have proved advantageous. Isolation of populations of sexually reproducing organisms produces diversity through the response of the collective genotype to differing environmental conditions, as well as resulting in the potential variation of genetic drift in small populations. Natural selection factors operate to cull unsuccessfully adapted individuals from a population, giving direction to and reinforcing the cohesion of the functional design. As the force of natural selection, or the biofeedback equilibrium between the organismic design and the designing environment, is never stable, the process itself assures that organisms will remain dynamic.

Culture has promoted human diversity through the results of differential mating criteria, isolation, the invasion of different environments, and even by the technological maintenance of individuals who could not survive otherwise. As there is a biological surplus of women in ratio to the number of men in human populations, which becomes increasingly marked following puberty, differential criteria in mate selection have, no doubt, been a subtle but continuous factor in directional selection. Of course, it should be added that many elements contribute to mate selection, and in many cultures polygamy and other practices have reduced strong physical selection. The ability to conceive and bear children successfully remains, no doubt, the single most important factor.

Cultural isolation has contributed to human biological diversity through reproductive barriers created by language, territoriality, systems of belief, and social stratification. The isolation of populations also has influenced cultural diversification, resulting in thousands of varying traits, linguistic differences, and other manifestations. Even cultural diversity has a biologically adaptive value because the greater the possibilities open to man for solving his environmental problems, the greater the probability that viable solutions will arise and that some will have high survival value in the event of change. For this reason, as well as those pertaining to aesthetics and subjective values, universal cultural homogeneity is to be lamented. There is no intrinsic implication in international cooperation that we must also share an international cultural sameness. Aside from the point of explicit survival, cultural diversity enriches the human potential by allowing innovations and insights arising from a particular society to diffuse into others. It may be argued that even were human culture to become homogeneous, human invention would not cease. That may be true of technological applications, as evidenced by the utilization of transcultural information today, but highly valuable cultural innovations have often been the products of the specific perception arising from a given cultural experience. If human society were to become more universally alike, the scope of possibilities might be expected to lessen.

The invasion of a variety of environments has caused some physical and physiological diversity among human populations, which we discussed previously as races. It does not seem reasonable that genetic drift *alone* would account for observable racial differences, although it undoubtedly had some influence on minor characteristics of isolated populations. Certainly primitive men were not free from the full force of natural selection any more than we are today. Dark skin in equatorial climates serves as a barrier to the absorption of vitamin D in harmful quantities, whereas lightly pigmented skin allows individuals, especially children, in far-northern latitudes to absorb enough of this critical vitamin to minimize rickets and other pathologies associated with vitamin D deprivation. As rickets in children is often permanently crippling, lighter skin, permitting maximal absorption, must have been strongly selected for among the hunters and gatherers who migrated into far-northern climates. Varying physical attributes between and among racial groups are surely the results both of natural selection and genetic drift. Unfortunately, human phenotypes do not conform ideally to environmental hypotheses. The light skin of northern Europeans best fits the adaptive hypothesis, but other examples do not support so clear a correlation. It is generally true that groups nearer to the equator have darker skins, but marked inconsistencies do exist. Among the world's most heavily pigmented peoples are those of tropical central Africa, in the Congo, the Cameroons, and Senegal. Yet many of them live in the tropical rain forest where solar intensity is considerably reduced. The Hottentots and Bushmen of northwest Africa, as well as the aborigines of northern Australia, all of whom are exposed to greater solar radiation than central Africans, are considerably less pigmented. One explanation is that any particular characteristic, whether black skin or a long nose, is not an independently modified feature (Brace 1969). Pigmentation may be influenced by factors other than solar radiation in many areas, such as the structure of the skin or its amino acid metabolism. There is a vast array of variables, and it is unlikely that human features are the products of singly operating factors, being instead mediated expressions of a variety of natural selection pressures. Further, as environmental factors are given to fluctuation, and since man is adept at modifying the environmental conditions affecting him, the effects of environment have changed, exerting less of an influence now than when man was a minimally cultural animal. And surely certain characters may have evolved in one environment, but have been less adaptive to new conditions arrived at through migration.

Culturally determined priorities may at times weigh more heavily in favor of certain poorly adapted physical types than natural selection can act against them, especially if the relevance of the features to survival is not critical. If in a small, isolated, and relatively primitive village, small, delicate women were considered more desirable as mates, then there would tend to be selection for women of a type less suited for childbirth and hard work, qualities far less important in a technological society. If the selection for females having a lower "fitness," biologically and in relation to their cultural role, were to continue to the point of endangering the welfare of the cultural group, the probability is great that a shift in priorities would take place. But logic does not always prevail, even when survival depends on it, as is evidenced by many of the values and priorities exerted within our own culture. In the majority of cultures, and especially in nontechnological ones, most patterns are founded more in advantageous than in detrimental practices. If a culture is extant, one may assume that not too many of its quirks have become counterproductive.

Neutral, nonadaptive diversity may occur in populations, as illustrated previously by the American Dunkers, through the process of genetic drift. As an evolutionary force, genetic drift can effect changes only in small populations. Certain nonadaptive characteristics may become fixed in large populations, a fact causing some geneticists to doubt the validity of drift as a causative factor in random variation. The explanation may be in the accelerated rate at which a given population may increase, retaining features already fixed through drift, although it could no longer operate within the expanding population. Even nonadaptive features caused by genetic drift might eventually prove to be of some value, given the hypothetical situation in which environmental conditions changed in such a way that the formerly neutral character becomes beneficial and subject to positive selection. A particular blood type owing its predominance to genetic drift may be of no value to the population expressing it until a formerly absent disease is introduced and the prevailing blood type happens to carry with it in its genetic complex a certain degree of immunity to the new disease.

Cultural circumstances may minimize as well as promote potential diversity. The adoption of clothing and housing from their most primitive forms began to lessen the selective force of environment. Today many individuals in technological cultures are able, if they wish, to avoid any but the briefest of contacts with their natural environment, replacing it with an air conditioned, heated, humidity-controlled microenvironment in apartments, cars, offices, enclosed shopping centers, and even mausoleums. It is possible for someone to live in an environmentally controlled dwelling, transfer to the car, to the office, and back to home without once coming into contact with "fresh" air—a practice not too unwise in many cities today. Such refinements are probably economically unsustainable as well as environmentally unsound, and few individuals wish to live quite so limited an existence. Man will no doubt continue to have to deal with his environment on basic levels for some time to come. Most artifacts of our culture, however, minimize the contact between man and environment and thereby minimize potential biological diversity. Those increasing man's mobility, such as cars, boats, and planes, are directly responsible for a decrease in both biological and cultural diversity. Had it happened that all human aggregates had remained at culturally primitive levels and that mobility were minimal over a long enough span, the cultural and biological isolation would be expected to reflect itself in broadening divergence between populations. This would lead eventually to true genetic incompatibility and the origin of valid species of man from his races. There is no biological reason that this could not have happened, except perhaps for man's predisposition to be an inveterate wanderer. That it did not is due primarily to the acceleration of intergroup contact, which is now integrating man in such a way that short of a holocaust vastly reducing the human population and technology and causing once again the genetic isolation of groups, there is no possibility of further trends toward speciation apart from directed genetic engineering. Rather, future man will become less distinguishable by racial or ethnic group, as interracial and interethnic marriage become more acceptable in all cultures.

Biologically and socially, racial amalgamation will benefit the human species through the phenomenon of *heterosis,* or hybrid vigor. Although there may be some concomitant disadvantages, as suggested by a higher infant mortality rate related to genetically diverse parental heritages, the net effect is beneficial. It is a fact, with man and all other sexually reproducing organisms, that variety in the gene pool carries with it biological benefits. Given the diversity that exists among races of man, there is little danger that interbreeding of races will ever result in too homogeneous a population.

The concept that contemporary races of man have descended from pure racial stocks which are being diluted by current integration and intermarriage is one of the most popular foundations for racism. Human races are counterparts to what biologists describe as subspecies in other animal populations. James King in *The Biology of Race* defines a species as "a group of populations with individual variation within them and geographical variation between them, with varying amounts of interbreeding among them, each tending toward genetic equilibrium but fluctuating around it." The populations in this definition are the subspecies, and the races of man accommodate the concept. Geographical variation is steadily decreasing throughout the world as a result of the diffusion of cultures and races from their centers, from those occupied at the time the races of man were forming. There never was a "pure" race, as was theorized of the Aryans. Certain groups of men have more phenotypic characteristics in common than other groups because of longer or more culturally stringent genetic isolation, but none are without some crossbreeding with neighboring groups. It would be more accurate to consider the long-isolated Australian aborigines a pure race than any historical or modern population exposed to frequent opportunity for interbreeding, as the aborigines have been isolated, on the Australian continent, perhaps longer than any population of man. The myth that racial "purity" confers an innate superiority is a persistent and troubling cultural concept with no biological basis. Even in modern Japan, long culturally isolated from "inferior" Westerners, there are paradoxical views on racial admixture. Although the standard of beauty of the half-Japanese, half-Western woman is highly valued by general cultural perception, and these women can secure highly paid jobs as actresses and models, they are considered inferior to pure Japanese stock and relegated to special occupations, especially in rural areas. Few tradition-conscious and mobile young Japanese men would jeopardize their positions by marrying a woman of mixed racial parentage. Children of mixed parentage born in Japan after World War II were especially scorned, much as the children of mixed black-white marriages once were generally and still are scorned in many areas of the United States.

One of the convenient aspects of racial differences for those desiring the perpetuation of social inequalities is that race may be equated with differences in status or class (see Chapter 10). Status differences are more readily accepted as discriminatory rationales than racism and the problem can thus be veneered and mollified conveniently. Plato put all this very nicely in his *Republic*. He justified three classes in his Utopia—the guardians, auxiliaries, and common people—and stated that all must be persuaded to believe that men are fashioned of gold (the guardians), silver (the auxiliaries), or bronze and baser metals (the common people). Each person's status in life was to be kept according to the metals of his construction (Plato 1955). Today we do not believe that the metal (or race) makes the man, but the notion of inferiority arising from one's class or racial heritage is equivalent. Racial variety is to the advantage, not the detriment, of mankind.

239

Man, the result of his culture, is also the product of the biofeedback between the neuroanatomy of his body and his environment. Without cultural biofeedback man would not have developed so proficient a brain, nor would the dexterity of his hand and generalized nervous system have become so great. Visual acuity and neural coordination and response are the results of interplay and feedback between cultural and environmental factors.

Not only neurological diversity but that of physiological response to stressors also characterizes human populations. This latter diversity may assume particular importance in the immediate evolution of human populations. If we assume that man-created environmental stressors will increase in their selective intensity in the ensuing decades, how would physiological human diversity maximize man's potential for survival, as a population, under increased selective pressures? A brief consideration of increased radiation illustrates this well. It would cause the proliferation of mutation not only in man but in all other organisms in the biosphere. The effects of these accelerated rates may be anticipated to appear first among those organisms exhibiting relatively more rapid rates of reproduction and mutation, such as viruses, bacteria, and insects. These mutant strains, acting potentially as human pathogens, would exert more critical stresses on man by broadening their genetic base for interaction with him. In such events—probably inevitable because of the increase in radiation resulting from nuclear fission and fusion reactor plants—physiological diversity is in itself probably the only protection a species has against increased generalized selective pressures.

It is not an engineered genotype or phenotype that man needs so much as the wisdom to value the diversity in individuals and populations as his best insurance for a biological future. If eugenics or euphenics is capable of easing or removing the burden of congenital abnormalities from man's genome, so much the better. But any program resulting in the diminishing of diversity or selection for a subjectively determined, culturally biased set of values is not in the interest of the experimental population, nor that of man as a whole.

There is, however, a built-in regulator in the nature of diversity that could counter any misdirected efforts of eugenic engineering. Mutations and recombinations of genetic material are recurrent. Whatever man is capable of accomplishing in the field of eugenics, the complete elimination of mutations or recombinations scarcely seems to be one of the plausible expectations. In spite of any genetic controls assumed by man, if the technology necessary for their perpetuation were to fail, there is no reason to assume that our species would not fall back under the control of basic evolutionary mechanisms. It is doubtful that these basic sources of variation could ever be eliminated from the genetic processes.

It is risky to assume that anything is impossible. During the past fifty years, science has accomplished advances previously thought impossible. Consider, however, the question of what could happen if mutation and the cell cycle could be controlled to eliminate the genetic components of variation. Only then would eugenics be capable of directing man along an arbitrary course designed for his supposed welfare. With no genetic change possible, it would be far easier to manipulate and predict man's genotypic and phenotypic expression. With the complementary eugenic techniques of artificial insemination, with control and genetic microsurgery, and the euphenic techniques of biochemical regulation of development and function, it would be possible to engineer a man quite apart from the forces of classical natural selection. These technological products, independent of any natural environment, would be incapable of survival without the continued support of the technology that created them. And if the supporting sociotechnological structure were to disintegrate for any reason, men would be incapable of adapting optimally to existing or changing environmental conditions. There would be no mutations or recombinations to confer resistance to newly arising pathogens or to allow survival under any new exigencies. Of course, deleterious mutations would not plague man, but with his reserve of variability lost and none to draw upon in the future, he would probably not be present for very long to enjoy that small benefit. Lack of variation would be possible only in the context of a highly engineered and predictable society. As such a world is now fantasy, it is of interest to man's future to value normal rates of mutation and resultant variations as key factors not only in the evolutionary process, but in his own survival.

The potential for variability in organisms is great, but its expression is not infinite. For this reason convergent evolution results in closely similar morphologies and survival strategies among unrelated animals. Or it might be better said that the physical and biological parameters of the biosphere impose limits to variation. We may assume that no plant or animal has evolved to a particular form or strategy by design. All organisms are the products of chance, having become what they are as a result of an interaction and feedback of circumstances. It is these interactions acting on variation that allow evolution in the biosphere. If biological diversity were to cease, the order in the biosphere would diminish markedly.

Psychological diversity, perhaps as critical to the evolution of man's culture as biological diversity is to the continued energetic order of the biosphere, is significant to man's well-being. Culturally, a world of people too similar in psychological makeup would create an unbalanced society. Such a problem could plausibly be the product of overzealous eugenic or euphenic practices. Both could predetermine a future of individuals with engineered psyches designed to be in the best interests of society. There is no evidence that psychological variation is any less beneficial than physical diversity in man. If nothing more, a wide range of personalities and perspectives enriches the human experience, infusing culture with greater potential insight for adaptive change.

At the moment there is no reason to suppose that any attempt to standardize man, psychically or biologically, would be successful or possible. Some aspects of the human genome might be better deleted, but in most respects variability is to our advantage for the continuation of our biological and cultural evolution. Environmental as well as genetic and cultural diversity remain the best survival strategy open to man. Diversity is as important an aspect of the quality of man's total environment as any other factor. Man's survival lies in variety and his ability to exploit it as a human resource, not in the controlled homogenization of his genotype or of his ecosphere.

Suggested Readings

Bajema, Carl Jay, ed. *Natural Selection in Human Populations.* New York: John Wiley & Sons, 1971.

Brace, C. Loring. "A Nonracial Approach Toward the Understanding of Human Diversity." In *The Concept of Race,* edited by Ashley Montagu. London: Collier-Macmillan, 1969.

Johnston, Francis E. *Microevolution of Human Populations.* Englewood Cliffs, N.J.: Prentice-Hall, Inc., 1973.

King, James C. *The Biology of Race.* New York: Harcourt Brace Jovanovich, Inc., 1971.

Plato. *The Republic.* Translated by H. D. P. Lee. Baltimore: Penguin Books, 1955.

Savage, Jay. *Evolution.* 2nd ed. New York: Holt, Rinehart, and Winston, 1963.

Scientific American. *Human Variation and Origins.* San Francisco: W. H. Freeman and Co., 1967.

chapter

12

MAN'S SURVIVAL

The progressive history of human cultural development has been dependent on man's ability to neutralize environmental constraints. It is the success in overcoming these physical and biological factors that forms the fabric of cultural adaptation and success. Man has now come to a juncture in his cultural and biological history when, because of his disregard for the intrinsic limits of his physical and biological world, his further cultural and biological evolution is threatened. Man has been myopic and disregardful of limiting factors, although lost civilizations

243

FIGURE 12–1

of the past and the present, as with the Sahel, hint at the price he pays—depleted water resources, man-made deserts, environmentally disruptive agricultural practices, and overextension of his urban communities. However, the successes have been more spectacular than the failures. Since the Scientific and Industrial Revolutions, man has achieved conspicuous success in pushing back the mental and physical constraints on his populations through cultural advances and the exploitation of all facets of his environment. The history of our present century affords a startling perspective of technological advance and dominance by man over his internal and external environment. During this period, as in those past, all of the hidden costs of his success and mastery went unnoticed, and an optimism of technological proficiency has dominated the human view of the world. It is not unnatural, as the negative costs have been largely unknown and as man has advanced to a level of environmental manipulation never before achieved, that he might expect such environmental mastery, material progress, economic growth, and technological breakthroughs to continue to provide the solutions to his problems, increase his material standard of living, and elevate his understanding of the world. Man has been conditioned by the apparent success of his material culture to assume the role of the technological optimist. No matter what the problem, technology, given enough time, money, and refinement, can provide the answer.

Is there any evidence that this position is unjustified in part? Many scientists are concluding that there are numerous questions that, per se, have no technological answers, their resolution coming instead from basic changes in ethics and values. In the Report for the Club of Rome's Project on the Predicament of Mankind, *The Limits to Growth*, the authors—mainly M.I.T. scientists—analyzed the world environmental crises of the present, and by computer analysis and projection attempted to answer questions critical to man's cultural and biological survival. What are the physical limits to population and economic growth intrinsic in the nature and distribution of natural resources and the biological carrying capacity of planet earth? How is man's population explosion and technological proliferation depleting these resources? Given no change in cultural values and environmental ethics, a continuous depletion of irreplaceable resources, and a continuing increase in human population, how much time is left to man before the biological and natural resource carrying capacities of his biosphere collapse around him? The Study Council showed that population and industrial growth will peak and then decline drastically for the planet as a whole sometime during the coming century, by 2100 at the latest. Assumption of a uniform world model was necessary for the computer program. It is important to remember that in some countries this crucial point has *now* arrived; it will come later to the developed countries, but it seems an inevitable conclusion.

Given a change in world ethics and values, how much time is left man to balance himself with his limited, closed system? The answer is, as much as he *chooses*. This outcome is variable depending on what values and priorities are changed and how quickly.

245

For some time in human cultural history, economy and ecology have been disconnected in thought and in practice. Economy has exploited the ecology of the planet and indeed the resource of human population itself, by its unlimited growth. Natural resources—whether coal, oil, or whales and other living things—were plentiful and duly exploited to advance the amassment and exchange of material wealth. The Judeo-Christian ethic, by placing man over his environment rather than within it, sanctions this world view in the West. From its earliest myths, man had dominion not only over the living, once-living, and nonliving resources of the earth but also over his own kind. Ecology, an integrated understanding of environment for man and all other living things, has always been "uneconomical." Man's immediate need and use coopted any reserve of resources from other living things or, indeed, from fellow humans of the future. Historically, technological advance has served the economic rather than the ecologic cause. From its earliest widespread applications in the Industrial Revolution of eighteenth century England, technology has furthered economic interests, leaving human incomprehension and social and cultural disruption in its wake. Man's loss of communion and contact with nature and his depersonalization by exploding cultural and technological expansion are written in the literature of the nineteenth and twentieth centuries, but it is only recently that this chronic complaint has been heard as more than a romantic longing for a simpler past. In payment for unlimited population and economic growth, man has realized only in the last decade that the price is somewhat higher than that of a lost past; in the bargain he is also eating himself out of house and home.

In past human philosophical reflections, there has been little awareness of a necessary balance between his desires and his resources. The Protestant ethic of work for its salutory value and the Faustian ethic that man must strive for the sake of infusing life with meaning have never been placed on a budget. Traditionally, man's horizons have been limited only by his desire and motivation, but we now find ourselves at a point in historical and biological time when very exacting budgets to man's cultural materialism and the procreation of his own species are imposed. This point in both time references is unique, critical to man's future and unfortunately little understood.

Inherent in our inability to grasp the dimensions of our present dilemma is a lack of comprehension and reckoning of the world about us. We are conditioned to think in terms of cause and effect, such as A, the cause, bringing about B, the effect. But we seldom think of

246

reciprocal actions between us and what we effect. Interactions between the physical environment and living organisms in the biosphere have been evolving since the origin of life. Evolution is in no way descriptive of simple cause and effect; it is interaction, with all agents, organic and inorganic, being changed in the process. There are also exceedingly subtle levels of regulation and control of such processes. A concept that was proposed by Norbert Weiner several years ago expressing this mutual control and regulation of interactions is cybernetics. Cybernetics, or feedback control, implies that not only is the nature of B changed and regulated by A, but that A is itself changed and regulated by B. Simply, we can express this concept on a level familiar to freshman chemistry students as the products affecting the reactants:

$$\text{not } A + B \rightarrow AB$$
$$\text{but } A + B \rightleftharpoons A_1 + B_1$$

A dynamic system of information transfer is established, and the functionality of the system is maintained by its interchange. Of course, any system in the living world is much more complex in its total information integration, reception, and transmission than $A + B \rightleftharpoons A_1 + B_1$, so complex that total description is not available for the most basic of living things. The ecosphere in which we live owes its functionality and balance to a summation of the uncountable biocybernetic interactions between, within, and among many organic and inorganic effectors that are each in turn effected, regulated, and limited. In a relatively simple biological model, we may partially visualize the biological components of these interactions determining a food chain. In a social model we may attempt to conceptualize our world as conceived by the M.I.T. study group.

The point is emerging with an unavoidable and alarming urgency that there are and always have been biofeedback interactions that determine the limits to any human expression, biological or cultural. There is a necessary balance between population, resources, and environment determining the quantity and quality of human life and these limits must be perceived and respected if man is to survive. In fact, man's survival depends wholly on his perception of and deference to these innate limitations on his increasingly restrictive biological and physical world.

Until this point in man's cultural and evolutionary history, growth has been the goal for his populations, his cultural activity, and his technology. Growth has been the goal in and of itself. There seldom

247

has been any question of its fitness and survival value, not only in the aspirations of material culture, but also in the implied ethic of growth for its own sake. Granted, tremendous diversity has been a product of our material expansion, and this has enriched the human experience. There is, however, a point at which this material increase becomes counterproductive to the critical interests of the human species.

As it becomes apparent that unlimited growth can hold no goal beyond the extinction of vast numbers of species, depletion of finite natural resources on which our material culture depends, and catastrophic collapse of the world population, economy and social order, man is forced to seek a new ethic to provide a foundation for his further cultural decisions and for the supervision of his own evolution. This ethic, which we shall call the ethic of survival, has been suggested by numerous authors. Charles Reich proposed it in *The Greening of America*: "The price of survival is an appropriate consciousness and social order to go along with the revolution of science and technology that has already occurred. The chaos we are now experiencing is the inevitable and predictable consequence of our failure to rise to this necessity." Van Rensselaer Potter in his book, *Bioethics: Bridge to the Future*, suggests much the same thing. Survival and quality of life should be underscored as the underlying ethic of future economic, ecologic, and eugenic efforts.

What must be realized to effect an ethic of survival for man in his interactions with his environmental and social orders? There are two primary controls that serve as underpinnings for man's survival potential in the imminent future and in the succeeding century.

1. *Human population on a global level must be balanced with the biological carrying capacity of the ecosphere.*

This means zero population growth where net births are equalled by deaths, not only for the United States and other developed countries that are already close to this goal, but for the underdeveloped countries of the world as well. If the United States has achieved zero population growth by 1975, and there were subsequently no net immigration, the U.S. population would still increase until the year 2037, leveling off at about 266 million. If we assume that the underdeveloped countries are not capable of contributing to this goal until the year 2000, at which time the world population would be 5.8 billion, the subsequent lag increase throughout the world would result in a final population of 8.2 billion, more than double the present world population. It is generally agreed that even if these goals are realized within the depicted

248

time span, there will be a general economic and agricultural collapse under the weight of so excessive a population and its depletion of dwindling natural resources, and a rise in the death rate due to bio-feedback on man from increased pollution, decreased health care, and a generally accentuating food shortage. Clearly, zero population growth for all peoples is a survival ethic of immediate importance.

2. *World economics must be balanced with a global, not national, ecology, resulting in some lessening of the rate of depletion of limited resources.*

It has been stated by the advocates of unlimited growth that ecology is uneconomical, and by conservationists that economy is unecological. Both are true, given the present world view. To quote Charles Reich again, "Suppose . . . we decide there should be more conservation. If at the same time we continue to believe in the basic values of economic and technological 'progress,' no program for conservation will be effective; conservation will always be 'too expensive' or contrary to the public interest. The values of technology and progress, which remain unquestioned, are the real destroyers of the environment, rather than man's carelessness or wantonness." Economy, or for that matter technological practice, does not have to be in opposition to the aims of ecology; it is only increasing human population that is de facto opposed to ecology. Economies and technologies are choices of manifest value systems in themselves; they are not cultural systems having an innate evolutionary direction. Man by an employed ethic can direct rather than be directed. To reduce world resource depletion and stabilize economies the ethics of not only the United States, but also of all other nations must be shifted to conservative, survival-oriented standards. In order to survive, economies must be made ecologies with an end to planned obsolescence, depreciation, behaviorally conditioned and created "needs," and with maximal recycling. Theoretically, as shown by the world model of the Rome Study Council, if no action were taken to integrate economy with ecology, material resources would be depleted almost entirely by the year 2100 and, consequently, industrial production would grind to a halt. The only hope for the capitalist remaining a capitalist through the twenty-first century is for him to become an ecologist as well. Ecology is everyone's business; economy and ecology cannot be in opposition and survive. Survival of our material culture depends on the initiation of this synergistic integration.

It is our contention that technologically dependent eugenics, aside from birth control, makes little sense under existing circumstances, creating a false hope for man's survival, as long as the aforementioned concerns of population control and economic integration are unrealized. There is every reason to believe the material and nonmaterial quality of life for the individual will not be bettered, but will decrease markedly in the absence of correction of the imbalance of these critical factors, consequently negating much of the potential in common and uncommon genotypes alike. As material resources decrease, technology must, perforce, decrease with them, and it is questionable whether we will enjoy the economic freedom to indulge our eugenic or euphenic flights of fancy. The realization of many of man's dreams depends upon a continuing, stabilized material culture. Thankfully, there are no limits to the growth of man's nonmaterial culture, except in his own imagination, although there is no doubt that feedback exists between material and nonmaterial cultures. However, were the food shortages and increased pollution projected by the World Model to be realized, chronic malnutrition would take its toll on the creativity of men's minds.

In Kurt Vonnegut's novel *Slaughterhouse Five*, the Tralfamadorian remarks that earth is the only planet in the universe where there is still talk of free will. Do we in fact have any power to change the course of events that have been cumulative in their impact since the Scientific and Industrial Revolutions of 300 years ago, or must we accept the now implicit message that man's time is fast running out? We are involved presently in an ideological dilemma, one of ethics and values. If the questions and answers have always been solely scientific and technological in their nature, we would never have come to this juncture of having *to decide* whether or not to survive. However, we can exit through the same door by which we entered. Ideology can make a difference.

The revolution we effect, if indeed we choose to do so, and there remains enough time on our side to realize our decision, must be a cultural revolution integrated with an ecological perspective. While we are presently a part of a technocratic culture and appear to have lost the ability to control our own destiny, as evidenced by every thread of the fabric of our society, we should bear in mind that technology does not necessarily direct culture; culture can direct technology. We live in an uncontrolled technological state where the technological optimists tell us that all will be well as yet another assault is made against the foundations of our ecosphere and civilization. By reformulating our cultural ethic to one of survival, we can regain control.

In reasserting that control, these conditions need to be met for the biological and cultural survival of man:

1. A maximal euphenic environment as a primary goal in the salvaging of Earth with:
   a. a balanced human population.
   b. a balanced ecology—economy for the material and aesthetic needs of man.
   c. optimal nutrition for all peoples of all countries.
   d. optimal education according to individual desire and ability.
   e. maximal protection from infectious and noninfectious disease.
   f. a *maximally diversified* biological and social environment.
2. A eugenic environment that enhances the survival and evolution of the human species (admittedly theoretical until the foregoing conditions are satisfied):
   a. freedom from congenital disease and abnormality.
   b. freedom from dictated or prescribed genetic uniformity in physical or intellectual characteristics—the right to genetic diversity.
   c. freedom to choose accessibility to technological, innovative eugenic practices as they are implemented.

These goals may be utopian for the world population, but they are neither unrealistic nor unattainable; they can be realized in the context of a set of changing social values, ethics, and priorities. Man's future, now as never before in his history, will follow the course of his own choosing.

Suggested Readings

Burch, William R. *Daydreams and Nightmares: A Sociological Essay on the American Environment.* New York: Harper & Row, 1971.

Chisholm, Anne. *Philosophies of the Earth: Conversations with Ecologists.* New York: E. P. Dutton & Co., Inc., 1972.

Dasmann, Raymond F., John P. Milton, and Peter H. Freeman. *Ecological Principles for Economic Development.* New York: John Wiley & Sons, 1973.

Falk, Richard A. *This Endangered Planet: Prospects and Proposals for Human Survival.* New York: Random House, 1971.

Fuchs, Walter R. *Cybernetics for the Modern Mind,* translated by K. Kellner. New York: Macmillan Publishing Co., Inc., 1971.

Meadows, D. H., D. L. Meadows, Jorgen Randers, and William H. Behrens, III. *The Limits to Growth*. New York: Universe Books, 1972.

Potter, Van Rensselaer. *Bioethics: Bridge to the Future*. Englewood Cliffs, N.J.: Prentice-Hall, 1971.

Reich, C. A. *The Greening of America*. New York: Random House, 1970.

Vonnegut, Kurt. *Slaughterhouse Five*. New York: Delacorte Press, 1969.

Wiener, Norbert. *Cybernetics*, 2nd ed. Cambridge, Mass.: M.I.T. Press, 1965.

index